'Modernising' Social Policy: Unravelling New Labour's Welfare Reforms

TOM BURDEN, CHARLIE COOPER, STEPH PETRIE

Ashgate

Aldershot • Burlington USA • Singapore • Sydney

Published by
Ashgate Publishing Limited
Gower House
Croft Road
Aldershot
Hampshire GU11 3HR
England

Ashgate Publishing Company
131 Main Street
Burlington
Vermont 05401
USA

Ashgate website: http://www.ashgate.com

British Library Cataloguing in Publication Data
Burden, Tom
    'Modernising' social policy : unravelling New Labour's
    welfare reforms
    1. Public welfare - Great Britain 2. Great Britain - Social
    policy
    I. Title II. Cooper, Charlie, 1952- III. Petrie, Steph
    361.9'41

Library of Congress Control Number: 00-133533

ISBN 1 84014 387 8

Printed and bound by Athenaeum Press, Ltd.,
Gateshead, Tyne & Wear.

Contents

Contents

1 The Emergence of 'New' Labour

Introduction

The 1997 General Election marked the prospect for a new epoch in British social policy. The British electorate, in thrall for so long to the 'neo-liberal' project of the Conservatives, followed trends elsewhere in Europe in the late 1990s and voted decisively for a new 'centre-left' government. Labour's landslide election victory was the largest in its history. According to some commentators, this turning point offered possibilities for establishing a 'third phase' in the post-war history of the welfare state (the first being the creation of the Keynesian welfare state, the second being the neo-liberal reforms of the 1980s and 1990s). The exultation that greeted Tony Blair's entrance to Downing Street on the morning of 2 May 1997 seemed to represent an extraordinarily deep-rooted sense of relief, shared throughout the nation, as if a huge dark cloud had lifted. Both *The Observer* (4 May 1997) and *New Statesman* (May 1997 Election Special), echoing Blair's own pronouncement, proclaimed Labour's victory as heralding the dawn of a 'new era'. This book critically explores this proclamation and considers the reality of, and options for, a new era of social welfare in Britain under New Labour.

The welfare state that the Labour government inherited from the Conservatives was in a critical condition. The National Health Service (NHS) was under strain due to a combination of an ageing population, increasing demand for new and expensive medical technology, and underfunding. The education system was facing numerous difficulties such as increasing school exclusions (even among primary-age children), decaying buildings and poor equipment, and an increasing sense of demoralisation amongst teachers. The nation's housing stock was falling into increasing disrepair; housing affordability, homelessness and rooflessness had become problems for increasing numbers of people. Social inequality was widening, and around one in four children lived

1

below the poverty line. The 'family', increasingly expected to meet the demands of care in the community, faced intense pressures brought about by cut-backs in social services, longer working hours, the risks and fears of unemployment, and poverty. Welfare institutions, no longer able to cope with inequality and ensure access to essential services, had become overseers of a rationed, substandard, residualised service. Social policy in Britain was unable to address these problems because of the perceived need for financial prudence forced on government by globalisation, world competition and voters resistance to tax rises.

Much of the existing material on future prospects for social welfare under New Labour tend to measure the degree to which strands in its thinking reflect 'Old' Labour or neo-liberal social values. Despite their claims to a distinct 'Third Way', provisional verdicts suggest that there is clear policy convergence in some areas between New Labour and the neo-liberals. This is reflected most notably in the continuance of public spending controls and economic prudence, limits to state intervention, welfare to work, voluntarism, and quasi-markets in welfare (Powell 1999). New Labour has also been seen to embrace a particular conservative and conditional brand of communitarianism, characterised by highly moralistic and prescriptive approaches to collective responsibility. In return for collective rights, individuals are bound by duties and obligations (Driver and Martell 1998).

This book takes a different approach to evaluating future prospects for social welfare in Britain by exploring what we call the dominant discourse of welfare. By this we mean the way in which the dominant power interests within discourses construct the welfare subject as a problem to be dealt with by courses of action, created, articulated and put into practice through policy intervention. Social policy intervention is central to the way in which sense is made of our social world. Its constructs reflect and recreate power relationships in society by shaping our understanding of 'reality'. Therefore, it is essential to analyse the discourse of welfare and discursive practices in social policy intervention to fully appreciate how constructed 'abnormality' enshrined in policy enables power interests to achieve legitimacy and maintain the *status quo*. Discourse limits the space within which policy debates are conducted and agendas are formed, excluding the lived experience of those without power. However, discourses, by their inherent contradictions, can become sites for emancipation, constructing and reconstructing opportunities for new forms of political resistance.

Despite years of state intervention in welfare, governments remain concerned with the question of social cohesion in society, more recently expressed as social exclusion. Our assessment of New Labour's policies to tackle social exclusion leads us to conclude that they are not going to lead to a more inclusive society because they inhabit a policy framework set within the same discourse of welfare that underpinned the policies of Old Labour and the neo-liberals. We show that welfare policies do not take account of the complexity of modern Britain in terms of social diversity and difference. Indeed, we share the view of Hayek in this respect in that governments cannot know enough to plan society according to some grand scheme, since no conceivable plan can truly reflect the complexity of human diversity (Hayek 1975). Because of this, welfare provision is failing to meet the needs and wants of those groups who fail to fit the model of the normalised family central to the policies of both the neo-liberals and New Labour. Social relationships in British society are not constructed around the same social values central to New Labour's agenda. In particular, we believe the language of New Labour is derived from distorted constructions about the welfare subject (defined in New Labour's policies as those likely to become dependent on welfare if not forced to enter the world of 'work').

In order to illustrate this we draw on the work of Leonard (1997) and his attempt to highlight how the dominant discourse of welfare has been significantly constructed by the partial or supplementary discourses of 'work', 'consumption', 'family' and 'sexuality', constructing 'difference' as 'deviance' under the neo-liberals and now, we believe, under New Labour. We question New Labour's attempt at presenting themselves as something 'new'. While they may represent something different (and perhaps better) than the previous neo-liberal government in terms of, for example, their acknowledgement of social exclusion, in respect of their welfare policies we would say they are little different. This is largely because they inhabit the same discourse of welfare as both Old Labour and the neo-liberals and, as a consequence, their policies exacerbate, rather than alleviate, social exclusion.

Moreover, our analysis is concerned with broad changes in the social, economic and cultural fabric of society, and the impact of these on social policy developments. We show that social policy has been used throughout its different phases as part of a welfare discourse, constructed and reconstructed over time as a means of promoting economic priorities and maintaining social order. We demonstrate how policies have become more excluding and that this is the legacy of the British welfare state. We argue for a new era of welfare – one that recognises and acknowledges difference, and encourages new forms of co-operation between divergent interests – that will reverse the growing social divide in British society and bring greater security to the majority.

Before going on to describe the structure and content of this book, the next section will offer a brief description of the emergence of New Labour into British politics.

The emergence of New Labour

New Labour's evolution owes much to Neil Kinnock's own 'modernisation' of the Labour Party following the stinging election defeats of 1983 and 1987. Kinnock's reforms involved both the dilution and abandonment of a number of policies, as well as the rebranding of Labour's presentation style (such as the thornless red rose and US-style electioneering). This effectively led the way for John Smith's and Tony Blair's reconstruction of Labour after the more surprising defeat in the 1992 election. Blair arguably pushed through a more radical agenda of reforms after John Smith, who replaced Kinnock in 1992, died in 1994. It was Blair who introduced the title 'New' Labour alongside the jettisoning of a number of socialist policy objectives on production – in particular, discarding the old Clause 4 on state ownership. This effectively eliminated Old Labour's commitment to Keynesianism, and giving the state a dominant role in stabilising market capitalism in the interests of greater equality and social justice. Blair's 1997 manifesto mirrored the neo-liberal agenda, with no increases in taxation and low inflation alongside stable economic growth key priorities. Blair promised welfare reforms and work schemes, tough policies on crime, and strong families and communities. Still, it had been Old Labour in government that had shifted towards the political right. In 1976, James Callaghan, then Labour Prime Minister, responding to pressure from the International Monetary Fund, announced that the era of tax-and-spend was over (Driver and Martell 1998).

The principles of Old Labour were effectively destroyed in 1983 with the defeat of Michael Foot's election campaign. This defeat had been partly due to the 'Gang of Four' – Roy Jenkins, Shirley Williams, David Owen and Bill Rogers – who broke from Labour in 1981 to form the Social Democratic Party (SDP). The founders of the SDP were keen to distance themselves from Old Labour prescriptions and embrace the European social market model. Foot's manifesto *A New Hope for Britain* remained committed to state ownership and economic planning, wealth redistribution, unilateral nuclear disarmament and withdrawal from the European Economic Community (EEC) – a document described by one Labour member as 'the longest suicide note in history' (cited in Powell 1999: 6). Kinnock's succession to Foot was to herald the beginnings of a shift in policy emphasis in the Labour Party. Initially, this was piecemeal, and Old Labour went into the 1987 election retaining plans for nationalisation and unilateral nuclear disarmament. Labour's third election defeat in succession, however, led to a policy review of greater magnitude and Labour effectively inhabiting the 'discourse' of the political right. The language of market competition and economic dynamism, efficiency and effectiveness, while present to some degree in Old Labour thinking, was now to pervade all areas of the party's agenda, marking a distinct shift away from the political economy of socialism and preparing the groundwork for Blair's own 'modernisation' project.

A key milestone in this development was the report of the Commission on Social Justice, published in 1994, which set out a programme for national renewal based largely on investment and education. The report argued that economic opportunity, achieved through education reforms and investment, is the basis of social justice. Statements endorsing any belief in a social insurance system providing for life's risks, or the desirability of promoting collective forms of welfare provision, were absent in the report. The way forward was to encourage individualised forms of private insurance. Quite clearly, the strategy was aimed at winning the vote in the south by enticing Middle Englanders away from the Conservatives through the promise of tax cuts. This required appealing to the values of, and being credible with, the comfortable middle class: the desire to progress in their careers; decent hospitals and schools; and freedom from crime and violence. As Giles Radice and Stephen Pollard wrote in one of a series of Fabian pamphlets published in September 1994:

> To be credible, the basic core of Labour's ideas – community, fairness and opportunity – has to be clearly linked to a few key policies such as crime, education, employment and health. Labour has also to demonstrate its economic competence by continuing to emphasise the need to control public spending and to ensure value for money. (Cited in Driver and Martell 1998: 25)

This was to become the Blair project on his succession to the Labour leadership – meeting Labour's core values in new ways. Central to this project is the redistribution of opportunity (rather than income and wealth) in return for people accepting their moral obligations to society. In tandem is the need for sound fiscal policies and keeping public spending under tight control. It is within this context that New Labour's welfare policies are evolving.

Structure and content of the book

The following Chapter Two of the book offers an historical perspective of key ideological positions on welfare, highlighting how different viewpoints came, as a result of key social, political and economic factors, to predominate at different moments in time, influencing the shape and direction of social policy developments. It shows how social policy developments in Britain were largely influenced by two distinct but interconnected bodies of thought: Liberalism (and subsequently, neo-liberalism) and Fabian socialism. Both perspectives were committed to the aim of perpetuating capitalism. They differed, however, on how this might best be achieved.

This approach represents one way of understanding the making of social policy, and how policies and their effects mirror the interaction of power relationships in society. It is also one that relies heavily on the belief that social policy is driven by ideology, and policy outcomes largely reflect the interests of those groups whose ideological stance gains predominance at particular moments in history. From this perspective, social policy is functional for the particular material interests of specific groups. It is, however, an approach embedded in the 'modernist' tradition, and does not fully explain why some policies either fail to deliver their expected outcomes or, indeed, exacerbate the condition they aim to alter.

Therefore, in Chapter Three, we offer a different understanding of how social relationships are mediated through social policy intervention. We do this by examining the dominant discourse of welfare, by which we mean how individuals and groups come to be marginalised and excluded through the construction of 'abnormality' and, thus by inference, the construction of what is 'normal' and therefore desirable. Thus, as social policies become more prescriptive, the more the 'normalised' state dominates, with no space or legitimacy for ways of living that are 'Other than' the 'normal'.

This leads us to argue that policies need to be developed within a different context, within a discourse of welfare that includes diverse agendas, diverse needs and varied ways of being, articulated and defined by individuals and groups themselves. This requires a new role for social welfare, one that facilitates dialogue and recognises contextuality. Effectively, a role that allows discursive practices to be fluid and relational by exposing and challenging the processes of exclusion and oppression, and encouraging active participation in policy making and implementation.

In Chapters Four to Eight, we apply this framework of understanding to what have been described as the five pillars of welfare in Britain – health, education, housing, income maintenance and family policy. The aim is to highlight how the discourse of welfare constructs the 'abnormal' and, thus, the 'normalised state', through the supplementary discourses of 'work', 'consumption', 'family' and 'sexuality'. Chapter Nine concludes by drawing together the threads of these analyses in a critique of New Labour policies. We question New Labour's claim that it has a new and distinctive project, one that represents a fundamental break with both Old Labour and the neo-liberals, and see instead the continuities rather than the ruptures with the past. In particular, New Labour continue to pathologise social problems by constructing 'normality' in a way that serves to objectify and exclude those individuals and groups whose lived experience is different. What is needed is a 'new' way of deconstructing this process of exclusion, and reflecting on its effect. Only then can we hope that welfare discursive practices, including policies, will become more inclusive.

References

Driver, S. and Martell, L. (1998) *New Labour: Politics after Thatcherism*, Polity Press, Cambridge.

Hayek, F. (1975) 'The Principles of a Liberal Social Order', in A. de Crespigny and J. Cronin (eds.) *Ideologies of Politics*, Oxford University Press, Capetown.

Leonard. P. (1997) *Postmodern Welfare: Reconstructing an Emancipatory Project*, Sage, London.

Powell, M. (ed.) (1999), *New Labour, New Welfare State? The 'third way' in British social policy*, The Policy Press, Bristol.

2 The Development of Social Policy

Introduction

The aim of this chapter is to provide the necessary background to understanding the current situation in the development of social policy. In order to do this the first part of the chapter will examine some significant features of the historical development of social policy that culminated in the mature welfare state of the post-war period. The second part of the chapter will look at a range of critiques, from both left and right, that developed as the conditions which sustained the post-war welfare state broke down in the 1970s.

Key phases of social policy development

The perspective employed in the account of the development of social policy which is given in the first part of this chapter is based on a Marxist approach. In this approach emphasis is given to the impact of the development of capitalism on policy. Particular attention is paid to the role of class conflict and to the balance of class forces in society. This approach highlights the way in which ruling groups represent powerful capitalist interests. There is a focus on how power is used to secure order and to maintain the stability of society in which powerful groups are able to retain their dominant position. There is also a focus on how subordinate groups attempt to influence policy in order to ensure that their interests are taken into account (Burden 1998).

The strength of this approach is that it is able to demonstrate the impact of broad changes in economic structure on the growth of social policy. It also avoids making the assumption that social policy is invariably benevolent and beneficial to those to whom it is addressed (Baker 1979). However, the approach is one which is largely structural. It does not give a

8

prominent place to understanding the subjective experience of those who are subject to social policies. It also tends to view policy as normally working to reinforce the power of dominant groups (Burden and Campbell 1985, Gough 1979, Ginsburg 1979). It does, however, provide a distinctive way of dealing with the unanticipated effects of policy.

Some alternative critical approaches to social policy put a great deal more emphasis on understanding the different forms of oppression that various groups are subject to. These approaches may place greater emphasis on a wider range of social divisions and social aspirations than those which Marxists normally emphasise. They may give much more prominence to issues connected with gender, race, disability, sexuality, age, and other social differences. Indeed, part of the account that will be developed in this book involves a recognition of the importance of 'difference'. This requires a significant move away from traditional approaches to understanding social policy such as that developed within Marxism.

We shall not attempt to give a chronological account of social policy here. Instead we will focus on five periods in which central and long lasting features of welfare policy were established. This section of the chapter will examine five key phases in the development of social policy up until the mid-1970s and identify the characteristic features which were established in each period. The five key periods we will examine are:

1. The Tudor Poor Law which was consolidated in a systematic form at the end of the sixteenth century.
2. The reform of the Poor Law in 1834.
3. The 'new liberal' reforms undertaken early in the twentieth century.
4. The radical social policy reforms of the Second World War.
5. The Keynesian welfare state consolidated in the long post-war boom.

The Tudor Poor Law

The Tudor Poor Law was established in a period in which the transition to capitalist relations of production was taking place. State policy towards the mass of the people was normally based on local gentry control. The Reformation had involved the closure of monastic houses and hospitals that considerably reduced the charitable resources devoted to the vagrant population. During the sixteenth century the treatment of the poor was changed as the older feudal traditions of charity and hospitality increasingly broke down. Workhouses and 'houses of correction' began to be set up to deal with vagrants. The laws dealing with the poor were eventually consolidated in the Poor Law Act 1601 (George 1973).

The major concerns of this Act were to secure order and to reinforce the obligation to work. This was the means used to maintain the social hierarchy within which paternalist relationships between the higher and lower classes were the normal form of domination. The Act was a response to the periodic disorders resulting from the existence of a substantial mobile, destitute population. This was due to agricultural enclosures, the threat of starvation arising from food shortages caused by bad harvests, population growth and inflation. Poor relief was to be the responsibility of individual parishes, controlled by the local Justices of the Peace and financed by the poor rate.

Vagrancy was considered a crime and it attracted severe penalties. Periodic round-ups of vagrants took place and they could be required to undertake labour services for a period of a year. They could also be drafted into the services in times of war. They were subject to severe bodily punishments such as branding and whipping. The settled poor were not considered to be such a threat though there were very many of them. They normally numbered around a quarter to a third of the population though their numbers could be swelled by bad harvests or local economic dislocation.

Many features of the present system of state income support can be traced back to the Poor Law Act 1601. This set up a national system of social regulation at an early stage in the development of capitalism. The legislation provided for separate treatment for each of three categories. The able-bodied were to be set to work with materials provided by the parish, possibly in a workhouse. Those who had proved unwilling to support themselves would be subject to a disciplinary regime in a house of correction. The impotent poor, unable to maintain themselves, would be maintained by income supports and/or the provision of almshouses. The scheme rested on the classification of the poor according to their adjudged ability to perform wage labour, a combination of income support and institutional provision, and the denial of any relief to the working poor (Golding and Middleton 1982).

Since control of poor relief was highly localised, enormous variations existed in the levels and forms of relief provided, and the provision of separate poorhouses, workhouses and houses of correction was not widespread. However, the framework provided by the 1601 legislation continued to govern the administration of poor relief at least until the end of the eighteenth century.

A major development occurred in 1794. A meeting of magistrates agreed to pay poor relief in cash or kind whenever the price of bread reached a threshold level. This early form of index-linked benefit was known as the 'Speenhamland system' after the place where the magistrates had met. The relief was paid whether or not the applicants were in paid work. This system was established at a time when wages in many areas were falling below subsistence level due to the inflation caused by the Napoleonic War and to a series of bad harvests. In addition, the authorities were concerned to minimise the growth of radicalism in the aftermath of the French Revolution.

This system was an attempt to re-establish a degree of economic security for the rural working class, based on gentry paternalism rather than purely capitalist values. The system led to increases in expenditure on poor relief, and thus to higher rates, that provoked the opposition of the ratepayers. It also led to low wages, since employers could pay them in the knowledge that they would be supplemented from the parish rates. The system also offended the tenets of classical political economy by interfering with the free determination of wages and by failing to impose the sole responsibility for paying for child care on parents.

Reform of the Poor Law 1834

The end of the relatively settled conditions of life of pre-industrial Britain undermined the ideological basis of the existing organisation of society and led to new pressures to reconstruct the state apparatus. From 1820 major changes took place. These changes were the culmination of a reforming campaign that had been taking place over several decades. The reformers wished to establish a modern state apparatus run on bureaucratic lines that would support the consolidation of the capitalist free market economy.

Many reformers felt that these new conditions required a more disciplined and orderly society – people needed to be made to adjust to the new demands of a competitive market economy. It was generally assumed that everyone should take complete responsibility for maintaining themselves without relying on the state. If there were people unable to fend for themselves, however, it was the job of the state to help, or even force, them to do this.

The intellectual centre of the reform movement was Bentham and his circle. Bentham's views were based on the philosophical system known as 'utilitarianism'. This system placed great faith in scientific investigation in policy-making, and sought to evaluate alternative policy options on the basis of which ones would produce 'the greatest happiness of the greatest number'. This rationalistic principle was combined with an acceptance of the arguments of classical political economy that the removal of restrictions on private property and the market would normally secure efficiency in the economic sphere. These notions developed out of the thinking of such commentators as Adam Smith, Thomas Malthus, David Ricardo and John Stuart Mill, all advocates of a minimal role for the state in welfare. State intervention was only desirable to protect individual freedom and free exchange between individuals (for instance, through law and order measures, or the removal of nuisances), or where markets failed to provide (such as the provision of parks, museums, or docks). The emphasis was on the laws of the market. Bentham's associates and followers subsequently played a major role in the reform movements. They were also represented by Parliament in the reforming tendency known as the 'Philosophic Radicals' (Corrigan 1980).

Victorian liberalism emphasised individualism and personal freedom so long as people were self-reliant. While the state should have a minimal role its power could be used to reinforce the disciplines of the market and to encourage people to take their responsibilities seriously. Various social problems and conditions that had previously been treated with a degree of tolerance were now to be dealt with by the state. New residential institutions were set up, specifically designed to reform or remoralise their inmates. A range of 'total institutions' – including prisons, lunatic asylums and reformatories – were set up to do this in the early period of capitalist industrialisation (Scull 1984).

Institutionalism was a key element in the Benthamite programme. Its earliest expression was in the prison reform movement which had an impact on policy from the late eighteenth century in the form of the Penitentiary Act 1779. A nationwide system of imprisonment regulated by the Home Office began to be established following the Gaols Act 1823. In prisons this involved the establishment of a disciplinary regime based on surveillance, hard work, long periods of solitary confinement, and the constant monitoring of behaviour. The provision of asylums for lunatics was another early success of the reformers. The County Asylums Act 1828, which was passed after a series of enquiries, established the base for a nationwide system of state 'madhouses' run in an organised and regulated fashion. The asylums were organised on a system of wards graded by the level of 'privileges' available. Compliant behaviour would lead to assignment to a ward with less unpleasant conditions.

The process of bureaucratisation was most visible in the construction of completely new arms of the state apparatus where the organisation could be set up in line with the reformers' conceptions without the need for the accommodation of existing interests. The Poor Law (Amendment) Act 1834 was based on the report of the Commission of Enquiry into the Poor Laws, itself the result of a massive nationwide 'scientific' investigation into their existing operation. The report embodied the ethos of the reformers. Its two main authors were Chadwick, a leading Benthamite, and the economist Nassau Senior (Checkland and Checkland 1974).

The Act transferred the responsibility for the poor to some 600 Poor Law Unions, run by Guardians elected by the ratepayers, from whom the necessary rates were collected. Central control was undertaken by a Poor Law Board using circulars and instructions to local Guardians, and through an Inspectorate. The Poor Law Board was an early example of bureaucratic organisation in the state. It employed a 'rational' form of administration based on statistical returns and careful monitoring of the effects of policy. It was equipped with powers to regulate the implementation of the Act at local level and to monitor its operation through an Inspectorate. It did this by laying down detailed rules governing every aspect of the internal organisation of the workhouses.

The basic principle of the amended or 'new' Poor Law was that as far as possible no cash payments ('outdoor relief') would be made and the only assistance for the poor would be the offer of a place in the workhouse. Conditions in this institution were designed to deter any but the most desperate from accepting the offer. The Act incorporated the notion that individual failings were the cause of destitution. It emphasised an institutional solution to the problem of 'pauperism' which would remoralise the deviant individual.

The Poor Law (Amendment) Act 1834 was the most significant achievement of the reform movement. The policies and institutions that it incorporated remained central to British social policy until well into the second half of the twentieth century. The design of the Poor Law administration became something of a template for future organisational changes in the state administrative structure. The punitive approach towards the poor was reinforced as the basis of policy. The emphasis on providing incentives to work was maintained. The concern to minimise state expenditure on the poor, and to provide benefits at a level of bare subsistence, became key principles of policy. The Victorian Poor Law also emphasised the degraded status of recipients of poor relief by removing the right to vote from those who possessed it and by requiring them to live in an institution run on authoritarian lines (Rose 1972).

The 'new liberalism'

The 'new liberalism', while not a coherent political theory, was a reforming tendency within the British Liberal Party that developed in the early part of the twentieth century and exercised an influence over policy in the Liberal governments of 1906-14 (Weiler 1982). Some leading Liberals felt the party could no longer continue to support Victorian *laissez faire* principles. There was growing evidence of deep-seated poverty and other social problems that seemed to result from an uncontrolled market. Seebohm Rowntree, a progressive industrialist from the Quaker chocolate manufacturers, demonstrated that wage levels were so low that they were insufficient to maintain a normal level of health and working efficiency for many workers. Rowntree's research studies were reported in *Poverty and Town Life* in 1899. They established the modern study of poverty using a 'scientifically' calculated poverty line (Kincaid 1973). This discovery of poverty led some new liberals to argue that it was the job of the state to promote a sense of 'citizenship' and make the working class full members of society. However, this change in liberal thought was largely:

> inspired as much by a desire to bring about moral and spiritual betterment and to generate a sense of solidarity between the middle and working classes as it was to improve the material conditions of the poor. (O'Brien and Penna 1998: 26)

Another factor influencing liberalism's evolving philosophy was the rapid growth of foreign competition through the development of industrial capitalism in such countries as Germany, France and the US. In particular, Germany's industrial base and trading markets, and subsequently its international political influence, were expanding during the late nineteenth century. This not only posed a threat to the British Empire but also drew attention to the state of the nation. Social problems – such as illiteracy and sickness – came to be perceived not just as individual problems but as the nation's problems:

> The capacity of the nation-state to compete in an aggressively imperialist world was seen to depend on the 'fitness' and 'development' of its human and technical resources. (O'Brien and Penna 1998: 32)

While the new liberalism is the ideological current most closely associated with reform in this period, other organisations and currents of opinion also played an important part. These included the 'national efficiency movement', Fabianism and eugenics (Hay 1975).

The new liberalism was closely linked to the 'national efficiency movement' which campaigned for policies to improve the health and strength of British workers to enhance industrial productivity and military strength. The Education Act 1902 was partly inspired by the concern for national efficiency. It was brought in by the Conservatives and provided for an extension of the period of compulsory education. Another effect of the concern with national efficiency grew out of the review of the experience of the Boer War. Many of those who volunteered to fight had to be rejected because of poor health. The government established a Committee on Physical Deterioration which reported in 1904 and recommended the provision of meals and medical inspections for school children. This was the basis for subsequent reforms in the area of child health and welfare. New institutions were developed including a child health service involving a system of national monitoring of child health (Searle 1971).

The Fabian Society played a major part in the process of reform associated with the new liberalism in the Edwardian period. It was formed by a number of socialist intellectuals in 1883. Fabianism has been the principle source of reformist plans and ideas within the British Labour Party. The early Fabians viewed the main defects of capitalism as waste and inefficiency, rather than inequality and exploitation. Two key figures in the movement were Sidney and Beatrice Webb, who played a major role in mobilising reforming opinion through personal contact with members of the élite. The Webbs also produced a massively detailed programme of reform in their *Minority Report* of the *Royal Commission on the Poor Laws* which reported in 1909.

The strategy of the Fabians was 'rationalist', 'élitist' and 'gradualist'. They were rationalist in that they believed that research and discussion could produce solutions to all social and economic problems. They were élitist in that they believed that a small number of dedicated intellectuals could alone create effective pressures for reform, and in that they sought to implement their ideas through 'permeation' – that is, by personal influence with decision makers. They were gradualist in that they sought a steady progress towards socialism rather than a sudden revolutionary shift.

An important feature of the general intellectual climate of the time was a belief in the hereditary character of social problems. Eugenics is based on 'scientific' laws of heredity showing that human characteristics are inherited and that social problems are caused by people who are biologically inferior. A belief in the biological inferiority of the lower classes was widely held at this time. It was closely related to 'social Darwinism', the application of Darwin's ideas on the role of 'natural selection' and competition between species in ensuring the 'survival of the fittest' (Jones 1980).

The Eugenics Society was founded in 1907, supported by many leading Fabians, such as Beatrice and Sidney Webb, and representatives of the new liberalism, such as Keynes and Beveridge. It had an important influence on legislation. For example, the Mental Deficiency Act 1913 viewed 'feeble-mindedness' as hereditary. It was seen as the main cause of poverty, unemployment, crime, prostitution, promiscuity, alcoholism and vagrancy. The Act classified mental defectives into four types: idiots, imbeciles, the feeble-minded and moral imbeciles. Under the Act, members of these categories could be, and often were, compulsorily detained (Searle 1976).

The new liberalism began the replacement of the Victorian Poor Law. This had largely rested on a system in which eligibility for benefits was based on the 'workhouse test'. Applicants had to agree to enter the workhouse and accept its rules before being given relief. The Liberal government developed new forms of income support. Its first move in this direction was the Pensions Act 1908. The Act provided a small non-contributory pension at the age of 70 to those with very low incomes. This scheme failed to become a model for the subsequent growth of cash benefits because of Treasury opposition to the non-contributory principle.

The major innovation introduced by the new liberals was National Insurance. This employs compulsory personal saving to provide a fund to supplement income when it is interrupted. It was first used in Germany in the late nineteenth century, and introduced in various other countries early in the twentieth century. In Britain the National Insurance Act 1911 introduced means-tested health insurance and a scheme of unemployment insurance. The scheme was paid for by a fixed weekly contribution from employees and their employers with the fund being topped up by a contribution from the Treasury. This provided compulsory sickness insurance for those paid below £3 per week and insurance against unemployment for around 2.5m workers employed in specified industries that were subject to seasonal fluctuations in employment. It works by redistributing income within an income group – healthy workers support the sick, those in work support the unemployed (Gilbert 1966, Hennock 1981).

The establishment of the system of National Insurance was a major innovation that gave the state a new means of integrating and regulating the working class. The system of insurance for sickness began the use of means tests. With a means test, eligibility for a benefit depends on having an income and/or wealth below a specified level. Means testing is designed to keep public expenditure down, encourage thrift and support the private provision of services.

The pensions and insurance schemes represented a move away from the deterrent approach of the Poor Law. However, considerable elements of continuity were maintained. The schemes were designed to restrict benefits to a category of 'deserving' individuals. Pensions could be refused to those who were unable to show that they had not habitually failed to work. The insurance schemes used the alternative approach of restricting the duration of benefit so as to exclude malingerers. The low level of benefits was designed to provide a continuing market for private insurance schemes. The division between recipients of insurance benefits, and those only given assistance subject to means tests or other conditions, has continued. The structure of the National Insurance scheme was retained as the scheme was progressively extended over the next four decades. It enabled the state to enforce the ethic and practice of self-help at little cost.

The establishment of the welfare state

During the Second World War there were major shifts in ideology and policy. The dominant class, under pressure of war and of the growth of popular radicalism, adopted the rhetoric of moderate reformism. The war profoundly unsettled some of the principal theoretical underpinnings of the dominant ideology. There was a considerable increase in the power and influence of the working class and its industrial and political organisations (Calder 1969).

A number of factors contributed to the growth of working-class radicalism. The experience of the 'blitz' increased social solidarity. The mass involvement in voluntary duties associated with the war effort such as air-raid precautions, fire-fighting, and home defence, gave many ordinary people an important social role for the first time. The experience of army life, particularly the involvement in education and discussion of social and political issues organised by the Army Bureau of Current Affairs, increased political consciousness. The presence of large numbers of affluent US troops highlighted the low living standards of working-class Britain. Many professionals, such as doctors, were required to undertake work in working-class areas and were brought face-to-face with working-class standards of life for the first time. The evacuation of children from urban areas also confronted many middle-class people with the evidence of the extreme poverty of urban life. Other families had soldiers 'billeted' in their homes with similar effects (Davies 1984).

Some radical changes to social provision were made during the war. Rationing involved a system of food distribution based on need rather than income. An Emergency Hospital Service, which had been planned before the war, was set up. It was designed to cope with what were expected to be the large number of civilian casualties from air raids. Various other groups were given entitlement to receive treatment, which was normally free, under the scheme. By 1941 it incorporated over 80 per cent of all hospital beds and formed in effect a free national hospital service. The Education Act 1944 abolished charges for secondary education. The wartime coalition government passed the Family Allowances Act 1945. Under this Act, an allowance of five shillings per week was paid to the mother for each child after the first. Family allowances were to be paid to all families on a non-contributory and non-means-tested basis.

A key role was played by the Beveridge Report of 1942 (Beveridge 1942). This proposed a comprehensive system of National Insurance based on a single weekly contribution that would finance a broad range of benefits set at subsistence level. The benefits and contributions were set at a single rate applying to everyone. It excluded those unable to work, such as the handicapped, and offered lesser benefits to women (Bland et al 1979).

Key features of the scheme were consistent with the values of capitalism. The insurance principle would reinforce self-help. Rules on the number of contributions necessary before benefits could be drawn would prevent abuse by malingerers. Contributions from the employer and the state would symbolise a concern for employee welfare and contribute to a sense of citizenship. Benefits set at subsistence level would keep the cost low, maintain work incentives and encourage the private provision of insurance.

While the Beveridge report is extremely important for establishing the principles and details of the National Insurance scheme, it has a wider importance in that it laid down the broad basis for the post-war welfare state. Beveridge argued that the success of the National Insurance scheme was based on what he called three 'assumptions'. These preconditions were: a National Health Service, full employment and a scheme of family allowances.

The Beveridge proposals were not fully endorsed on publication, despite considerable popular support for them, However, in 1944, a White Paper on social insurance was produced which accepted many of the details of the Beveridge scheme, although it rejected the central provision that benefits should be set at subsistence level. Other detailed proposals for reform were published in a series of White Papers in 1943 and 1944. These included *Educational Reconstruction, A National Health Service* and *Employment Policy* that proposed to commit the government to an interventionist policy to secure full employment, against all the traditions of the Treasury and the doctrines of orthodox liberal economic thinking (Marwick 1970).

A new feature of the wartime reforms was universalism. This was the name given to the principle that social benefits be made available to everyone in an eligible category. Family allowances were paid to all families with two or more children, regardless of income. The proposed health service available free to all in need was another universal benefit. In the National Insurance scheme benefits were also universal, although they had to be 'earned' by contributions.

The wartime reforms also involved a shift in the direction of what has been termed 'decommodification'. A commodity is something which is distributed through sale at a market price. The wartime plans and reforms substantially increased the free provision of social benefits. Decommodification has been viewed as a defining feature of a radical social policy that meets needs, or distributes essential goods and services to those who require them, rather than on the basis of willingness and ability to pay.

The post-war Keynesian welfare state

The term 'Keynesian welfare state' refers to the kind of policies established in many western capitalist countries after the Second World War. It involved a system of managed capitalism in which limits were placed on the rights of private property owners. The adoption of these policies has been seen as part of a 'post-war settlement' which was able to resolve social antagonisms and form the basis for a period of social harmony (Krieger 1986).

The two key thinkers whose ideas under-pinned the post-war settlement were Keynes and Beveridge. Both were associated with the new liberalism and both worked within the Liberal Party. Keynes' theories involved a system of government intervention to increase spending in order to create jobs, whilst preserving the market and individual economic and political freedom. He argued that the free market is not self-regulating – guided, as Adam Smith suggested, by the 'hidden hand' of market forces – and that national economies are subject to uncertainty and risk, particularly as the behaviour of individuals in the market (producers, consumers, investors, savers, and so on) is not always predictable. Keynes, therefore, emphasised political choice in economic affairs, and the ability of governments to manage economic forces. The state should act to regulate cycles of investment, production and consumption by investing in public programmes in times of economic downturn. The key was to maintain full employment and aggregate demand for goods, measures that would provide opportunity for economic growth. Both Beveridge and Keynes:

> emphasised the centrality of employment as a means of tying individuals into both the capitalist economic structure and its social benefits. Employment was both the individual's contribution to the society and the vehicle through which individuals would be insured by society ... The proper balance between

individual freedom and collective government, it seemed, had been struck. (O'Brien and Penna 1998: 36)

Beveridge's proposals for the welfare state were contained in his report of 1942. Much of the legislation for the British welfare state was brought in by the Labour government of 1945-50. However, when the Conservatives were re-elected in 1951 they maintained the commitment to Keynesian full employment policies and the welfare state.

During the long boom, the Keynesian welfare state became viewed as an established and essential feature of society. The existence of a wide-ranging system of social services had considerable support across the political spectrum. The social services are generally taken to include social security cash benefits, the provision of education, welfare support for those unable to look after themselves (the personal social services), subsidised housing, and health services.

The post-war welfare state rested on a 'technocratic' base. Both the new liberalism and Fabianism, its two main ideological sources, can be characterised as technocratic. Technocracy is the term used to describe the exercise of power by experts. Technocrats often claim to be pursuing social welfare, efficiency, economic growth and stability, in a non-ideological fashion. Decisions are made on 'rational', 'scientific' grounds and not on the basis of political ideology.

The long boom was a period of growing prosperity accompanied by political moderation, low levels of ideological conflict, economic growth and a belief in continuing progress. For some authors, the emergence of the Keynesian welfare state reflected a 'logic of industrialism' (Kerr et al 1973). This rested on a theory based on technological determinism. It suggested that as modern industrial methods of production come to predominate in any society, certain requirements are created which have to be met to ensure sustained economic expansion. These requirements consist of a system of competitive recruitment to occupational roles based on competence, and a high level of consent to the existing order among the population. In order to meet these requirements, every industrial society was seen as under pressure to develop a similar income and occupational structure underpinned by social policies. These included a mass educational system in order to ensure that required skills and knowledge were available, and that employers had the widest possible pool to draw from. It required health services to ensure a healthy and contented workforce. Social services, therefore, are needed to reduce dependence on the extended family, so allowing the social and geographical mobility required for the efficient use of labour.

The operation of the Keynesian welfare state was not subject to powerful fundamental challenges during the period of the long boom. However, even its strongest supporters perceived that there were problems which needed to be addressed.

One problem concerned the efficiency of the administrative arrangements employed to implement a range of social policies. It was believed that administrative reorganisation would provide solutions to persistent social problems. The administrative deficiencies identified included inadequate planning, unclear goals, departmentalism, administrative failure, duplication of services, overlapping or unclear responsibilities, lack of inter-agency co-ordination and the failure of different professional groups to work together. Administrative reorganisation used a 'rational' approach to organisational design to improve the delivery of policy without increasing costs. In Britain, major administrative reorganisations of social work and health care were undertaken in the late 1960s and early 1970s.

A second response to the problems that began to emerge in the welfare state in the 1960s was to attempt to reduce alienation and opposition from the public through promoting schemes for 'participation' in various areas of social policy. In Britain, participation enjoyed a vogue in the late 1960s and early 1970s. This was partly a response to disillusion with local authority slum clearance policies. Older, urban working-class housing was demolished and residents were re-housed in peripheral housing estates, often with substantial quantities of deck-access and high-rise accommodation. The new estates were seen to lack the community spirit of the older working-class areas they replaced. Participation was an attempt to make decision-making in planning more responsive to local needs. The Planning Act 1968 required participation in the planning process, including the use of a 'community forum' involving local groups.

In the Seebohm Report (Seebohm 1968) on the re-organisation of social work services, participation was identified as a means by which any stigma associated with the receipt of social benefits might be eliminated. Participation was also an element in other British social policy reforms around this time. In the 1974 reform of local government, the Ministry of Local Government recommended the establishment of 'Neighbourhood

Councils'. Similar ideas lay behind the provision for Community Health Councils in the 1974 reorganisation of the health service.

A third significant critique which took place within the intellectual framework of the Keynesian welfare state focused on the continued existence of pockets of deprivation, often to be found in cities. In Britain in the late 1960s, a number of area-based policy initiatives were started. Areas were identified in which high levels of deprivation were present. Educational Priority Areas were established in some poor inner-city areas and extra resources were channelled to the schools in them. General Improvement Areas and Housing Action Areas were also designated. The problems of the residents were viewed as compounded by the general deprivation of the area in which they lived. Some radicals saw this as a means of channelling resources to the poor without using individual means testing.

Critiques of the welfare state

In order to understand why, and how, specific social policies develop over time, we need some appreciation of the theoretical and ideological thinking shaping these developments. That is, we need to understand the ideas and values – or ideologies – which fashion society's views on how social problems should be interpreted and, subsequently, the way society should be organised to remedy these. As Alcock argues:

> The power of ideology cannot be overestimated in social science; ... in social policy ideologies of welfare have shaped and structured all perceptions of welfare policy and the development of all policy planning. (Alcock 1996: 119)

When the long boom finally came to an end in the 1970s, the political consensus between the Labour and Conservative parties, on which the post-war Keynesian welfare state had rested, also came to an end. The forces of the left in the Labour Party increased in strength. The Conservative Party moved to the right, particularly following the accession to the leadership of Margaret Thatcher. Both the Labour Party and the Conservative Party became influenced by the ideas of 'neo-liberalism' (see below). The ideological turbulence which developed in the 1970s also led to a major realignment in British politics with the emergence of the Social Democratic Party (SDP) in 1981.

Towards the end of the long boom a range of critiques of the Keynesian welfare state emerged. The critiques had both a political and an academic dimension. The critique that was most politically influential came from the New Right, or what is sometimes referred to as neo-liberalism. Its political importance in Britain, as elsewhere, arose from the existence of a government prepared to implement some of the features of the New Right programme developed by academics and New Right think tanks.

Other critiques developed from a radical direction. A range of radical viewpoints became more significant at this time. Marxism re-emerged as a significant voice in the study of social policy. However, other radical viewpoints were also important, including the 'critical theory' developed by Habermas, the radical pluralism associated with the notion of new social movements, a revived feminism and the environmentalist anti-industrialism associated with Illich.

The neo-liberal critique

The perceived failings of the post-war welfare state allowed liberalism to reappear in Britain at the end of the 1970s as a powerful and popular force. What emerged was a rebranding of liberalism, or 'neo' liberalism, built on a critique of almost 30 years experience of collective state welfare and Keynesian managerialism. Neo-liberalism challenged the Keynesian view that nation states had autonomy in the conduct of economic policy, particularly in the light of a growing recognition of 'globalisation'. The International Monetary Fund (IMF) defined globalisation as:

> The growing economic interdependence of countries worldwide through the volume of cross-border transactions in goods and services and of international capital flows, and through the more rapid and widespread diffusion of technology. (IMF, cited in Mullard and Spicker 1998: 120)

According to Giddens, globalisation means 'the era of the nation state is over' as states have lost most of the sovereignty they once had (Giddens 1998). Finance institutions and investors can now shift vast sums of money around the globe at the click of a mouse. This means that public policy at the national level can no longer control market forces. There is, therefore, a shift in power from the nation and communities to transnational companies and global capital. The 'power of the market' becomes *the* economic and political idea that no one dares to challenge, leading to such notions as the end of political ideology. Whoever is elected to political power will have to be preoccupied with introducing policies that increase the confidence of investors: reductions in taxation and public expenditure, the erosion of the welfare state, and the drive to create flexible labour markets through minimising wage demands and eroding working conditions. The concept of globalisation has been a useful one for both right and 'centre-left' parties. For the political right it has confirmed the need to create competitive and flexible markets, and to attack collectivism and labour union rights. For the political centre-left, like New Labour, it has served to justify expounding the limits to state intervention. So globalisation is an attractive concept for many governments in today's world.

Political crisis became particularly acute in western Europe during the 1970s, when instability in the international financial system, inflation and growing global competition led to a decline in economic growth. Public pressure, from welfare organisations and their users, was placed on governments to maintain or increase public spending at a time of economic downturn. In attempting to address this crisis, capitalist regimes have followed different paths, including a number of different types of welfare restructuring (Esping-Andersen 1990). In Britain, in 1979, the electorate opted for Mrs Thatcher's neo-liberal/New Right agenda, an agenda founded on an economic, political and moral critique of the post-war welfare state.

The economic critique of the Keynesian welfare state was largely founded on 'monetarism'. Monetarism is basically a revival of classical political economy, only reformulated as a response to the perceived failings of Keynesianism. As we saw above, Keynesianism emphasised the ability of government to manage the economy through 'demand-side' economic policies. That is, Keynesianism was an attempt at sustaining economic growth by maintaining sufficient effective demand for goods through state spending on public programmes, such as road and house building, to create employment and thereby wealth. Monetarists challenged the view that nation states had sufficient autonomy in the conduct of economic policy for Keynesian 'demand management' to work. They argued instead that only 'supply-side' economic policies were viable. They therefore prescribed sustaining economic growth by controlling inflation and making goods profitable to export. This involved the control of the 'money-supply' by manipulating interest rates, ensuring wage restraint and cutting back on state borrowing (Barratt Brown 1987). This prescription influenced Conservative policies in the early 1980s, which witnessed efforts to cut back public expenditure, reduce taxation and welfare entitlements, and diminish trade-union powers.

Neo-liberalism's political critique drew heavily on the ideas of New Right academics and their 'think-tanks', such as the Adam Smith Institute and the Institute of Economic Affairs (IEA). One of the most important influences on Mrs Thatcher was Friedrich Hayek, whose work was promulgated by the IEA after it was established in 1956. Central to Hayek's thinking is the notion of political 'freedom', by which he means freedom from coercion or control by others. For Hayek, this freedom was the overriding principle of liberalism. Consequently, he believed that state intervention was generally harmful to society. People in control of the state machine would invariably abuse their position of power for their own ends, leading to totalitarianism and, thereby, constraints on freedom. Consequently, Hayek believed in the 'spontaneous' orderliness of market forces rather than 'man-made' order (Hayek 1975).

Linked with this strand in neo-liberal thought is the idea of the 'overloaded government' (King 1975). The concept of overloaded government criticises the expansion of the state. It argues that there are inherent tendencies for state social provision to expand. Sometimes this is augmented by government responses to an emergency such as war. Subsequently, it proves difficult to cut expenditure back down to its previous levels because numerous vested interests have been created. A number of processes are at work. Political parties seek votes by promising more public spending, especially on social services. Each party will try to outbid the others, thus raising the proposed extent and level of benefits. The expectations of the electorate will tend to increase over time, leading to more demands for increased expenditure.

The liberal theory of motivation that focuses on the rational pursuit of self-interest has been applied to political and administrative behaviour. These ideas have been used to create predictions about the behaviour of bureaucrats seeking to maximise their incomes and status. A 'rational choice' model of bureaucracy has been developed (Niskanen 1971). This model of bureaucratic behaviour is based on neo-classical economic theory. Every individual is seen as seeking the greatest possible rewards for themselves. Civil servants running public sector organisations will seek to expand their departments. A higher budget will provide more jobs and improve career prospects for bureaucrats. Pressure for increased expenditure also comes from professionals who provide services, such as teachers and social workers.

Hayek set out three conditions under which state welfare activities could be regarded as legitimate (Hayek 1975). First, welfare services must not be delivered by monopoly providers, but there should be a plurality of service providers. Second, resources for welfare programmes should be raised in a uniform way, through a regressive tax system, and not in a way that would seek to redistribute income from the rich to the poor. And third, the 'wants' to be satisfied by welfare programmes should be the 'collective wants' of the community as a whole, and not merely the needs of particular groups in society. Welfare programmes, therefore, should not aim to redress inequalities faced by a particular class, gender, racial or sexual group. Hayek did see the need for the state to guarantee a basic 'social minimum' for extreme needs, such as the aged, the unemployed and the sick, through a social insurance scheme. However, individuals should cover the cost of this provision through compulsory contributions.

Hayek was keen to stress that any state action must be limited, otherwise it will expand beyond manageable proportions. This expansion is inevitable because of the behaviour of welfare bureaucracies themselves – that is, welfare professionals, in pursuing their own interests, will campaign for the growth of welfare organisations – and the nature of politics – that is, political parties will promise ever-increasing welfare provision to win votes. The over-expansion of the welfare state will lead down the 'road to socialism', which Hayek equates as the 'road to serfdom' – effectively, equality by coercion. People will have to accept those monopoly welfare services provided by the state because, having paid taxes to maintain these, they will have no money left to seek alternative choices in the private sector. In Hayek's view, state welfare generates a disincentive to the development of other more efficient and effective forms of service provision.

The economic and social policy implications of Hayek's perspective are most clearly worked out by Milton Friedman (Friedman 1962, Friedman and Friedman 1980). In principle, he argued, all services should be provided by the market since then people can express their preferences freely in terms of what they are willing to pay for. Competition between providers in a free market will ensure that services will be produced efficiently. However, if for practical or historical reasons state social provision exists, it must be run on lines which are consistent with market principles. Consumers must be able to choose between providers; providers must compete with one another. The recipients are seen as consumers (buying a product) rather than clients (receiving a professional service).

A third dimension of neo-liberalism was its moral critique of the welfare state and this again draws largely on Hayek's work. Hayek believed that state planning held inherent moral dangers:

> To the extent that the market is distorted by centralised planning and state intervention, the natural path of social development is deflected, with the consequence that moral values are undermined, the socialisation process ceases to operate effectively, the function of the head of the family in accumulating capital is impaired, and there emerges an erroneous faith in the scientific control of social development together with an overestimation of human capabilities. (O'Brien and Penna 1998: 87)

Hayek's discourse on morality consisted largely of pro-religion, pro-heterosexual patriarchal family and pro-capitalism, 'traditional' values transmitted by established social institutions – the church, the family, schools and so forth (O'Brien and Penna 1998). These values are shared by various neo-liberal theorists who, particularly through IEA publications, have promulgated their views on a range of personal morality issues. For some, the perceived breakdown in traditional moral values has led to the emergence of an 'underclass' in British society (Murray 1990), characterised by illegitimacy, violent crime and drop-out from the labour force. 'Definitive proof' of an underclass lies in the large number of young, healthy males who 'choose not to take jobs' (p. 17) and fail to see the importance of work for their self-respect. Unable to support a family, a dependency culture of lone-parent families emerges, exacerbating the problem. Men who cannot support a family are not 'real' men, and they therefore look for alternative ways to prove their 'masculinity' – such as through violent behaviour and crime. In the words of Murray, these men 'remain barbarians' (p. 23). The underclass discourse of the radical right had evolved by the mid-1990s into the 'social exclusion' debate, reflecting welfare theorists' concerns with the widening social divide.

Reformist critiques

One response to the growing dominance of neo-liberalism has been an attempt to revive and rework the traditional reformist approach to the welfare state. This has involved a rejection of the statism characteristic of much Fabian thought. Instead, there is an emphasis on partnership between a range of agencies. The state has a role not as an exclusive provider, but as a partner with other agencies in building welfare services. These agencies are also sometimes seen as emerging from a revived sense of community, or from a more dynamic civil society. The kind of citizenship offered by the Keynesian welfare state has been criticised as passive and disempowering (Keane 1988). Keane calls for a revival of 'civil society' invoking a form of active citizenship of the left, based on autonomous organisations such as firms, households and voluntary agencies.

The concept of 'welfare pluralism' has been advanced by some reformists. Welfare pluralism is concerned to reduce the role of the state in the provision of welfare – it is also sometimes known as the 'mixed economy of welfare' (Beresford and Croft 1984). Welfare provision results from the combination of activities undertaken in four sectors that operate in different ways:

1. The statutory sector is based on legislation and operates through state welfare organisations.
2. The voluntary sector uses voluntary effort but may be co-ordinated and partly financed by, and operate under contract to, the state sector.
3. The private sector operates for profit under contract and sometimes in partnership with other sectors.
4. The informal sector consists mainly of families who provide care to dependent members and members of the community who assist others.

Another new development is 'communitarianism'. This is critical of liberal individualism, although it retains a strong attachment to traditional morality (Etzioni 1993). The main idea of communitarianism is to balance individual rights and community responsibilities. Unrestrained individualism is seen as having undermined family and community relationships. The goal of communitarians is to promote community rather than equality. They believe that the modern state must have a broad sense of purpose greater than the sum of individual and group interests. Communitarianism has become a key idea in those versions of reformism that downplay economic egalitarianism and emphasise moral improvement. The solution to social exclusion needs to include the return to traditional community values. For communitarians like Etzioni, a strong community requires traditional nuclear family structures, providing strong parenting, achieved in part by making divorce more difficult. It also requires members of communities to accept their duties and responsibilities in the form of service to others, effectively prioritising civil duties over civil rights.

Radical critiques

Marxism views state welfare provision as a means by which ruling groups stifle dissent and reinforce their own dominance, whilst failing to make any substantial reductions in inequality. They see capitalist society as based on exploitation, inequality and class conflict.

One approach of Marxism to the growth of social policy is based on the idea that capitalism passes through different stages as it develops. In the early phase of 'competitive capitalism' firms are small and the technology employed relatively simple. Educational provision is often restricted. Appropriate policies would be those designed to enforce labour discipline and support the market, perhaps through the use of the workhouse or similar polices.

In the later phase of large-scale capitalism, sometimes called 'monopoly capitalism', firms become much larger and use more advanced technologies. Scientific and technical training, as well as the general level of education, becomes more important. Health and working efficiency may also be considered important with services initiated to improve them. Trade unionism and organised political action will grow along with pressure for more democracy. At this stage, moves may be made to integrate the working class into society through social policies designed to reduce poverty and economic insecurity.

Marxism assumes that social policies will be strongly influenced by the need to ensure the survival of capitalism. One version of Marxism starts by asking what functions social policy performs for 'capital' – that is, the survival of the capitalist system. This approach is sometimes called a 'capital logic' or 'state derivation' theory. This is because the nature of the welfare state is 'derived', that is, deduced, from the needs of the capitalist system. The role of the state in liberal democracies is to fulfil two functions, 'accumulation' and 'legitimation'. Accumulation refers to the ability of private capital to remain profitable, while legitimation refers to the need for states to retain social cohesion and win votes (O'Connor 1973). It has also been argued that welfare is central to notions of political citizenship in liberal democracies (Bauman 1998). All public spending is, therefore, seen as achieving either one or more of these objectives.

An alternative Marxist approach puts greater emphasis on the distinctive character of the historical development and the 'balance of social forces' found in different capitalist societies. Social policies are seen as resulting from the political process within a capitalist society. Various factors may affect the social policies initiated by ruling groups including: the types of political parties and other significant social movements; historical legacies such as a strong or a weak labour movement; and international factors such as imperial possessions.

The work of Habermas is closely related to a Marxist perspective. Habermas introduced the concept of 'legitimation crisis' (Habermas 1976). He depicts society as made up of three sub-systems: the economic, the political and the socio-cultural. Each sub-system has to operate effectively for the society as a whole to continue to function. When unmanageable problems arise in the inputs or outputs of any of the sub-systems there is a crisis. These crises can take several forms which are often related to social policies.

A rationality crisis can occur when the state is incapable of implementing effective solutions to serious policy problems. A fiscal crisis can occur when the levels of taxation needed to finance social policies damage the general profitability of capitalist enterprise. A motivation crisis can occur if institutions involved with social policy, such as schools and families, do not succeed in socialising the young into the values necessary for the continuation of the society.

In combination, these specific crises can lead to a generalised legitimation crisis that threatens the survival of the society in its existing form. Social policies can thus be viewed in terms of the role they play in contributing to, or resolving, crises.

Radical critiques of modern society have in recent years moved away from the exclusive emphasis on class inequality characteristic of Marxism. The common element in much of this critical literature is a focus on individual identity and experience, and its importance as a basis for a new kind of politics. This is evident in that branch of the radical literature which rejects industrialism. This viewpoint is commonly a feature of the environmentalist or green political perspectives that are becoming significant in the study of social policy. Identity is also an important factor in the ongoing feminist critique of conventional social policies and the social policy literature. The issue of identity is also at the forefront of the literature on new social movements (Fagan and Lee 1997). Taken together, these strands of critical opinion constitute a comprehensive critique of the idea of the welfare state.

Some radicals criticise industrialised societies for failing to offer a genuinely human experience due to their scale, technology, complexity and specialisation. They seek to move to a society based on simpler technology and smaller organisations, in which people could live in closer harmony with nature and with each other. Three aspects of modern industrial societies are criticised: advanced technology, large-scale organisation and occupational specialisation. Advanced technology is seen as being out of control since it destroys many formerly meaningful human activities, such as work. Large-scale organisation is opposed because it is seen as bureaucratic and impersonal. Occupational specialisation, especially in the form of professionalism, is also opposed. Illich argues that professionalism in areas of social policy, such as health care and education, prevents these activities from being controlled, or even influenced by, those who are subject to them. He argues that modern medicine dehumanises patients and is itself a major threat to health. He supports a recasting of education and has advocated 'deschooling' society (Illich 1973, 1977).

Since the 1960s, the feminist perspective in the study of social policy has grown and developed. It is argued that social policy and the welfare state cannot be properly understood without understanding how it deals with women. Feminists have claimed that gender should be viewed as a fundamental social division as significant as class (Williams 1989). Taking this view seriously requires a substantial reorientation of the traditional approach in social policy which tends to focus, where it deals with the issue of inequality at all, on the question of class. The approach of feminism to the development of social policy argues that conventional histories neglect the role of women in the process through which policy eventually comes to be made. Women are seen as 'hidden from history'. Conventional accounts of social policy have also neglected the role that it plays in reinforcing gender inequalities (Dale and Foster 1986).

The term 'new social movements' has been used to describe a range of social movements which became influential in the 1980s (Scott 1990). Many of these movements dealt with issues central to social policy. These included groups campaigning for the rights of women, ethnic minorities, the disabled, the old, and those with a minority sexual orientation. In contrast to Marxist theories of politics, these movements are not based on class membership and do not pursue class interests. Many new social movements are distinctive in rejecting orthodox lifestyles. They have been seen as expanding the boundaries of political debate to include new issues involving questions of 'identity' and what is sometimes called 'personal politics'.

Some authors have argued that welfare professionals, in order to work effectively with these groups, need to emphasise the idea of 'empowerment'. Empowerment involves helping oppressed or passive groups to become aware of their rights and of ways to enforce them. Professionals should attempt to reduce, or eliminate, the inequalities of power and status affecting groups and categories which are systematically disadvantaged. This approach rejects the traditional professional-client relationship based on the passive receipt of, and compliance with, professional or expert treatment and advice. The clients are seen as active agents who should be encouraged to 'challenge' oppressive behaviour and to organise to pursue their demands (Freire 1972).

Conclusion

Our discussion of the five key phases in the development of social policy illustrates that the structures of the state, at both local and national level, have normally been retained over long periods. These parts of the state apparatus retain significant characteristics that were present at a time when they were founded, and which reflect the particular balance of social interests that underlay their establishment. The apparatus of administration, the procedures employed in dealing with social issues, the occupational groups established, the networks and contacts with existing social interests, all help to sustain these organisations and their characteristic mode of operation over long periods.

The mature Keynesian welfare state of the long boom, so far as the social services were concerned, involved a rather disparate pattern of social provision in the different social policy areas. Services which existed differed substantially in their scope, their impact on social inequality, the principles on which social benefits were to be distributed, and the administrative apparatus employed to implement policies. Many of these differences related to the different periods in which particular services had originally been established, and which continued, therefore, to affect the character of the service.

The end of the long boom, and of the political and academic consensus on social policy which it sustained, led to the emergence of a range of critiques of orthodox social welfare theories and policies. The Fabian tradition began to move away from a reliance on state action to promote welfare and moved towards support for a mixed economy of welfare. A revival of Marxism led to an emphasis on the failure of the welfare state fundamentally to reduce class domination and class inequality. Indeed the welfare state was portrayed as playing a key role in its maintenance. The work of Habermas broadened the factors that could be viewed as contributing to social breakdown in capitalist societies. Whilst Marxism emphasised economic conditions as crucial, Habermas also referred to political and administrative breakdown, and to failures in what he called the 'socio-cultural system'.

A further range of critiques rested on alternative views of lifestyles and identity. These included a broad rejection of industrial society as a whole, a view which is now often identified with radical versions of environmental thought. Other authors attempted to widen the range of social divisions which were seen as fundamental to the nature of inequality. The key role here was played by feminism, which highlighted the nature of inequalities of gender. However, others pointed out that race, disability, age and sexual orientation were also significant bases of inequality. Emphasis on this broad range of social divisions was also linked to a focus on the new social movements that were being formed to advance the interests of these groups. Others pointed to the implications for the practice of social welfare professionals in taking these critiques seriously.

The overall situation emerging in the wake of the end of the long boom was one in which a series of significant critiques of the welfare state as it had developed were emerging. The question arises as to whether these critiques actually offer a fundamental alternative to existing thought on the welfare state, or whether they merely offer a radical version of the existing orthodoxy. A key argument which will be put forward in this book is that postmodernist thought, which builds on but goes beyond these critiques, can be the source of a fundamental alternative – not only to orthodox welfare statism, but also to the critiques which emerged following its breakdown.

References

Alcock, P. (1996) *Social Policy in Britain*, Macmillan, Basingstoke.

Baker, J. (1979) 'Social Conscience and Social Policy', *Journal of Social Policy*, Issue 8, pp. 177-206.

Barratt Brown, M. (1987) *Models in Political Economy, A Guide to the Arguments*, Pelican, Harmondsworth.

Bauman, Z. (1998) *Work, Consumerism and the New Poor*, Open University Press, Buckingham.

Beresford, P. and Croft, S. (1984) 'Welfare Pluralism: The New Face of Fabianism', *Critical Social Policy*, Issue 9, Vol. 3, No. 3, pp 19-39.

Beveridge, W. (1942) *Social Insurance and Allied Services*, HMSO, London.

Bland, L., McCabe, T. and Mort, F. (1979) 'Sexuality and Reproduction: Three 'Official' Instances', Chap. 4, M. Barrett, P. Corrigan, A. Kuhn and J. Wolff, (eds.) *Ideology and Cultural Production*, Croom Helm, London.

Burden, T. (1998) *Social Policy and Welfare*, Pluto, London.

Burden, T. and Campbell, M. (1985) *Capitalism and Public Policy in the UK*, Croom Helm, London.

Calder, A. (1969) *The People's War*, Cape, London.

Checkland, S.G. and Checkland, E.O.A. (eds.) (1974) *The Poor Law of 1834*, Penguin, Harmondsworth.

Corrigan, P. (ed.). (1980) *Capitalism, State Formation and Marxist Theory*, Quartet Books, London.

Dale, J. and Foster, P. (1986) *Feminists and State Welfare*, Routledge and Kegan Paul, London.

Davies, A. (1984) *Where did the Forties go?*, Pluto, London.

Esping-Andersen, G. (1990) *The Three Worlds of Welfare Capitalism*, Polity Press, Cambridge.

Etzioni, A. (1993) *The Spirit of Community: Rights, Responsibilities, and the Communitarian Agenda*, Fontana, London.

Fagan, T. and Lee, P. (1997) 'New Social Movements and Social Policy', Chap 8, M. Lavalette and A. Pratt (eds.) *Social Policy*, Sage, London.

Freire, P. (1972) *Pedagogy of the Oppressed*, Penguin, Harmondsworth.

Friedman, M. (1962) *Capitalism and Freedom*, University of Chicago Press, Chicago.

Friedman, M. and Friedman, R. (1980) *Free to Choose*, Penguin, Harmondsworth.

George, V. (1973) *Social Security and Society*, Routledge and Kegan Paul, London.

Giddens, A. (1998) *The Third Way: The Renewal of Social Democracy*, Polity, Cambridge.

Gilbert, B.B. (1966) *The Evolution of National Insurance in Great Britain*, Michael Joseph, London.

Ginsburg, N. (1979) *Class, Capital and Social Policy*, Macmillan, London.

Golding, P. and Middleton, S. (1982) *Images of Welfare*, Martin Robertson, London.

Gough, I. (1979) *The Political Economy of the Welfare State*, Macmillan, London.

Habermas, J. (1976) *Legitimation Crisis*, Heinemann, London.

Hay, J.R. (1975) *The Origins of the Liberal Welfare Reforms 1906-14*, Macmillan, London.

Hayek, F. (1975) 'The Principles of a Liberal Social Order', Chap 9, A. de Crespigny and J. Cronin, (eds.) *Ideologies of Politics*, Oxford University Press, Cape Town.

Hennock, P. (1981) 'The Origins of British National Insurance and the German Precedent 1880-1914', Chap 5, W.J. Mommsen, (ed.) *The Emergence of the Welfare State in Britain and Germany*, Croom Helm, London.

Illich, I. (1973) *Deschooling Society*, Penguin, Harmondsworth.

Illich, I. (1977) *Limits to Medicine*, Penguin, Harmondsworth.

Jones, G. (1980) *Social Darwinism and English Thought*, Harvester, Sussex.

Keane, J. (1988) *Democracy and Civil Society*, Verso, London.

Kerr, C., Dunlop, J.T., Hall, F.H. and Myas, C.A. (1973) *Industrialism and Industrial Man*, 2nd edn., Pelican, London.

Kincaid, J. (1973) *Poverty and Equality in Britain*, Penguin, Harmondsworth.

King, A. (1975) 'Overload: problems of governing in the 1970s', *Political Studies*, Vol. 23, pp. 284-96.

Krieger, J. (1986) *Reagan, Thatcher and the Politics of Decline*, Polity, Cambridge.

Marwick, A. (1970) *Britain in the Century of Total War*, Penguin, Harmondsworth.

Mullard, M. and Spicker, P. (1998) *Social Policy in a Changing Society*, Routledge, London.

Murray, C. (1990) *The Emerging British Underclass*, IEA, London.

Niskanen, W.A. (1971) *Bureaucracy and Representative Government*, Aldine-Atherton, New York.

O'Brien, M. and Penna, S. (1998) *Theorising Welfare*, Sage, London.

O'Connor, J. (1973) *The Fiscal Crisis of the State*, St Martin's Press, New York.

Rose, M.E. (1972) *The Relief of Poverty 1834-1914*, Macmillan, London.

Scott, A. (1990) *Ideology and the New Social Movements*, Unwin Hyman, London.

Scull, A. (1984) *Decarceration*, 2nd edn., Polity Press, Cambridge.

Searle, G.R. (1971) *The Quest for National Efficiency*, University of California Press, Berkeley.

Searle, G.R. (1976) *Eugenics and Politics in Britain 1900-1914*, Noordhoff, Leyden.

Seebohm, F. (1968) *Report of the Committee on Local Authority and Allied Services*, Cmnd. 3703, HMSO, London.

Weiler, P. (1982) *The New Liberalism*, Garland, New York.

Williams, F. (1989) *Social Policy, A Critical Introduction.* Polity, Cambridge.

3 'Welfare' Perspectives

Introduction

The previous chapter highlighted a number of key perspectives of welfare that came to have a major sway on policy at different periods in time. These perspectives represent a particular approach to understanding social policy and power relationships, one that is embedded in the 'modernist' tradition. It is an approach that inclines towards the notion that policy developments are primarily driven by ideology, and that policy outcomes will largely reflect the interests of dominant power holders. This is because, as Eagleton argues:

> Ideology is a matter of 'discourse' ... of certain concrete discursive effects, ... It represents points where power impacts upon certain utterances and inscribes itself tacitly within them. (Eagleton 1994: 223)

Ideology as discourse works to legitimate social order by silencing the voices of political resistance, conflict and confrontation. However, at the same time, the inherent contradictions within discourse open up possibilities for challenging dominant power interests and their discursive practices. In order to illustrate how these dynamics of power relationships are played out within the welfare system, this chapter proposes another way of looking at social policy developments, using an analytical framework built on concepts drawn from what are loosely-termed 'postmodern' commentaries on social welfare; debates which challenge our understanding of ways of being in postmodern (or late capitalist) societies. While recognising that the very notion of postmodernism is a contested concept, we believe it opens up possibilities for widening our understanding of social policy by offering another vantage point from which to identify the characteristics, and consequences of, welfare reforms.

Particular attention is given to the concept of a 'discourse of welfare', by which we mean how the 'welfare subject' is constructed and de-constructed over time, and how these constructs influence the discursive practices of welfare, including policy and service developments. Discourse can be understood as:

> a systematic set of beliefs, ideas or knowledge and practices specific to particular situations or locations ... Discourses and discursive practices limit the ways in which we experience the world, and therefore our subjectivity. (Billington et al. 1998: 245-246)

We are all subjects in discourse, constituted through and by it, yet active not passive. Discursive practices, such as welfare policies, are actions emanating from, and congruent with, a particular discourse; actions that reflect the power interests predominant at any one time. A simple example would be to think of three people sharing the same experience. If all three were asked about the experience, it is likely that each person would describe it slightly differently. This is not surprising as their personal characteristics, such as gender, age, racial origin and so on, and physical factors such as their individual locations, will construct a differential meaning for each of them. This, in itself, has potential for mutual enrichment: however, if one individual has power over the others, and constructs the experiences of the others as 'abnormal', exclusion and marginalisation occurs. If others must see as he/she sees, understand as he/she understands and be as he/she is, in order to be part of the experience, then their own unique meaning becomes invisible and the fullness of experience is lost to all three.

Discourse, however, is generative not static, constructing and de-constructing subjects over time, and so another way of understanding discourse is:

> as a means of constituting the subject within a historical and cultural location. Within any discursive field, a number of discourses will offer alternative states of subjectivities and identities. However, some will be more legitimate than others and will validate the 'status quo', others will challenge dominant interests ... Those less dominant discourses, subjectivities, identities, are likely to be marginal but will be crucial in defining what is dominant, central, 'mainstream'. Within bodies of knowledge and their related institutions there are competing interests, different subject positions allow for the accommodation of diverse and contradictory interests and resistance to the predominant discourse [sic]. (Plant 1999: 115)

In any dominant discourse there are inherent contradictions because power ebbs and flows and the voice of the 'Other', that is those outside the current construction of 'normal', is not always silenced or unheard. One example is the Martin Fitzpatrick ruling (discussed in Chapter Six). Welfare can, therefore, be thought of as a discourse that is socially constructed and which is fluid and changing according to how power is exercised at any one given moment. The welfare subject is constructed as an object of charity, a welfare recipient, a client, a service-user, a customer, a consumer, and so on, by the dominant discourse of welfare at various points in time. In order to show how this discourse constructs subjects, the term 'welfare subject' will be used in a generic way. However, the term is provisional and contingent as there is no single subject which is an ever changing construction and re-construction. The recipient of welfare is constituted as an object of charity, or welfare customer, or 'scrounger', and so on, often simultaneously, in response to dominant discourses which are themselves always changing.

For the purposes of this book, we apply our framework to an analysis of the welfare policies of neo-liberalism and New Labour. By adding this dimension of understanding we are able to detect strong similarities between New Labour's and the neo-liberal/New Right's discourse of welfare, irrespective of their apparent ideological positions. In particular, we argue that because New Labour and the neo-liberals inhabit the same discourse certain individuals and social groups are excluded. Welfare discourse, mediated through the discursive practice of welfare policies, defines the boundaries that mark the margins of society by constructing the 'Other' (those outside the normalised state). 'Normality' is constructed by defining, characterising and constructing 'abnormality'. We are constructed as normal by the construction of what is abnormal. This is evident in the way in which the supplementary or partial discourses, or narratives, of 'work', 'consumption', 'family' and 'sexuality' (identified by Leonard (1997) as critical to the construction of the welfare discourse) constitute the welfare subject for both the Conservative and New Labour parties. These are significant elements in the determination of welfare eligibility and ineligibility, increasingly linked to judgements about those who are 'deserving' and those who are 'undeserving'.

We conclude that social policy-makers and practitioners need to critically reflect upon the dominant discourse of welfare when establishing processes to design and implement policies. Unless these policy processes take account of how discourse defines the Other, which excludes 'difference', they will continue to marginalise those who do not conform to society's notions of normality, and perpetuate welfare as a mechanism of exclusion. This understanding is particularly important at a time when societies are experiencing greater differentiation and diversity, due to changes in modes of living, social movement and globalisation. It is also one that we find useful for our analyses of the different welfare discursive practices 'health', 'education', 'housing', 'income maintenance' and 'family' policies, to be explored in the subsequent chapters.

Modernism, postmodernism and welfare

Within a modernist framework it is assumed societies follow a linear, historical advance towards progress and civilisation. Modernism holds to the concept that, through rational scientific discourse and the application of 'truth' and objective knowledge, we are able to influence, through collective action, both the present and the future. Metanarratives, or 'grand theories' such as Marxism and Liberalism, upon which state welfare systems of various types were predicated, fall within the modernist tradition of 'rationality', 'objectivity' and 'absolute truth'. A major critique of these grand theories is that they largely reflect the power interests of particular dominant discourses, offering a viewpoint of knowledge and understanding that excludes the lived experience of others:

> It is evident that the scientific discourse of modernity has been one forged predominantly in Europe, with the non-European as its object. And by men, with women as their object. And by the wealthy, with the poor as their object. (Smaje 1996: 7)

Postmodernism, on the other hand, is largely concerned with the ambiguous nature of society beyond modernism. Postmodern concepts may appear confusing because their gestation spans many decades and disciplines, and have been used to describe almost contradictory phenomena. However, as Bertens suggests, 'If there is a common denominator to all these postmodernisms, it is that of ... a deeply felt loss of faith in our ability to represent the real' (1995: 11). This in turn raises questions about the possibility of making social changes for the common good that are generally based on a notion of social justice, constituted as an expression of universal human rights. Accepting there is no single reality suggests there is no one universal truth but many truths, and therefore, determining universal rights becomes elusive.

However, a number of social theorists (Jordan 1996, Leonard 1997 and Bauman 1998) argue that recognising individual truths, and therefore the many varied and valid ways of being in postmodern societies, is not incompatible with aiming for social justice. Although these theorists suggest a number of ways for social justice to be pursued in postmodern or late capitalist societies, common to all is the need to become aware of the inherent contradictions in the current welfare discourse, always present within any dominant discourse. These become evident when the voices of the Other are heard and discursive practices are changed. The public acceptance that HIV/AIDS was not a retributive disease only infecting gay men, for example, was due to the constant lobbying and raising of awareness by many gay and sympathetic groups and individuals, countering public and political prejudice by presenting information and generating debate. In other words, developing a critical and reflective society in which 'knowledge' and truth are regarded as provisional and contingent. A crucial aspect of membership in such societies is that the boundaries of belonging are permeable, not based on exclusive and unchanging characteristics, so that on-going negotiation and power-brokering between interests at all levels takes place. Rather than building welfare policy on metanarrative notions of universal reality, the uniqueness of lived experience is recognised through contextualising and deconstructing discourses of welfare and discursive practices, enabling dominant power interests to be uncovered. We are then able to recognise how the Other becomes subject to exclusionary processes. This perspective offers the opportunity to build new forms of social co-operation that allow many and varied identities to participate in the policy-making processes and service delivery. Individuals can articulate their felt needs and negotiation takes place, rather than their needs being defined by dominant power interests and used as criteria to judge individual worth.

The development of social policy revisited

In Chapter Two, we were primarily concerned with key economic and social events that can be identified as milestones in the development of social policy and the welfare state within a modernist perspective. We will now revisit this history, albeit chronologically, using the concept of discourse to illuminate how the welfare subject has been constructed and de-constructed over time. In particular, we will be exploring the degree to which the socially included have benefited from the discourses and discursive practices that constructed the poor as welfare subject and excluded them.

In pre-modern Europe, social organisation was based on the feudal community and church. Those 'in want' belonged to their lord or were the objects of charity:

> His [sic] safeguard, if it existed, lay in the communal nature of society and its ethical canons, expressed – though not always observed – in the teaching against usury, on the duty of almsgiving, on the efficacy of the corporal works of mercy. (Heywood, cited in Hoggett et al. 1996: 573)

The discourse of poverty constructed the poor as providing the affluent with a means of salvation, that is, helping the rich to save their 'souls'. The value of the poor was independent of individual behaviour or failings, or particular family structure. However, as society moved into its modern phase there was the rejection of the 'power of the dead over the living' (Bauman 1998: 87) and the poor became constructed as a social problem. Notions of giving as a purely beneficent act, however, remain in some philosophies, as in the Muslim concept of 'Zakat':

> Zakat is a voluntary act of love ... To employ a metaphor that is often used for the purpose, Zakat taps the parts of the body where the blood is congested and transfers it to those parts which are weak or anaemic. (Dean and Khan 1997: 197-98 – original emphasis)

A similar notion was explored by Titmuss (1970) in his examination of the British Blood Transfusion Services, based entirely on voluntary donations. However, in postmodern or late capitalist society, this construct is no longer dominant and the fear of the poor, recast as the 'underclass' (Novak 1997), has re-emerged. The Poor Laws (beginning with the Elizabethan Poor Relief Act 1601) were an earlier expression of this fear. They set the pattern of welfare to the poor until finally repealed in 1948. The Poor Laws reflected the state's concern to reinforce the 'work ethic' (where the absence of work was viewed as morally enfeebling) and to differentiate between the 'eligible' and 'ineligible', constructed as deserving or undeserving of assistance. Categorisation of this kind ensured that the two groups received different treatment, and any assistance was designed to be sufficiently unpleasant so as to deter all but the most desperate.

Liberal policies in the early part of the nineteenth century reflected the belief that the state should not take utilitarian action to deal with poverty and sickness as the unfettered operation of the free market would produce the greatest benefits for the greatest number. The Poor Law Act 1834 effectively institutionalised the poor, without alternatives, in the workhouse. This was seen as a provision of last resort. Foucault's analysis of the disciplinary power of institutions and systems showed that labelling and segregating difference provided the necessary stimuli for the development of internal supervision (Rabinow 1984). Seeing the exclusion of 'Others' induces fear of social exclusion. The potential to become excluded is, therefore, a sufficient stimulus to induce the self-policing of deviance. The desire to be 'part' of, rather than 'excluded' from, serves the construction of the normal. The more successfully the socially included distanced themselves from those identified as being outside the normalised condition, the less the state needed to display its powers of physical coercion to enforce conformity. Those constructed as poor and insane were segregated from the rest of society, not only as physical beings but also because their voices were silenced. This process of segregation is well documented elsewhere in relation to other marginal groups, such as the black slaves in the US, and the Jews during the rise of fascism in Europe in the 1930s. Similarly, throughout the period of industrialisation, the voice of the 'Other', that is, the subjugated knowledge of those who were socially excluded, remained silenced. Liberal policies at this time also served to normalise a new form of patriarchy in society, reinforcing gendered roles – men in the public realm, women in the domestic realm.

In the second half of the nineteenth century, Liberal discourses evolved to embrace liberal-democracy and the idea that increased state involvement in managing social problems was possible without undermining the notion of individual responsibility. This change was largely due to the growing strength of the organised labour movement, the extension of the franchise, and also, partly, a result of the influence of the philanthropic movement and charitable organisations:

> inspired as much by a desire to bring about moral and spiritual betterment and to generate a sense of solidarity between the middle and working classes as it was to improve the material conditions of the poor. (O'Brien and Penna 1998: 26)

A second major influence was, however, international competition, particularly from Bismarck's Germany, which drew attention to the state of labour. Problems – such as illiteracy and sickness – came to be perceived as the nation's problem, particularly at the time of the Boer War (1899-1902). The welfare of the nation depended on the welfare of its individuals, and vice versa. Although this appeared to usher in a greater acceptance of mutuality, this merely reflected the dominance of an economic construction of welfare subjects. Without welfare the quality and availability of labour would be reduced. This discourse, which we termed 'new liberalism' in the previous chapter, was to particularly influence Lloyd George's budget of 1909, which in addition to raising revenue for extra military expenditure also raised funds for social welfare programmes. By the end of the nineteenth century, the characteristics of modern society – industrialisation, bureaucratisation and the application of technical solutions to social problems – were firmly established. Since then, the welfare debate has centred on the extent to which the state should take responsibility for promoting and producing the social wellbeing of its citizens, and on what basis welfare should be distributed.

As capitalism moved into the early twentieth century in Britain the nation's need for healthy warriors and workers intensified, and scientific methods were increasingly applied to solve the problem of adults unfit to work or fight. To some extent this changing discourse reflected recognition that poverty could be caused by social and economic factors, and not just by individual incompetence, and so was constructed as a social problem that could be solved. Within this discourse welfare subjects became problems to be solved, although they were not expected to be part of their own solution, but were to be the passive recipients of social science interventions. As we saw in the last chapter, Rowntree 'scientifically' identified the point at which poverty occurred (the 'poverty line'); the Fabians were concerned with the inefficiency and wastefulness of capitalism in relation to human resources; the National Efficiency Movement targeted the health and strength of male workers in order to improve industrial productivity; and the Eugenics movement tried to ensure that social and moral weaknesses were not passed from generation to generation. The identity of those needing welfare was recognised only in relation to their potential to work in industry or war. However, unlike cogs in a machine, these welfare subjects were understood to have economic, psychological and social needs too; a return to positivist, epidemiological thinking. In other words, the sick social body was to be healed by the application of social science in the form of economics (particularly the theories of free markets), psychology (notably psychoanalytical theories) and sociology (particularly studies of urban life). The key feature of this period was the belief that poverty could be eradicated if only the correct solutions for the poor could be found. Those unable to make the transition into work and a socially acceptable life were considered intractable, and the major concern was to prevent them 'infecting' others. Dr Barnardo, for example, believed that the influence of poor parents on their children was pernicious: 'parents are my chief difficulty everywhere; so are relatives generally ... because I take from a very low class' (cited in Petrie and James 1995: 314). As a result, many poor children in charitable care endured forcible emigration to British colonies.

In the period following the First World War, liberal philosophy largely shifted its position on free-market economics, particularly due to the influence of Keynes. Work, as a philosophical concept, is clearly central to Keynes's thesis. For Keynes, work:

> strikes at the heart of community values and the spirit of excellence. Jobs provide people with the basis for the practice of excellence in a very important sphere of their lives. For our society and others, occupations also play a part in creating individual roles and developing personal dignity. (Cited in Mullard and Spicker 1998: 21)

Keynes was largely concerned to ensure capitalism ran smoothly without extreme divisions of wealth and poverty that would threaten social cohesion. His theories provided the 'scientific' grounding for both Roosevelt's 'New Deal' in the US in the 1930s, and Beveridge's post-war welfare state in Britain. Liberals had now become 'reluctant collectivists' for the sake of protecting capitalism, although work, rather than social rights, was central to the post-war scheme. The welfare consensus after the war, therefore, can be viewed as a 'new deal', a form of what has come to be called the post-war settlement. The post-war welfare state was conceptualised in the 1942 Beveridge Report, *Social Insurance and Allied Services,* and was closely associated with the model of economic management prescribed by Keynes. Such a system of welfare has been identified as a key characteristic of all western-liberal democracies at similar stages of economic development (Kerr et al. 1962) and the apotheosis of benign social engineering (Lavalette and Pratt 1997). Keynes argued that mass production needed high levels of mass consumption, maintained by state-induced demand management. The welfare state was a particular model of social protection designed to ensure a fit and healthy population, echoing concerns earlier in the century, although this time the nation required wage-spenders not warriors. The welfare subject was constructed by this welfare discourse. As Powell states:

> The Beveridgean citizen was the fully employed (and insured) married, white, able-bodied, male worker, with other categories of people – including women, ethnic minorities, disabled people, children and elderly people – experiencing highly conditional forms of welfare exclusion outside the 'normal' universalism. (Powell 1999: 2)

So even in the context of a welfare system that rested on the notion of 'universalism' (as this was an expression of the social democratic metanarrative) many were excluded. Those household structures that did not conform to the Beveridgean notion of family formation largely lost out from the post-war settlement. However, these difficulties did not undermine the system in place until increasing global competition, in the 1970s, led to rising unemployment and economic decline, and pressure to control the level of public spending. The fragility of social commitment to universalism and collective responsibility became evident as the numbers of poor began to increase. The dominant discourse of welfare reconstructed the welfare subject by employing notions of eligibility, linked to criteria that were increasingly associated with the behaviour, or status, of potential claimants. For example, by the late 1980s, the discretionary elements of the social security system were reduced and the criteria for benefits were more tightly defined; loans were introduced instead of grants. This was an attempt to reduce expenditure on welfare benefits by excluding more people. The exposure of the vulnerability of Keynesianism to expanding international markets challenged the fundamental values underpinning the welfare consensus (Mullard and Spicker 1998). Moreover, new technology and the globalisation of labour markets meant that fewer workers were needed in Britain as cheaper workers could be found in other parts of the world. In such situations governments distance themselves from taking responsibility for the consequences of unemployment and poverty.

Welfare systems have been critiqued and classified since their very beginnings, often by the same theorists responsible for welfare policy development. However, the change of attitude towards the provision of welfare, and the welfare subject, that has taken place since the end of the so-called welfare consensus in the 1970s, has been significantly different from anything else that has taken place since the main elements of the welfare state were established in 1948. The idea that welfare can be harmful has gained ground within both major political parties during the last twenty years. Welfare, it is argued from a right and centre modernist perspective, has damaged both the economy and society. Economic changes in Britain, in particular the shift away from a mass-producing manufacturing economy towards a service-sector economy with flexible labour markets, means that labour must be ready and willing to enter and leave the labour market when required. Financial welfare provides a measure of security for those without employment, removing the incentive to enter the insecurity of the labour market and thereby depriving capital of a cheap and flexible workforce. This is exacerbated even more in the context of global markets. Cheap and productive labour can be found in many parts of the world and capital is now able to move operations to wherever that labour can be found. To remain in the market place, therefore, labour must not have expectations that are too high. From this perspective, it can be argued that the provision of welfare generates unemployment, because labour is no longer willing to respond to the needs of the market. In the long-term this is to the detriment of labour as national wealth is undermined and poverty increases. Welfare will no longer be affordable at all, it is argued, if capitalism fails.

The change in economic context is described by some commentators as a shift from 'Fordism', the organisation of heavy industrial production around scientific management techniques with a strict demarcation of labour into specialist tasks, to 'Post-Fordism', small-scale production organised around flexible labour markets. Post-Fordism has been interpreted as the end of the modern period (that is, the end of an era of economic production that started with the industrial revolution and finished with the collapse in mass production around the 1970s) and is associated with adaptable and changing markets and flexible employment patterns – for many, part-time, temporary, non-unionised, service-sector jobs. Social protection has been abandoned in this context of diversity, fragmentation and change, in the interests of economic goals. As argued by Loader and Burrows (1996), this economic transformation has had a profound impact on welfare discursive practices. Economic change is perceived to be inevitable and even desirable. On the other hand, changes in ways of living, particularly changes in gender roles and family life, are seen to be highly undesirable:

> We are witnessing a renewed emphasis on the family as the one institution which *should not* change, even though it is taken for granted that everything else around the family is changing radically ... [There is] an irony in this rush to embrace the restructuring of society according to market forces, and that is the way in which, *at the level of political rhetoric*, it is always assumed that the family should stand aside from this turbulence and should not become a location of client/provider exchanges or internal markets. (Smart 1997: 302 – original emphasis)

The discursive practices of welfare, including policies, are now aimed at removing barriers to economic activity whilst at the same time resisting certain changes in social organisation. On the one hand, many areas of life affecting the welfare subject have been deregulated, or reduced in scope and availability, as government, it is argued, has little power to swiftly and effectively reduce levels of poverty, or ameliorate its consequences without supporting the market economy. On the other hand, government is increasingly involved, through policies and legislation, in regulating the private lives of individuals in order to support normalised family life and the rearing of children.

At the end of the twentieth century, therefore, there is again an element of political consensus around the nature of welfare and the role of the state:

> In one country after another the majority of voters give their support to parties that explicitly demand the curtailment of welfare provisions, or promise more benign taxation of individual incomes ... The astounding unanimity on this point among the parties across the political spectrum served some analysts as a main argument to assert the advent of a new 'solidarity' of sorts; of a new political consensus 'beyond left and right' ... It is this change of axis around which democratic consensus is built that needs explaining. (Bauman 1998: 5)

The debate is now about how to reduce expenditure on welfare, categorise welfare applicants for purposes of new eligibility criteria (primarily to determine who should not receive welfare), manage welfare markets more efficiently and eliminate welfare 'dependency'.

Framework for analysis

Examining the current dominant discourse of welfare, which constructs the welfare subject (as 'eligible' or 'ineligible', 'high priority' or 'low priority', 'in need' or 'not in need'), allows us to identify the processes of inclusion and exclusion. According to Leonard, the dominant discourse of welfare is constructed from four supplementary discourses or narratives that are fundamental to the construction of the welfare subject. These supplementary discourses of work, consumption, family and sexuality are interconnected and related:

> Out of the many dominant discourses which exist we can identify four which appear critical in the formation of contemporary subjects of late capitalism and are especially relevant to current debates on welfare: the discourses of work, consumption, family and sexuality. These discourses are the means by which, on a daily basis, the social relations of class, gender, ethnicity, age, disability and sexuality are maintained and reproduced as elements in the subject positions of individuals. (Leonard 1997: 35)

Leonard argues that these supplementary discourses of welfare construct difference (that is, any departure from the normalised state arising from class, gender, age, race, impairment and sexual identity) as negative and a threat to social stability. Those who are not in waged work, depend on state benefits, live in other than a normalised family and are not heterosexual are outside the current construct of normality and are often subject to exclusionary processes. Conforming to the norm has become an increasingly important eligibility criteria for welfare services in postmodern society, with welfare provision becoming more selective and 'targeted' on those deemed most in need. There is hardly a single area of welfare provision where moral judgements about the welfare subject do not influence eligibility, and this is common with the formation of any dominant discourse. Recent debates have considered the eligibility of smokers for medical treatment for tobacco-related illnesses, income support for lone parents who do not work, and health information and contraception for those sexually active under the age of 16 years (the age at which sexual activity is legal between men and women). In each of these areas the concern has been to ensure that the provision of such services will not encourage recipients to continue to behave in a way that is judged morally and socially undesirable.

If we examine each of Leonard's four key partial discourses or narratives in turn, we can see how judgements are made about those defined as welfare subjects. In the case of the first, 'work', this theme has been central to social policy debates since the nineteenth century. Work has always been part of how the worth of the welfare subject has been constructed (Bauman 1998, Jones and Novak 1999), with only waged work offering social status. Still, and notwithstanding the indisputable evidence that work is in short supply (Turok and Edge 1999), the major political parties persist in engaging in discursive practices that rest on the notion that individuals can, if they are motivated, find work. The constructed culpability of the unemployed for their own predicament has, therefore, been legitimised and incorporated into the discourse of welfare. Moreover, those undertaking voluntary or caring work within the home or local community are not seen to be contributing to society's common wealth; whilst those excluded from work by reason of age, impairments or parenting responsibilities, have little value. Worse still is that much of the policy debate, from both left and right of the political spectrum, has centred on developing measures to police and control these groups to ensure that social cohesion is not threatened.

The welfare subject, therefore, is only constructed as deserving of support if paid work eludes them for reasons that are socially acceptable, such as being an elder. Those who are unable to work because of changes to the economic and demographic context in which they live are still expected to find paid work, or accept work created for welfare subjects, which is likely to be compulsory. Although the latter activity has neither the value, status nor income of waged work, it is accepted that it is better for society if the welfare subject is not allowed to be idle. Even reasons for being without paid work which were constructed as natural and normal, and thus perceived as acceptable in the past, are no longer tolerated. For example, being a non-working parent, or rather mother, of school-age children was not only socially acceptable, but socially desirable a decade ago. But no longer, as New Labour proposals to bring lone parents into the labour market demonstrate. Consequently, as we can see, the dominant discourse shaping attitudes to work is a clear factor in defining the welfare subject in postmodern times.

Leonard's second theme, 'consumption', is such a powerful narrative that it is almost impossible to imagine how our social world could be organised without it. Throughout the globe, capitalist notions of supply and demand, and the social subject as consumer, are the fundamental paradigm for economic and social planning. Even children are constructed primarily as consumers, certainly in the western world – consumers of education, consumers of leisure, and consumers of fashion – targeted by market research and advertising. Poor children are excluded by this discourse for while, on the one hand, the discourse of consumption embraces them (marketing aimed at children is indiscriminate), their lived experience excludes them. Although they live in the same consumerist culture (Seabrook 1988), the poor are not expected to desire the same goods and activities accessible to the affluent. Moreover, poor parents are to be held accountable if their children steal; punishment for their failure to instil their children with values outside the discourse of consumption.

Changing the welfare subject into the welfare consumer was a paradigm shift brought about by neo-liberal governments. It is one that remains embedded in welfare policy and practice as a result of legislative changes, in particular, the NHS and Community Care Act 1990. The neo-liberal belief that welfare, provided by markets, achieve economy, efficiency and effectiveness (the 3 'Es'), and value for money (VFM), imposed a model of welfare that equated the welfare subject as 'consumer/customer' rather than 'client/citizen'. However, as Le Grand and Bartlett (1993) argue, welfare markets cannot be considered pure markets but are, at best, 'quasi-markets' (virtual markets). This is because the welfare subject rarely has real purchasing power (consumer demand is not expressed in money terms) and services are usually purchased by a third party, such as a local authority or health purchaser, on behalf of the welfare subject. The welfare subject is not, therefore, a consumer with choice, but an 'ersatz' consumer with little or no potency to negotiate in the market. The choice of the welfare subject is likely to be between one service or no service, as choice of provision is rarely available. What little choice there is may still be denied the welfare subject by virtue of notions of ineligibility, constructions which change in the interests of a fund-holder's budget.

This latter aspect reflects the rise of 'managerialism', or 'new managerialism', in welfare services, representing, in essence, the rise of the professional manager over the welfare professional. Managing state welfare in such a context is perceived as little different to managing any other enterprise. This has brought about a radical shift in the culture of welfare organisations. Prior to this change, the responsibility of the welfare-state professional was to make decisions about the eligibility of the welfare subject for services with little or no mandate to manage the costs of such services. As budgets were held centrally, decision-making about service eligibility was, therefore, distanced from decisions about finance. Consequently, the focus of the professional was primarily on the welfare subject rather than the cost of the service. Now, resource considerations are paramount, due to pressure to provide a service at the lowest cost. The worth of the welfare subject is held directly in the balance against the cost of the service. The operation of the market means, therefore, that the aged and others with little economic value are likely to have lower priority for services than those who are potentially economically active. Managerialism creates the conditions within which the welfare subject becomes another unit to be managed at the lowest cost. The introduction of devolved budgets and management of unit costs means the minimisation of difference between welfare 'units' if financial comparisons are to be made. So, for example, much attention was devoted to the definition of a 'social' bath compared to a 'health' bath, following the imposition of welfare markets into social care brought about by the NHS and Community Care Act 1990. This was because the former service to elders and disabled people in the community involved costs to social services, and the latter to the health authority. Baths for pleasure were presumably not to be paid for by either agency.

The affluent in society, however, are able to act like welfare customers, with some power to make choices within the private sector. Therefore, whilst markets may have brought empowerment and choice into welfare provision for those with purchasing power, a two-tier welfare system has been created with the poor receiving a residual state service:

> [D]issatisfaction with state welfare is not driven by experience of improved standards of consumption in the non-state sector, so much as by the concerns and needs of the less privileged groups in relation to state provision. The traditional agenda of a redistributive welfare state, designed to meet the needs of those least able to look after themselves in the market, may still strike a chord with public opinion. (Taylor-Gooby 1998: 472)

Market concepts in welfare are deeply flawed (Petrie and Wilson 1999), although they continue to be propounded. As Jones and Novak (1999) argue, New Labour's acceptance of the market differs little from that of the New Right. Global markets are accepted as the final arbiter in economic and social life and, as far as welfare is concerned, New Labour propose a continuation of internal markets in state provision. The welfare subject is embraced and seduced by the narrative of consumption, but what is constructed as choice is experienced as disempowerment. Despite discursive practices turning the welfare subject into the welfare customer, the socially excluded remain where they have always been, without power and without choice.

Moving on to Leonard's third theme, the 'family', available evidence shows that the normalised family, the heterosexual, two-parent marital relationship, sustainable until death, is only one of many different family forms. By 1993, for example, more than 30 per cent of children were born outside marriage (Hoggett et al. 1996) and this trend continues. Both major political parties, however, continue to draft policies aimed at supporting or returning to the social construct of the nuclear family as normal, on the grounds that this is the best way to bring up children and to maintain social cohesion. Those who do not live in such groups are not only constructed as deviant, but are marginalised, particularly lone parents. Certainly, there is great resistance to developing services to support these alternative groups, and indeed there are policies which actively seek to discourage them (for instance, the Child Support Agency and a 'cooling-off' period in divorce cases). The construct of the normalised family, a wage-earning male and nurturing female, a family structure that is self-contained and self-reliant, is so pervasive that it affects almost every aspect of welfare. Yet there is a wealth of evidence demonstrating changing couple relationships across all postmodern, or late capitalist, societies as a response to changing social conditions:

> This lack of concern [with marriage] is nothing new among groups accustomed to forming and dissolving informal unions without coming into contact with legal institutions. Among these groups legal marriage is but an aspect of the irrelevance of traditional American family law, law that is viewed as being property-oriented and organised around the ideals of a dominant social group. Lack of concern with marriage law has been growing, however, among many who definitely are not outside the mainstream of American life. Until recently these converts accepted unquestioningly the traditional structures of the enacted law, but now they find that on balance the enacted law offers no advantages over informal arrangements. (Glendon, cited in Hoggett et al. 1996: 37)

Yet, alternatives to the normalised family, such as the family networks of lone parents, particularly lone mothers, are constructed as dysfunctional and harmful to society (Edwards and Duncan 1997). These women are held responsible not only for the behaviour of their own children, but also for the disintegration of the social fabric of society. These notions reflect commonly held beliefs that lone parents conceive children in order to unfairly acquire scarce resources, such as financial benefits and housing. Rearing children without a husband is viewed with hostility and suspicion. Family life that differs from the marital, heterosexual, long-term, monogamous relationship with children model has become the target of social policies designed to enforce normality.

The normalised family is also expected to provide welfare for its members. Major changes in welfare programmes, such as Care in the Community, designed to keep those constructed as needing care out of institutions, depends on the unpaid labour of family members, mainly women (Williams 1995). It is accepted by both major parties that the family should look after those needing care, and welfare is there to support, not replace, those families constructed as caring. Even so, there is evidence to show that the level of support for carers is woefully inadequate, and those who fall through the family-support net must rely, at best, on a residual state service. For some, such as those with enduring mental illnesses, the prison system may act in lieu of other forms of provision (ONS 1998). For many young care leavers, the street becomes their only form of housing provision (Kincaid 1999).

The discourse of family, as with Leonard's other themes, is profoundly interconnected with his fourth narrative, 'sexuality'. Concepts of couple relationships and sexuality have been powerful mediators of welfare policy since industrialisation, with heterosexuality constructed as natural, and thereby, awarded a privileged status position:

> [I]f we examine the UK welfare state through the lens of sexuality we can see that its foundations are firmly constructed on the basis of normal heterosexual relations, with the heterosexual family form central to the provision of welfare and women's major role as mothers and carers seen as 'natural' and 'normal'. (Carabine 1998: 127).

Sexuality at the end of the 1990s is even more closely allied to the formation of adult couple relationships within family structures and gendered roles than ever before (Bernardes 1997), particularly in the context of HIV and AIDS. The latter led to the development of new disciplinary procedures which allowed the reaffirmation of dominant patriarchal heterosexual power structures, reconstructed in both the neo-liberal, and New Labour's, reassertion of normalised family values:

> The sexual epidemic is rife with opportunities for conflicting political inscriptions. The anxiety induced by the regulatory production of the epidemic is conducive to conservative political agendas. The anxiety that becomes mobilised around the connection of sex to death in AIDS entails increased fetishization of life as such. Hence, the anxiety produced through the epidemic is displaced and condensed in the regulation of sexual reproduction and the promotion of the family as the supposedly exclusive site of safe sex. (Singer 1993: 29)

As Singer argues, in the age of AIDS, sexuality has been reconstructed as a site for further investigation in our lives. Sexuality is not only redefined in terms of its dangers and risks, which enables capitalist growth through the development of the safe sex industry – such as the dating services offering assurance of contact with pre-screened clients, telephone sex services, cyber-sex, home-based markets in erotica, and so on; it is also redefined in a way that seeks to discipline pleasures, and impose ideological concepts about sexual desires and relationships, seeking to contain these within the confines of safe sex within the heterosexual nuclear family (Singer 1993). Such strong social disapproval of difference in relation to sexual behaviour is hypocritical, given that political parties are frequently in the position of having their politicians publicly exposed for living hidden sexual lives, and having sexual relationships that are constructed as abnormal and undesirable. It may seem that homosexuality is now tolerated more readily than in earlier decades, but welfare policies, such as those discouraging adoption by gay men and women, demonstrate only too clearly the processes whereby gay men and women remain excluded.

The idea that there is a 'once and for all romantic love' that is to be found is embedded in much of the legislation and policy relating to normalised family life (Giddens 1992). For example, collective ways of living and rearing children are barely acknowledged, and certainly not supported. Other ways of establishing couple relationships are viewed negatively. Arranged marriages, for example, are often seen as oppressive to women, and those racial groups who value this practice are viewed with suspicion. Judgements are made about the nature of their couple relationships that are sweeping and indiscriminate:

> The male-dominated nature of family life creates a very different experience for women within ethnic minority cultures ... The reason for the attempt by ethnic

minorities to control the lives of women lies in the need to maintain family honour. (Wilson, cited in Hoggett et al. 1996: 16)

The marriages of people from black and other racial minority groups are subject to scrutiny during immigration processes to ensure they conform to white ethno-centric constructs of family or relationship.

The discourse on sexuality also has a vivid age dimension. For instance, older people, and disabled bodies, are not expected to maintain their sexuality. Sexual health information, particularly about HIV and AIDS, is not targeted on older people, yet research in California shows an increase in HIV infection amongst this group, linked to the unrecognised use of prostitution and lack of health information (Kooperman 1994). Sexuality also excludes the young as sexual activity is only legitimate for heterosexuals aged 16 or over and gay men aged 18 or over. Sexual activity under this age is criminalised if with an adult, and pathologised if taking place between young people themselves. The social construction of non-heterosexuality is supplemented by the construction of deviance, thus generating a social construction of sexuality.

Changing the welfare discourse

The discourse of welfare is constructed as a binary of 'Other than' and 'normal'. For example, the 'sick' and the 'healthy', and the 'unemployed' and the 'employed', and so on. These categories are usually rigidly defined, often in statute, and become the threshold condition for access to, or ineligibility for, welfare. Those who cannot lay claim to constructed normality through paid work, a recognised family role, heterosexual relationships and the resources to function as a consumer, are likely to be constructed as welfare subjects. Within the current dominant discourse most welfare subjects are constructed as non-productive, draining the resources of those who work, and without careful monitoring and judicious negative incentives, are likely to become 'welfare dependent'. Targeting those who 'really' need help has become the accepted approach to welfare resource distribution of both the neo-liberals and New Labour. Welfare distribution by 'tick-box', whilst giving the appearance of consistency, efficiency, clarity and fairness, is value-laden and judgmental. Even more worryingly, such approaches ignore and undermine many people's lived experiences. This makes survival with dignity impossible, and impoverishes the rest of us by excluding those individuals, and their actual and potential value, from our society. If, as we shall argue, policies arising out of the discourse of welfare are inevitably flawed, it is necessary to become critical of the welfare discourse and change discursive practices.

As has been shown there are many theorists who, accepting the notion of discourse and fragmented power, are still concerned to explore the possibility of collective action for the common good. Although we do not intend to debate the merits of this perspective – as opposed to Marxism, for example – as a way of dealing with power relationships in society as a whole, these ideas highlight ways in which the current discourse of welfare can be challenged. The commonality of these approaches is to suggest that there are always contradictions within discourse. Recognising contradictions invites challenge. Using an environmental metaphor, this enables us to view the landscape from another hillock and recognise that some needs, such as the need for water, transcend territorial boundaries. Freire, as long ago as 1972, promoted the value of pedagogy as a means by which the poor and oppressed could understand their own discourse and become empowered. He calls this 'critical consciousness' (Freire 1972). Foucault talks of 'reverse discourse' (Foucault 1984); Giddens of 'reflexivity' (Giddens 1992); Bauman of 'Being-for the Other' (Bauman 1995); and Leonard of becoming the 'resistant moral agent' (Leonard 1997):

> For modern welfare to flourish ... it must be the basis for the kind of welfare which no longer excludes the Other because it understands that its knowledge as an agent of welfare is not absolute or universal but based upon cultural discourses and practices which are always open to critique. It is a form of welfare in which the subject is not seen as potentially homogeneous but as reflecting diversity and constituted by resistance. A conception of the subject as a *resistant moral agent* provides one means by which a welfare project can be reconstructed. (Leonard 1997: 162 – original emphasis)

The idea of a modern welfare project, defined as 'a design which can be chosen and justified in its choice, to which society aims and struggles' (Sarup 1993: 167), is an interesting one. This notion implies a process, involving contextuality and relationality, rather than stasis; a condition to be aimed for, rather than a goal to be arrived at, once and for all. Two prerequisites for a modern welfare project are, according to Leonard, 'interdependence' which enables mutuality to be achieved without excluding on the grounds of difference, and what he calls, with echoes of earlier feminist political activity, 'consciousness-raising'.

Necessary to this welfare project is 'collective resistance', which Leonard defines as a coming together of welfare subjects to challenge dominant discourses. He also argues that aiming to meet common human needs enables solidarity among diversity. The most basic human needs for food, shelter, social contact, and so on, transcend race, gender, age, sexuality, disability, culture, geography and time, and provide the basis for welfare policy:

> The idea of common needs implies an optimal level of protection against serious harm and suffering, a protection which requires not only the curative elements of health and social care but also measures to prevent avoidable harm and suffering. (Leonard 1997: 167)

Changing the discourse of welfare, therefore, suggests participation in decision-making and challenging role differentiation. For example, pressure by women, in different places and times, through networks and alliances, together with some medical professionals (who recognised their knowledge as a partial, not total discourse), has led to less medical intervention in the birth process, and more control for the mother in labour. This process can happen outside of (or even despite) pressure to the contrary. For example, notwithstanding racist public opinion and social and economic policies during the last 20 years, Britain is now more overtly multi-racial than ever before in all aspects of social life. Liverpool City Council and the Housing Corporation (Merseyside Region) have recently commissioned research to examine the increase in self-classification as Black Other; the hypothesis being that this means second and third generation Black British. This mirrors debates in the US arguing that single-race classifications are no longer useful in multi-racial societies, as they ignore and undermine individual mixed-race narratives, notwithstanding, continued racism. What is required then, is the recognition of individual truths which inevitably brings awareness of contradictions within discourse and discursive practices. Welfare can then become a site of resistance and potential liberation. Valuing and protecting difference and diversity is part of the process of challenging the power interests within dominant discourses, whilst at the same time interdependence, notwithstanding difference, ensures collective action is possible. Leonard calls this 'a continuation of the narrative of emancipation, reconstituted to fit the Postmodern conditions of late capitalism' (Leonard 1997: 49).

Under the neo-liberals difference was often framed negatively and, although New Labour welfare policies can appear to reflect a more positive acknowledgement of difference – such as, an apparent acceptance of different family forms by increasing resources for childcare to support lone and working parents – the welfare discourse of both political parties is manifested in strategies of exclusion. Lone-mother families are undesirable families to both Conservatives and New Labour on both moral and economic grounds. They are not seen as contributing to social wealth, but are constructed as second-best families and an economic burden. The postmodern perspective, by exposing oppressiveness and exclusiveness within the values of grand theories, or metanarratives, and deconstructing welfare discourse and discursive practices, particularly social policy development, offers a different lens through which processes of social exclusion and unequal power relationships can be understood.

Therefore, in relation to legislation and central government policies, a change in emphasis is required. First, as Jack and Jordan (1999) argue, social capital must be rebuilt by reducing the inequality gap between rich and poor, by distributing collective wealth more equitably. Second, there must be a move away from detailed and prescriptive legislation and central government policy which focuses on difference towards the promotion of a dialogical concept of welfare. Policy and practice detail must be delegated to local areas and communities of interest. The characteristics of local discursive practices, therefore, will reflect local needs. It can be anticipated that such welfare services are not likely to be static, but will change as local needs change. There are many and varied proposals, but the main barrier to change is the popular resistance to constructing the welfare subject as anything other than a threat to, and a drain on, society. The nature of the welfare discourse and construction of the welfare subject is an important factor as to the degree of exclusion welfare policies bring about. Any policy is likely to have unforeseen consequences to a greater or lesser extent, but state intervention into social life is especially unpredictable because of the rapidly changing nature of personal and social relationships in the late capitalist society (Giddens 1992).

By deconstructing power interests within the dominant discourse of welfare, the postmodernist position offers social policy-makers, and practitioners, insight into policies and practices that meet the needs of a society characterised by fragmentation, diversity and difference. Social policy needs to develop within a different context, within the context of a discourse of welfare that embraces broader social agendas, reflecting diverse needs, articulated and defined by the individuals and groups concerned. This requires a new role for welfare, one that aims to facilitate dialogue and recognises contextuality; a role that enables discursive practices to be fluid and relational by exposing and challenging the processes of exclusion and oppression, outlined above, and encouraging active participation in policy-making and implementation. The subsequent chapters will examine key welfare discursive practices, including policies, in relation to health, education, housing, income maintenance and family, with this perspective in mind.

References

Bauman, Z. (1995) *Life in Fragments: Essays in Postmodern Morality*, Blackwell, Oxford.

Bauman, Z. (1998) *Work, consumerism and the new poor*, Open University Press, Buckingham.

Bernardes, J. (1997) *Family Studies – An Introduction*, Routledge, London.

Bertens, H. (1995) *The Idea of the Postmodern*, Routledge, London.

Beveridge, W. (1942) *Social Insurance and Allied Services*, HMSO, London.

Billington, R., Hockney, J. and Strawbridge, S. (1998) *Exploring Self and Society*, Macmillan, Basingstoke.

Carabine, J. (1998) 'New horizons? New insights? Postmodernising social policy and the case of sexuality', in J. Carter, (ed.) *Postmodernity and the Fragmentation of Welfare*, Routledge, London, pp. 121-135.

Dean, H. and Khan, Z. (1997) 'Muslim Perspectives on Welfare', *Journal of Social Policy*, 26 Part 2, April, pp. 193-209.

Eagleton, T. (1994) *Ideology – an introduction*, Verso, London.

Edwards, R. and Duncan, S. (1997) 'Supporting the family: lone mothers, paid work and the underclass debate' in *Critical Social Policy*, Vol. 17. No. 4, pp. 29-49.

Foucault, M. (1984) *The History of Sexuality, An Introduction*, Peregrine Books, Harmondsworth.

Freire, P. (1972) *Pedagogy of the Oppressed*, Penguin, London.

Giddens, A. (1992) *The Consequences of Modernity*, Polity Press, Cambridge.

Hoggett, B., Pearl, D., Cooke, E. and Bates, P. (1996) *The Family, Law and Society – cases and materials*, Butterworths, London.

Jack, G. and Jordan, B. (1999) 'Social Capital and Child Welfare' in *Children and Society*, Vol. 13, pp. 242-56.

Jones, C. and Novak, T. (1999) *Poverty, Welfare and the Disciplinary State* Routledge, London.

Jordan, B. (1996) *A Theory of Poverty and Social Exclusion*, Polity Press, Cambridge.

Kerr, C., Dunlop, J., Harbison, F. and Myers, C. (1962) *Industrialism and Industrial Man*, Heinemann, London.

Kincaid, S. (1999) *A new approach to homelessness and allocations*, Shelter, http://www.shelter.org.uk/news/essay.html, 28 October.

Kooperman, L. (1994) 'A Survey of Gay and Bisexual Men Age 50 and Older. Aids Related Knowledge, Attitude, Belief, and Behavior', *Aids Patient Care*, Vol. 8, No.3, pp 114-17.

Lavalette, M. and Pratt, A. (1997) *Social Policy – A Conceptual and Theoretical Introduction*, Sage, London.

Le Grand, J. and Bartlett, W. (1993) *Quasi-Markets and Social Policy*, Macmillan, Basingstoke.

Leonard, P. (1997) *Postmodern Welfare – Reconstructing an Emancipatory Project*, Sage, London.

Loader, B. and Burrows, R. (1996) 'Towards a post-Fordist welfare state?' in R. Burrows and B. Loader, (eds.) *Towards a Post-Fordist Welfare State?*, Routledge, London, pp. 1-10.

Mullard, M. and Spicker, P. (1998) *Social Policy in a Changing Society*, Routledge, London.

Novak, T. (1997) 'Poverty and the "Underclass"' in M. Lavalette and A. Pratt, (eds.) *Social Policy – A Conceptual and Theoretical Introduction*, Sage, London, pp. 214-227.

O'Brien, M. and Penna, S. (1998) *Theorising Welfare: Enlightenment and Modern Society*, Sage, London.

ONS (Office for National Statistics) (1998), *Report on Mental Health of Prison Population*, ONS, London.

Petrie, S. and James, A. (1995) 'Partnership with Parents' in K. Wilson and A. James, (eds.) *The Child Protection Handbook*, Balliere-Tindall, London, pp. 313-34.

Petrie, S. and Wilson, K. (1999) 'Towards the Disintegration of Child Welfare Services', *Social Policy and Administration*, Vol. 33, No.2, pp. 181-196.

Plant, J. (1999) *Regulated instability: deconstructing childhood in residential child care*, unpublished thesis.

Powell, M. (1999) *'New Labour, New Welfare State?: The 'Third Way' in British Social Policy'*, The Policy Press, Bristol.

Rabinow, P. (1984) *The Foucault Reader – an introduction to Foucault's thoughts*, Penguin, London.

Sarup, M. (1993) *An Introductory Guide to Post-Structuralism and Postmodernism*, Harvester Wheatsheaf, London.

Seabrook, J. (1988) *The Race for Riches: The Human Cost of Wealth*, Marshall Pickering, Basingstoke

Singer, L. (1993) *Erotic Welfare: Sexual Theory and Politics in the Age of Epidemic*, Routledge, London.

Smaje, C. (1996) *Social Policy, Postmodernism and Race*, paper to conference 'Postmodernity and the Fragmentation of Welfare', University of Teeside 9th-10th September 1996.

Smart, C. (1997) 'Wishful Thinking and Harmful Tinkering? Sociological Reflections on Family Policy', in *Journal of Social Policy*, Vol. 26, Part 3, July, pp. 301-21.

Taylor-Gooby, P. (1998) 'THINGS CAN ONLY GET BETTER: expectations and the welfare state,' in *Policy and Politics* Vol. 26, No. 4, Oct., pp. 471-76.

Titmuss, R. (1970) *The Gift Relationship: From Human Blood to Social Policy*, Allen and Unwin, London.

Turok, I. and Edge, N. (1999) *The jobs gap in Britain's cities?*, The Policy Press, Bristol.

Williams, F. (1995) *Social Policy – A critical introduction*, Polity Press, Cambridge.

4   Health Policies

Introduction

As has been shown in Chapters Two and Three, the 'health' of welfare subjects has been a concern for governments at various points in history. Following the Boer War (1899-1902), the government raised money for social welfare programmes to deal with the poor physical health of men destined for the armed forces. The Keynesian welfare state set up after the Second World War established a particular model of social protection designed to ensure a fit and healthy population. This chapter will begin by highlighting key features in the historical development of health care in Britain to show how these continue to impact on the construction of contemporary health provision for welfare subjects. In order to better understand how changing constructs of 'ill health' and 'health' constitute the welfare subject, the health policies of the Conservatives and New Labour will be examined using the concept of a dominant discourse of welfare within which the supplementary discourses of 'work', 'consumption', 'family' and 'sexuality' are critical to the formation of the subject in postmodern times (Leonard 1997). It will be argued that these constructs of 'ill health' and 'health' arise as much from social and moral imperatives as from biological states. Furthermore, it will be argued that the constructed culpability of the welfare subject for their state of well-being emerges whenever the health-care issues of marginalised individuals or groups arise. As the welfare subject is rarely seen holistically, health policies tend to focus on different aspects of health at different times.

Throughout the chapter, health policies will be viewed as involving more than just the provision of personal health care. Major advances in health have come from government intervention involving public health measures and housing improvements, rather than from personal medical services (McKeown 1976). In addition, this chapter deals with the related issue of community care for elders and disabled people, and the broader issues of public health policy. The policies of the Conservatives and New Labour will, therefore, be considered within two broad programmatic themes. These are health policies aimed at individuals, including medical treatment and health promotion in hospitals and the community, and policies aimed at social behaviour or aspects of social life in order to improve the health of society as a whole.

Health policies and the state

The welfare subject and personal health care

Much of the present-day organisation of medicine was established in the second half of the nineteenth century. The features of health provision with Victorian origins include:

- the existence of a range of medical specialisms
- the dominant position of the medical profession in general and of hospital doctors in particular
- the exclusion of general practitioners (GPs) from hospitals and their inferior status within the profession
- the practice by which patients could only obtain consultation with a hospital doctor through referral by a GP.

These features have remained substantially in place despite all the changes in ownership, organisation and delivery of health care over the last century (Doyal 1979). They reflect a positivist and patriarchal approach to health care. Firstly, the welfare subject is constructed as either 'healthy' or 'unhealthy', a binarism that rarely reflects the lived experience of most people. Secondly, the unhealthy body is constructed as a problem that can be solved by the application of 'expert' knowledge. Finally, the medical expert has usually been male, white and affluent.

The radicalism associated with the Second World War played a major role in the creation of the National Health Service (NHS). This development also reflected the dominance of the bio-medical model of health, with 'good health' defined in relation to the absence of ascertainable diseases or abnormal pathology. Furthermore, these constructs were intimately connected with the social and gender roles that the subject was expected to carry out:

> [Good health can] be seen in terms of the ability to carry out certain physical tasks or to perform certain social roles. These may be related to age, sex and

gender, occupation, ethnicity or other social division, so either doctors or lay people may describe an individual as being 'healthy for their age', or, 'healthy, given a particular disability'. (Allsop 1998: 116)

The government planned for a huge expansion of the number of hospital beds in an Emergency Hospital Service designed to cater for the large numbers of bombing victims that the war was expected to produce. The wartime policy also involved attempts to equalise the geographical distribution of medical staff and equipment. It provided a 'universal' and free system of health care covering hospital medicine and general practice, organised in three branches. For acute hospitals, the organisational framework that had developed in the voluntary hospitals was adopted, except in mental hospitals where the system used in the former local authority hospitals, which were run by a Medical Superintendent, was retained. The ability of the affluent to purchase private health care did not change when the NHS was established. Consultants kept control over 'their' beds, with the right to practice privately and to use NHS facilities for this purpose; they received salaries for previously unpaid hospital work as well as the chance of substantial 'merit awards' dispensed by their representatives. The second branch of the NHS encompassed general practice, along with dentistry and ophthalmic services. This was provided through Local Executive Committees. GPs remained self-employed and contracted their services. Apart from some controls over the distribution of GPs, few changes were made in the form of service provided apart from the abolition of charges. The third branch of the NHS was assigned to local authorities, whose health committees became responsible for a number of services that did not involve the extensive use of doctors, such as home nursing, health visiting, ambulances, health centres, midwifery, and the care of the mentally and physically disabled.

In effect, the NHS combined a largely, but not wholly, bureaucratic system of administration with a degree of operational control by the key professionals responsible for health care. In this apparent context of 'radicalism', however, the welfare subject was exposed to exclusionary processes that marginalised many women, racial minority groups and other groups:

When Beveridge announced his attack on the five giants – Want, Squalor, Idleness, Ignorance and Disease – he hid the giants Racism and Sexism, and the fights behind them, behind statues to the Nation and the White Family. (Williams 1995: 162)

Embedded in health-care organisation from Victorian times to the NHS, constructions of 'work', 'consumption', 'family' and 'sexuality' have been central to the provision of services. As has been shown in Chapter Three, the welfare state assumed the normalised family, a heterosexual couple with children, dependent on a family wage earned by the male breadwinner whilst the woman remained, unwaged, in the domestic sphere.

Health policy developments have been largely founded on exclusionary discourses of welfare drawn particularly from notions of perfection and superiority, with the reference point for this being 'the white, often male, physically and mentally-able person' (Sibley 1995: 14) – ideally the heterosexual family man, in paid work, with a responsible attitude to 'consumption'. By incorporating the aetiology of illness and disease into the welfare discourse, the medical system has been able to categorise and problematise individual ways of behaving. Foucault, for instance, identified the way medical science's focus on the body facilitated the increasing extension of surveillance and control over, and into, our lives. The medical discourse was increasingly used to define the body into narrower terms, thereby establishing 'norms' from which deviations could be identified and corrected. Foucault specifically cited the medicalisation of sexuality, which created four 'objects' for treatment: the hysterical woman, the masturbating child, the Malthusian couple (socialised procreative behaviour) and the pervert (the pathologisation of perverse pleasure) (Foucault 1984). All kinds of 'social problems' (obesity, unwanted pregnancies, childlessness, idleness, the criminal mind, and so on) and individual pathologies (the child batterer, the alcoholic, the schizophrenic, the promiscuous gay, and so on) have been named and defined by the medical profession (Allsop 1998).

In relation to 'mental ill health', a range of discursive practices and constructions of 'images of difference' have been played out throughout the development of British health policy. For example, in the late nineteenth century, the criminologist Cesare Lombroso produced photographic representations of criminality and madness, demonstrating 'the historical importance of physical categorisation in the cultural construction of normality and deviance' (Sibley 1995: 17). Lombroso's photographs:

Point to a connection between visual images of physical imperfection, according to his scale of being which differentiates the normal and deviant, and mental illness or disability, conditions which threaten the boundaries of the self. (Sibley 1995: 19)

This early obsession with identifying the physical characteristics of 'mad' and 'bad' served to delineate the boundaries between 'normality' and the 'Other', permitting the latter to be excluded in institutions. This process has continued throughout this century, albeit using more subtle forms of exclusion within the 'community', particularly through the use of the 'disease metaphor' in medical science. However, in the fields of mental illness and disability, and social welfare generally, a significant move from institutionalisation took place beginning with the Mental Health Act 1959. This Act encouraged an 'open door' policy based on voluntary admissions but, as will be shown, this did not lead to greater social 'inclusion' of those labelled mentally-ill. By the 1990s, there was an increase in powers of control and surveillance in the community and a re-casting of mental ill health as something dangerous and to be feared (Payne 1999).

The NHS became part of the post-war political consensus. There was no attempt to abolish it when the Conservatives were re-elected in 1951, and for the first twenty years of the NHS the main thrust of policy remained expansionary. It was widely expected at its inception that the operation of the NHS would lead to a healthier population, albeit within the notion of the medical model of health, and an eventual reduction in expenditure not only on health, but also on the costs of lost production:

It is a logical corollary to the payment of high benefits in disability that determined efforts should be made by the State to reduce the number of cases for which benefit is needed. It is a logical corollary to the receipt of high benefits in disability that the individual should recognise the duty to be well and to co-operate in all steps which may lead to diagnosis of disease in early stages when it can be prevented. Disease and accidents must be paid for in any case, in lessened power of production and in idleness. (From the report on Social Insurance and Allied Services, cited in Allsop 1998: 294)

Lower expenditure did not occur, however. Concerns were increasingly expressed at the variations that existed in health expenditure and in health costs from one area to another. The historical legacies of variations in health expenditure were initially supposed to be tackled following the reorganisation of the health service in 1974. The NHS (Reorganisation)

Act 1973 established a new structure for health provision, and was implemented in 1974 with support from both Labour and the Conservatives. While the NHS plans were strongly influenced by the principles of administrative science and managerialism, reflecting a positivist approach to the health concerns of the subject, the major role of medical professionalism was not seriously questioned at this time. The three branches of the existing service were brought within a single organisational framework. However, professional dominance over delivery was maintained through 'management by consensus' at the various levels of control, which amounted to a medical veto. As medical intervention was often able to preserve the lives of patients who then required further regular and more expensive treatment, expenditure actually increased due to the rising numbers of old people in the population. Medicine was seen as primarily technologically driven, with skilled staff and equipment increasingly concentrated in hospitals where treatments took place. However, hospitalisation may deprive us of our freedoms and leave us docile:

> When subjected to hospitalisation, one occupies the paradoxical position of losing one's usual site of validation in a system of gazes and regards. One is outside one's world and, hence, invisible in one's world, while also remaining perpetually on display ... Such mechanisms help to produce and circulate a kind of paranoia in the realization that we can be controlled by what others know about us, without our knowing what or that they know. (Singer 1993: 104)

The domination of the medical model, medical expert and hospital treatments was evident throughout the 1970s, and more and more individuals and conditions were drawn into the construct of ill health. Increases in health-care expenditure led to periodic alarms and reviews, though no serious attempt to restrict the scope of the services was made. Costs continued to rise – a major factor in this was the continuing advance of medical science and technology. The increased capital intensity of hospital medical procedures was also associated with the growth in the paramedical professions such as radiography, physiotherapy, occupational therapy and dietetics, thus further increasing staff and expenditure on equipment. As a result of the increasing cost of hospital provision, the proportion of the health budget devoted to it has increased during the post-war period. As economic dislocation continued in the 1970s, and in the aftermath of the financial crisis of 1976, the Labour government formulated plans for cuts in expenditure. Health spending was budgeted to rise at its slowest rate since the inception of the NHS (Webster 1998). Substantial changes in the pattern of care have taken place since the war. In physical medicine, the dominance of hospital treatment has continued. However, there has been a trend towards shortening the length of hospital stay required for many treatments.

Public health and welfare subjects

While the state has played a major role in the provision of personal health care throughout the twentieth century, far less emphasis has been put on public health measures, unless disease has been seen as a threat to the dominant power interests:

> Disease is a more potent danger if it is contagious. The fear of infection leads to the erection of the barricades to resist the spread of disease, polluted others. The idea of a disease spreading from a 'deviant' or radicalised minority to threaten the 'normal' majority with infection has particular power. (Sibley 1995: 25)

This idea permitted the early interventions of the British state in the nineteenth century to control the spread of what were perceived as 'working-class diseases', such as typhoid, cholera and syphilis, into middle-class areas:

> The poor as a source of pollution and moral danger were clearly identified in contemporary accounts of the nineteenth-century capitalist city. As socio-spatial segregation became yet more pronounced, the distance between the affluent and the poor ensured the persistence of stereotyped conceptions of the other. Social and spatial distancing contributed to the labelling of areas of poverty as deviant and threatening ... [The poor's] degradation was connected in Chadwick's view with their lack of control over desire: 'short-lived, improvident, reckless and intemperate, with an habitual avidity for sensual gratifications'. (Sibley 1995: 55-56)

Besides protecting the middle classes, health intervention has, since the nineteenth century, largely aimed to ensure that individuals are physically and mentally capable of performing their appropriate role in society – women as mothers and carers, men as producers and soldiers, children as pupils and home-helpers, and so forth. The Chadwick Report on public health, in 1842, was largely concerned with the effects of ill health on the 'labouring classes'. Arnold White's assessment of the population in 1901,

Efficiency and Empire, was primarily concerned with breeding strong mothers and men capable of defending the nation in wartime:

> Spectacled school-children hungry, strumous and epileptic, grow into consumptive bridegrooms and scrofulous brides ... If a voice be raised in protest against the unhealthy perversion of the command, 'Be ye fruitful and multiply' it is drowned in a chorus of sickly emotion ... In the Manchester district 11,000 men offered themselves for war service between the outbreak of hostilities in October 1899 and July 1900. Of this number 8000 were found to be physically unfit to carry a rifle and stand the fatigues of discipline. Of the 3000 who were accepted only 1200 attained the moderate standard of muscular power and chest measurement required by the military authorities. (White 1901, cited in Allsop 1998: 285)

One of the most important aspects of health policy concerns the extent to which it is designed to reduce inequalities and the particular inequalities on which the highest priority is placed. Inequalities in health can be viewed in a variety of ways. Statistics can be used to depict the pattern of 'class', 'gender' and 'race' inequality in relation to mortality and morbidity; that is, in relation to both death and disease. These forms of inequality can be viewed as measures of the outcomes of health policies although, as we have argued above, it needs to be remembered that health involves much more than provision for personal health care. Indeed, there is considerable evidence to show that personal health care is not a major factor in producing the existing pattern of social inequality in relation to mortality and morbidity. Far more important are a range of other social factors, such as housing, income and environmental conditions (Acheson 1998).

Neo-liberalism, health policies and welfare discourse

The welfare subject and personal health care

When considering the health policies of the neo-liberals it becomes clear that the supplementary discourse of 'consumption' was critical to the formation of the welfare subject as internal markets within health, and later social care, became the paradigm for service distribution. Government health policies since the late 1970s embraced New Right economic and political principles, based on tight controls on public spending and the encouragement of private provision. The election of a Conservative government in 1979 intensified the move towards neo-liberal policies. Competition and market forces were introduced to increase the efficiency of the delivery of services. The New Right also argued that policy formulation had become too responsive to the state bureaucracy and to health professionals, and this led to the accommodation of special interests and the over-expansion of state provision.

The Conservative government's NHS Act 1980, ended the phasing out of pay-beds, reduced restrictions on the development of private hospitals, and required health authorities to seek co-operation with the private sector. It allowed health authorities to undertake fund-raising activities and ended the commitment of the 1946 Act to fund all essential expenditure. The Conservative government also initiated an element of privatisation by encouraging the private provision of domestic services in the NHS. Other moves took place towards a less bureaucratic and more market-based approach. The administration was now seen to involve considerable duplication and, from 1982, 200 new District Health Authorities (DHAs) replaced the Area Health Authorities. The new Conservative government became concerned to introduce business methods into the running of the NHS. Attempts to limit the autonomy and power of the medical profession began with the introduction of private-sector managers and management techniques. However, these changes were seen to have failed to exert sufficient managerial control over the doctors (Cox 1991).

The government was, therefore, prepared to adopt a more radical solution in the form of a quasi- or provider market. The proposal for this was outlined in the White Paper *Working for Patients* (DoH 1989b). This argued that 'value for money' (VFM), rather than more funding, was the solution to the problems of health care. The White Paper proposals involved both marketisation and managerialisation, and can also be viewed as an attempt to 'roll back the state' by opening up more of the welfare state to competitive market forces. The purchaser/provider split within the NHS was enforced by the NHS and Community Care Act 1990. It involved a move towards a 'mixed economy of welfare' in health care, in so much as those that could afford to do so, the consumers, were encouraged to exit the NHS in favour of private health-care provision (Harrison et al. 1990). Since this 'market' is established by the state, rather than developing as a result of the actions of individual private consumers and producers, it is sometimes known as a 'quasi-market'. A feature of this particular quasi-market is that the consumers are not the people who actually receive the service, that is, the patients, but rather the health authorities and GPs who act on their behalf (Cutler and Waine 1997). Within quasi-markets 'contracts' exist between purchasers and providers, and do not include the patient. The welfare subject is effectively disempowered as health managers decide what services they should receive and from where:

> NHS contracts will be enforced primarily through an administrative process. They will amount to a system of imposed public sector contracts which has no obvious precedent in English contract law... there may be unexpected and closer parallels in the planned economies of Eastern Europe. Certainly, problems that have arisen with these contracts – the proliferation of pre-contract disputes, the need to shift the emphasis in remedy from monetary damages to specific performance, and the tendency to blur legal and administrative controls – are also likely to surface in the NHS. (Hughes, cited in Kennedy and Grubb 1994: 51)

Hospitals and GPs could obtain some freedom to operate as semi-autonomous units. NHS hospitals could become trusts by applying to the Department of Health (DoH) to opt out of DHA control and obtain a range of new powers and freedoms. However, there was no genuine attempt to introduce user-control in health-care provision. For instance, in respect of hospital treatment, Singer argues that:

> Patients are not told that they are ... consenting to an erasure of privacy, as staff doctors and nurses enter their rooms unannounced at any hour of the day or night to perform procedures and surveillances without explanation or rationale. They are also not told how completely their schedule and body will be disciplined by the institution's schedule and organisation, and that the significant points of temporal punctuation are provided not by the rhythms of one's body and its needs, but by the organisational demands of the particular institution. (Singer 1993: 102)

Hospitals are just one element of a network of institutional mechanisms authorised to observe, interrogate and objectify us within the dominant discourse. Moreover, this process extends beyond the walls of the institution into the realm of what Singer calls 'hospital-without-walls ... the invisible architecture of incarceration' (p. 104). How we live our lives is constantly investigated, and our inner sense of identity and 'normality' is shaped by how we compare with what is prescribed as 'normal'. In respect of health care, our sense of identity is determined by whom, in the eyes of the medical discourse, is deemed 'at risk'.

Those GPs who applied for 'fundholder' status were given practice budgets and could purchase hospital services for the patients on their list, thus becoming the primary determiner of need. By 1993, they could also purchase community services for their patients from psychiatric community nurses to chiropodists. There was a separation between the role of the hospitals in supplying hospital services, and the job of the DHA and fundholding GPs in purchasing hospital services for the population of a defined area. A DHA, in its purchasing role, contracts to buy the services it estimates its population will need from the hospital which offers the best bid, subject to quality standards. DHAs are able to purchase services from private as well as NHS hospitals. Tax relief for health insurance premiums encouraged further expansion of private provision for people over the age of 60. Not only were health services to be provided through market operations, but also the welfare subject became another unit to be managed at lowest cost within the supplementary discourse of consumption.

The *Patients Charter* (DoH 1991) reinforced the emphasis on the patient as a consumer rather than a client in receipt of professional services, with its emphasis on individual rights. Similarly, a victim-blaming approach, which implies that individuals who suffer ill health or experience welfare needs do so as a result of their own deficiencies or because of their lifestyles, tended to individualise health and welfare problems by blaming them on personal choices in consumption (Blaxter 1990). This perspective leads to prescriptions to transform people into 'model consumers':

> What is implied is that people harm themselves or their children by the excessive consumption of harmful commodities, refined foods, tobacco and alcohol, or by lack of exercise ... Some would argue that such systematic behaviour within certain groups is a consequence only of lack of education, or individual waywardness or thoughtlessness ... What is critical, it is implied, are the personal characteristics of individuals, whether innate or acquired – their basic intelligence, their skills obtained through education and training, their physical and mental qualities, and their personal styles and dispositions. (Townsend et al. 1992: 118)

This has echoes of the Beveridgean concept of the welfare subject as one who, in return for high benefits in disability, recognised the 'duty to be well'. Within this perspective, materialist or structuralist explanations of ill health, including poverty and inequality, are dismissed.

At the same time as internal markets were introduced into the health-care services, they were also introduced into social-care services. Under the Conservative governments, expenditure on residential and hospital care was increasing. The gross current expenditure on community-care services rose from £1,169m in 1979-80, to £3,444m in 1987-88, an increase of 68 per cent in real terms. Local authority personal social services' spending grew by 37 per cent in real terms during the decade up to 1989-90. Social security support for people in independent residential care and nursing homes rose from £10m in 1979, to over £1000m in 1989. The reasons for this were identified as an increase in the proportion of dependent elderly, and very elderly, in the population and the inefficiency of the services provided for them. However, during this period poverty increased dramatically and, in particular, the gap between the rich and the poor widened more dramatically than in any other European country. Inequality has been shown to have a greater bearing on health outcomes for a population than any other single factor (Ahmad 1993, Wilkinson 1997).

A key document in the promotion of community care was *Community Care: Agenda for Action* (Griffiths 1988). This report attempted to managerialise, marketise and individualise community care. It recommended a reorientation of the role of social services so as to ensure that individual needs are identified, care packages drawn up, and care managers assigned. These ideas formed the background to the White Paper *Caring for People* (DoH 1989a) which reaffirmed the government's commitment to promoting care in the community for older people and those with mental illness, disabilities or learning difficulties, preferably in their family home, thereby cutting costs. The construction of the normalised 'family' can be seen to be central in the construction of the welfare subject and community care. Community care was to be family care. However, almost immediately, the Audit Commission's costings between domiciliary and residential care were questioned as being an inaccurate projection of the actual costs, even in the context of unpaid labour by women in families, leading to serious underfunding of the programme and an underestimation of the costs to carers:

> The expectation that a woman will provide the necessary care within the family whatever the cost to herself, still underpins the reality of community care. Cuts in health and social services and cash benefits intensify the demands placed on carers, they mean there are less physical resources to aid them, less alternatives to relieve them, and less money to support them. Savings in public expenditure

increase the cost to carers in terms of her social life, her employment prospects and ultimately her physical and mental well-being. (Equal Opportunities Commission 1990, cited in Allsop 1998: 94)

Women were not the only carers, however, as increasing numbers of elders were cared for by their spouses and, by 1992, of the 6.8m carers in the UK, 13 per cent were men (Taylor 1999).

The legislation was to be phased in over a three-year period. Community care allowed costs to be cut by shifting the responsibility for patients from the state to the 'community': that is, where available, the family of the patient. The subtext behind this development implied that those without family support were in some way deficient – only those 'Other than' normal, such as gay couples, would not have family care to rely upon in old age or infirmity. The Act recommended a transformation in the role of local authority Social Services Departments (SSDs) from that of service providers to enabling agencies, concerned with assessing need, planning services and promoting consumer choice among a range of public, private and voluntary organisations. The government also wished to promote choice and to make maximum use of the independent sector.

Community care as a policy goal was originally adopted some 40 years ago, at a time when it had wide support within the post-war consensus. The adoption of the policy owed something to contemporary academic critiques of the oppressive culture of 'total institutions' (Goffman 1968, Illich 1976), as well as to a desire to reduce public spending. 'Community' as a concept, however, is complex and problematic. For instance, geographically, communities are:

not naturally homogeneous and will be divided into communities of 'interest' or 'identity' formed around social, cultural, economic and/or political concerns. This fragmented nature of 'community' raises difficult issues for people who do not fit in neatly within 'mainstream' notions of community ... or who find themselves having competing or conflicting interests with those in the majority. (Cooper and Hawtin 1998: 85)

Consequently, certain groups may experience 'community' as excluding and oppressive. This is no doubt why, as we saw above, community care has largely been based on a 'family model of care' which assumes that, as far as possible, those being cared for should be looked after by their families and in their own homes. The debate about community care has involved a conflict between concerns about the inappropriateness of institutional care, and the New Right social doctrine emphasising the obligations of the individual and his/her family. The New Right also wished to reduce state interference in the private domain, to give individuals greater 'choice' in running their own lives, to limit the power of state-employed professionals to control the lives of 'ordinary people', and to promote voluntarism. In this ideology, collective state provision is replaced by 'the community' in which caring is undertaken, generally by women, within the family, and unpaid:

> It is important to understand how the work of women and men is prescribed and proscribed by ideas from the New Right which emphasise traditional family values. In this world the family is viewed as the ideal source of care, and minimal backup or last resort services are justified on the basis of preserving the rights of the family to make their own decisions and be protected from state intervention ... This perspective denies the existence of alternate family structures including single-parent families, or lesbian or gay families. It also assumes the women are at home and free to provide care, and denies the reality that care in the family is frequently not loving and often abusive. (Taylor 1999: 69)

An unresolved issue concerns the borderline between NHS and local authority community care provision. Hospitals are increasingly unwilling to cater for chronically sick patients. In January 1994, the Health Ombudsman required Leeds Health Authority to compensate a stroke patient who they had discharged to a nursing home. This had resulted in an annual bill of over £6,000 per annum to meet the gap between his social security entitlement and the fees for the home. By the end of the Conservative period of government, elders in need of long-term care were subject to an assets test, under which any assets in their ownership worth more than £16,000 had to be spent on their care. As many hospitals were trying to reduce the number of people in long-stay wards, the number of elders subject to this provision increased. Throughout the period, since the establishment of the welfare state, elders had come to expect that care in old age would be provided free. Indeed, one of the most hated aspects of the workhouse was that it was seen as a place where pauperised elders were sent to die. Re-introducing charges, taking resources which elders wished to leave to their families, echoed the punitive aspects of the Poor Law for many. In 1997, the White Paper, *A New Partnership for Care in Old Age*, proposed that elders could be encouraged to take out insurance to cover care costs for a fixed period (DoH 1997). In return, they would be exempted from handing over all their assets if they required care for longer than the period paid for by their insurance. As is discussed in Chapter Seven, elders were perceived in purely epidemiological terms, and as an economic burden because of their absence from the world of work. 'Caring', within care in the community, is conceptualised as a one-way relationship; the carer 'giving' and the 'cared for' receiving. It is seen as essentially a private relationship with the state in a supportive role, if evident at all. Both 'carers' and those 'cared for' are excluded from 'work': carers because their 'work' is not regarded as, or remunerated as, waged work; and, in an ageist and disablist society, there are few opportunities where those cared for can contribute.

Public health and welfare subjects

Public health policies were also largely based on individualism and managerialism (Clarke et al. 1994). The 38 targets of the World Health Organisation (WHO) (European Region), in their contribution to the international *Health for All 2000* strategy, were never endorsed by the UK (Ahmad 1993), although they were adopted by some health authorities. The principles underlying the strategy were equity, health promotion, community participation, mutli-sectoral collaboration, primary health care and international collaboration. The Conservative government sought to promote health generally through establishing individualised targets and monitoring the extent to which they were achieved, relying on positivist quasi-scientific methods. Most public health measures implemented by governments form part of the remit of other departments than the DoH. However, there are some aspects of public health which are put into effect by the medical profession, or are least involve some of the supplementary medical professions. The most important of these measures are vaccination, inoculation and screening. The use of screening, in particular, has been increasing – it is important for some women's diseases such as breast cancer and cervical cancer. In the case of both these diseases, early diagnosis and treatment significantly increase the chances of a successful outcome. However, there were problems with the quality of the screening undertaken for both these diseases in some areas of the country (House of Commons 1995).

The Green Paper, *The Health of the Nation* (DHSS 1992), continued the use of targets centred on individual behaviour such as smoking, and specific diseases such as strokes. This involved strategies such as health checks, carried out by GPs under financial incentives in the new contracts embodied in the NHS reforms. Performance-related contracts for GPs led to record levels of childhood immunisation. In the case of whooping cough, the figure increased from 75 per cent to 90 per cent of the child population in the period 1989 to 1991. Those reluctant to have their children immunised against whooping cough, for fear of possible brain damage, were characterised as socially irresponsible. There was a continued emphasis on the responsibility of individuals to improve their health through adjusting their lifestyle. They could do this by adopting a more healthy diet, taking exercise, regulating their weight, and avoiding dangerous habits such as smoking or excessive drinking. Other targets in this document related to mental ill health. It was identified that 14 per cent of certificated absences, 14 per cent of in-patient costs and 21 per cent of pharmaceutical costs were accounted for by mental illness. It was also recognised that there was a worrying rise in suicide among young men (Buck 1997). Government targets were to improve the health and social functioning of mentally-ill people and, by the year 2000, to reduce the general suicide rate by 15 per cent, and for mentally-ill people by 33 per cent. There was no mention, of course, of the evidence linking poverty and unemployment to mental ill health, and 'work' was seen to be the passport to constructed normality. 'Enabling people with mental illnesses to return to work or find employment for the first time is a key part of their rehabilitation' (DoH 1994, cited in Buck 1997: 81).

In relation to health promotion and advice relating to such concerns as HIV/AIDS and contraceptive information for young people, the supplementary discourse of 'sexuality' was critical to the construction of the welfare subject. Any sexuality other than heterosexuality within a marital relationship became the object of public concern. The House of Lords ruled in 1985 (the Gillick ruling) that, providing the child (a young woman under sixteen years) has sufficient maturity and understanding of what is involved, her consent to contraceptive advice and treatment is legally valid. The parliamentary debate, however, revealed the extent to which constructed sexuality is embedded within the law and affects public policy:

> Parliament has for the past century regarded, and still regards today, sexual intercourse between a man and a girl under 16 as a serious criminal offence so far as the man who has such intercourse is concerned. So far as the girl is concerned she does not commit any criminal offence, even if she aids, abets or incites the

having of such intercourse. (Lord Brandon, cited in Kennedy and Grubb 1994: 681)

So, although Lord Brandon's argument was ultimately rejected, it reflected the common notion that 'normal' young people should not be sexually active.

As is shown in Chapter Eight, there was resistance to recognising HIV/AIDS as anything other than a disease of gay men, brought upon themselves by an immoral lifestyle, for several years after the first cases were discovered. One of the early public health responses of the Conservative government was to modify the Public Health (Control of Diseases) Act 1984 to include AIDS (although, surprisingly not HIV). Section 38 of the Act (modified by regulation 5) gives public authorities the power to detain in hospital those who may spread disease (Kennedy and Grubb 1994). 'Furthermore, the Act and the regulation make no reference to treatment and thereby appear to be oppressive without any saving therapeutic grace' (p. 84). The supplementary discourse of sexuality in medical science has remained a potent instrument in promoting a vision of moral order. Throughout the 1980s, the discovery of AIDS resulted in homosexuals and Black Africans being the target of a moralising discourse that called for policy prescriptions aimed at exclusion and treatment:

> It is, therefore, not all that surprising that those people who fancy themselves as members of some moral majority can feel threatened by the existence of gays, intravenous drug users, and other local subcultures which they will never see and with whom, knowingly, they will likely have little or no contact. At the same time, those who are targeted will feel at risk as that policy agenda, in all its hegemonic varieties, encroaches progressively upon their world, directly and at a distance. (Singer 1993: 104)

It is not difficult to see, therefore, how the processes of marginalisation and exclusion are regulated through discursive practices within the health system.

The impact of neo-liberal health reforms

One measure used by the Conservative government to assess their reforms was the size of waiting lists. Using waiting lists as a performance indicator was a continuation of the quasi-scientific approach to determining the quality of health care. It was complicated by the fact that patients not only wait to receive hospital treatment after it has been recommended for them by a hospital consultant, but also they may wait long periods before their GP is able to get them an appointment to see a consultant in the first place. The reduction in waiting-list time, however, was achieved through political intervention, and not through the operation of the market, since Ministers directly intervened to put pressure on health authority chairs and general managers to meet the government's targets. The impact of the exercise of discretionary ministerial power on the health service makes it very difficult to identify and assess the precise impact of the autonomous operation of the internal market. This internal market has encouraged a more entrepreneurial culture in parts of the health service, especially amongst GP fundholders; there are some indications that fundholders manage to keep prescription costs down more than non-fundholders.

The relationship between the NHS and the pharmaceutical industry is a significant one (Collier 1989). The cost of drugs to the NHS more than doubled between 1991 and 1997, rising from £3,104m to £6,360m. The Pharmaceutical Price Regulation Scheme, established in 1957, regulates the revenues which pharmaceutical companies receive from the NHS. This does not give the health service any control over the actual prices charged for drugs. The resources devoted to the scheme of price regulation are extremely small, consisting of 14 officials and the equivalent of four full-time accountants. The way the scheme works is that the health service requires companies to set an overall price for their drugs that gives a return on capital of between 17 and 21 per cent. This is a generous return, but some companies have been exploiting the rather lax regulatory system by selling on the right to produce particular drugs to smaller companies, which then substantially increase the prices charged to the NHS. When new drugs come on to the market the health service is frequently under pressure, as a result of publicity, to make these drugs available. In contrast to the US, British drug companies are not permitted to advertise drugs directly to consumers. However, through effective publicity and public relations, with the press always eager for stories of dramatic new treatments, companies do manage to obtain very high levels of publicity for new treatments, thus increasing the pressure on doctors to provide them. Drug companies often charge very high prices for new drugs in order to exploit these favourable selling conditions to the maximum. When Viagra came on to the market in 1997, the company initially wished to charge £10 per tablet. Although this was later reduced to just below £5, it still represents a massive price in relation to production costs.

Patients of fundholders also benefited from shorter waiting times for hospital treatment. Therefore, this aspect of the internal market contributed to increased inequality between patient groups (Le Grand et al. 1998). The entrepreneurial culture among GP fundholders, it has been argued, has been particularly inappropriate for community health services:

> [F]rom the standpoint of GPs, patient empowerment and health gain are marginal activities. GPs lack the incentive to provide a holistic approach and 'don't understand how social conditions and social care impact on health'... There is considerable evidence that GPs do not fully appreciate the nursing role and tend to impose a medical way of thinking. (Tinsley and Luck 1998: 484-86)

In any case, improved primary care increased the demand for hospital-based treatment rather than reduced it (Tinsley and Luck 1998), yet the reforms led to a substantial number of hospital closures.

A major effect of these reforms was to put pressure on those managing the NHS to cut costs by reducing the number of acute beds. The consequent rationalisation of hospital care involved considerable political controversy. Strategic plans for major cities, including London, Birmingham, Bristol and Newcastle-upon-Tyne, involved shifting resources into community and primary services, and closing hospital beds and duplicated services such as casualty departments in neighbouring hospitals. Conservative policy for London assumed that it had too many hospital beds. The Tomlinson inquiry was set up to review the situation (Tomlinson 1992). This recommended a considerable degree of rationalisation involving many closures. There was a reduction of about 28 per cent in the number of acute beds in London between 1986 and 1991. Bed closures continued across the country because of cost constraints and changes in the pattern of care provided, especially the use of 'keyhole' surgery, which considerably reduced the time patients needed to spend in hospital. Between 1981 and 1991, the number of acute beds in England fell from 145 000 to 114 000. The average length of stay was six days in 1991, compared to eight days in 1981. From 1990 to 1995 over 300 hospitals were closed. The government refused to take responsibility for this, arguing that local management, responding to specific market conditions, made these decisions.

The figures show that around a third of these closures involved psychiatric hospitals, which were being shut down as part of the policy of community care. The pattern of care for those with enduring mental illnesses, whilst shifting care from hospitals to the community, became sporadic with little continuity of care. Whilst the number of psychiatric in-patient beds had fallen by more than half since 1959, and the number of psychiatric in-patients by more than 300 per cent, yearly admissions increased (Payne 1999). This reflected a high level of re-admissions and short-term stay, a 'revolving door' of psychiatric care. 'The real shift in mental health policy has been the increasing role of community care for those with severe and enduring mental health problems' (p 190), but community care was seriously underfunded and depended on the unwaged work of family members, largely women. Furthermore, community-based services for the mentally-ill were seen as shifting the focus from the severely ill to the 'worried well'. The results were catastrophic:

> By the 1980s and 1990s those policy changes had produced a system which was verging on collapse, with too few beds for emergency admissions without the precipitous discharge of other, severely ill patients, and too little money to provide community psychiatric care for all those in need. (Payne 1999: 191)

This fuelled the construction of the mad as dangerous (referred to earlier), and eventually led to greater restraint for patients in the community through new orders brought about by the 1995 Mental Health (Patients in the Community) Act:

> Mental health policy took the specific direction it did – greater restraint rather than increased funding – for a variety of reasons. The timing of the changes was the cumulative result of highly-publicised incidents involving young mentally disordered men. There were other factors which became important in this period and which increased the difficulties faced by young men: higher rates of youth unemployment, increased levels of involvement with the criminal justice system, dramatic increases in suicide and changes in the structure of family life. (Payne 1999: 201)

Neo-liberal approaches to health were primarily based on defining conditions requiring treatment, identifying eligible individuals (and those not eligible), and delivering health care through the mechanism of welfare markets, measured and monitored by quasi-scientific and business measures. Neither Conservative or New Labour health policies have aimed to promote a holistic concept of health, such as the 'social model' of health defined by the World Health Organisation (WHO) as 'complete physical, mental and social well-being, and not merely the absence of disease or infirmity' (WHO Alma-Ata Declaration 1978, cited in Allsop 1998: 327). However, the health policies of both the Conservatives and New Labour have continued to be directed at ensuring a fit and healthy population to 'work' in both the public and private (domestic) spheres of society, and, when required, to fight in combat. The two factors considered central to the reduction of health inequalities are equity, and recognising that health gains can only be made through broad-ranging strategies (Ahmad 1993).

One important environmental factor is the quality of the air that people breath. Since the mid-1950s, the reduction in the use of coal as an industrial and domestic fuel has reduced this form of air pollution. However, the increase in road traffic, and especially the increased numbers of heavy goods vehicles, has meant that, in urban areas, air pollution is now a major threat to health. In particular, it may be responsible for a massive increase in the number of people suffering from asthma. Some industrial processes also create a health risk in the environment in which they operate. This is especially true where there are dangerous emissions of various kinds. In recent years, there has been significant debate as to the health risk posed by nuclear installations and household waste incineration.

Another well-known source of health risk is the workplace itself. Legislation on workplace safety dates back to the first half of the nineteenth century. The current health and safety at work system is based on the Robens Report of 1972 (Robens 1992). There is a Health and Safety Executive responsible for administering the health and safety legislation. The economic and human cost of workplace ill health is substantial: it has been estimated that around 20m working days each year are lost as a result. The most recent figures show around 1.6m industrial accidents a year, and 18m lost working days as a result. Some 11.5m days were lost through work-related ill health. Each year, 5 000 people have to leave work permanently as a result of accidents, and 16 000 retire early. More than 2m people reported ill health caused partly or wholly by work. The most common complaints are repetitive strain injury, back injuries and stress. The total cost has been estimated at £16bn. Some critics have argued that the way in which the Health and Safety Executive enforces the law is ineffective. Very few prosecutions are instituted and the executive prefers to negotiate with employers in order to improve the safety of working conditions (Kinnersly 1973). In recent times, attention has been given to the hazards of the domestic home as a workplace for women. The poor physical quality of many homes, the chemicals women have to use, the hard domestic labour they undertake, the isolation that causes depression, and the associated hazards of economic dependency and child-birth, have all been show to adversely affect women's health (Doyal 1979).

There is overwhelming evidence of the link between social class and mortality. This has been well documented for several decades and reported in detail in numerous studies (Townsend et al. 1992). The factors involved in the link between class and mortality include: occupation – where hazardous conditions or substances are encountered at work; the living environment – where dangerous substances or circumstances such as road traffic are encountered; and inadequate diet, poor housing, excessive hours of work and stress at work. These studies tend to show that persistent class inequalities have continued throughout the twentieth century. It has also been shown that class inequalities increased from 1980, and that there was a fall in the life expectancy of men in semi-skilled and unskilled occupations (Townsend et al. 1992). Inequality between richer and poorer areas, as measured by mortality rates, also increased in this period (Dorling 1997).

In the last few years, clear evidence has been found of a link between the extent of social inequality itself and death and disease. Research carried out by Wilkinson has demonstrated that it is not just poverty, poor housing and other aspects of material poverty which cause ill health, but the actual extent of inequality. It appears that when inequality increases, even if poverty does not increase, then those at the lower end of the income distribution will experience increased rates of illness and premature death (Wilkinson 1997). The explanation put forward for this is that increased inequality affects life expectancy through the increase in stress, reduction in personal status, and the low levels of self-esteem associated with this. It is interesting to note that this increased inequality is also linked to increasing crime, school failure and family breakdown. The policy implications of taking seriously the link between the degree of inequality and death rates amongst poorer people are important. Health can be improved not only by raising the living standards of those towards the bottom of the income scale, but also by reducing the gap between their living standards and those of the better off. More recently, evidence has shown that these inequalities have increased, along with the increase in poverty that has taken place, over the last two decades (Wilkinson 1997).

Another aspect of inequality, which has frequently been studied in relation to health, concerns access to, and usage of, health facilities. There is evidence that health services are less accessible to poor people and people from racial minorities (Northway 1997). The increase in the use of charging for aspects of health provision, particularly dental charges and charges for eye care, have also contributed to a decrease in the use of these services by poor people. The area of health care where private practice developed most extensively and most rapidly was dentistry. From being an entirely free service based on need at the inception of the NHS, dentistry moved towards a situation where, in many areas of the country, private practice became the dominant form of provision. Around 40 per cent of dentists no longer accept new NHS patients. The proportion of patients who pay privately for some or all of their dental care has, as a result, risen substantially. The acceleration in the growth of private provision occurred after 1992, when the Department of Health cut the fees paid to dentists for work done on NHS patients. As a consequence, 80 per cent of the British Dental Association's members voted to refuse to take on new adult NHS patients.

The strategy outlined in *Health of the Nation* in 1992 (DoH 1992) did not realise its full potential according to a subsequent evaluation by the DoH. It had little impact on the activities of trusts and providers of primary care. It did not succeed in drawing in other government departments alongside the DoH. At local level, local government played little part in the implementation of the strategy that tended to be heavily disease-based rather than being based on the promotion of a positive view of health. Critics also point to a lack of control of public funds and to extravagance and waste. The Commons Public Accounts Committee criticised the Wessex Regional Health Authority for wasting, on their own admission, at least £20m on buying and running a failed computer system at the expense of patient care. The West Midlands Regional Health Authority was criticised over contracts placed for a computer information system for patient care that cost the authority more than £43m before it was abandoned.

Trusts have to sell their 'products' as if they are businesses. However, their cash flow is largely beyond their control and some experience financial difficulties. A leaked report from the NHS Management

Executive Committee, in 1992, stated that the number of hospitals that were more than £100,000 in deficit had risen from 79 to 86, with 65 per cent of hospitals expecting to close beds and cut services. There is a continuing debate on the impact of the reforms on the size and cost of management in the NHS. In the UK as a whole, the number of NHS managers rose from 6091 in 1989-90 to 20 478 in 1992-93. Over the same period, administrative and clerical staff rose from 144 582 to 166 363 – a 15.1 per cent increase. Taking together managers, administrative and clerical staff, the rise over the whole period was 36 168. The salary cost of managers more than trebled from £174.2m to £532.9m in the period 1990-93. Regional Health Authorities account for only 12 per cent of the increase in managers between 1989 and 1992. The real growth in NHS management has been in self-governing trusts. At the same time, the number of nursing and midwifery staff, expressed as whole-time equivalents, fell by 27 235 from 1989 to 1993. Ministers argue, however, that some of the fall in nursing numbers comes from the re-classification of senior nurses as managers. In addition, more than 18 000 student nurses have been removed from nursing numbers since 1990.

There has been controversy about the administrative changes introduced. Critics have pointed out that many trust and health authority boards have been packed with Conservative supporters. More broadly, the growing number of these trusts is seen as part of the general expansion of 'Quangos' (Quasi Non-Governmental Organisations) and the increase in the role and power of non-elected appointees ('the quangocracy') over the disposition of public funds. Democratic control of health provision has been lacking since the establishment of the NHS and the decision to exclude local authorities from playing a major role in the delivery of personal health care. Throughout its history, there has been no general move to establish democratic elective structures in any area of NHS provision. Control has always been exercised by appointed boards of one kind or another, the members of which are normally appointed by the Minister. Nominations for appointments are usually received from local political parties and other interested organisations. There is clear evidence over the last two decades that Labour governments tend to appoint a preponderance of Labour supporters, and Conservative governments do likewise. While the system ensures some local representation, it allows for little or no democratic accountability. Since the establishment of self-governing trusts under the Conservative government, the extent of democratic influence has been further eroded.

There has been a debate as to whether the steps taken through the reforms introduced by *Working for Patients* were part of a long-term strategy by the government to dismantle or privatise the NHS. Certainly, there are those on the right of the Conservative Party who would view this as a desirable goal. There is no doubt that the policies were designed to stimulate private provision in both health and community care. Indeed, an expansion of the private sector, in the form of nursing homes and hospices as well as acute hospitals, has taken place. It is the private acute hospitals that are the focus of the most intense political dispute. Critics claim that these undermine the approach of the NHS, in which treatment is generally linked to 'need' rather than ability to pay. Even though need is a social construction, it offers an opportunity for contextualising health in a more flexible way than the criterion of wealth. Private hospitals, by contrast, provide a (growing) minority of people with a means of avoiding queues for services, and of enjoying a higher level of amenities than is generally available in the NHS. One result of the long period of Conservative rule which ended in 1997 was a change in the character of the public debate about health services, and the role of the state in providing them. Support for various aspects of private provision – such as private insurance, charging for various aspects of service, private practice within the health service, and partnerships between public and private-sector providers of health care – is now frequently voiced.

Despite the considerable attention given to health by the Conservatives and the extensive restructuring of the NHS, the proportion of national output devoted to real health needs has not risen, and Britain spends less, as a proportion of GDP, on health than it did in the mid-1970s. The reforms have not been accompanied by any more resources, except in the run-up to the 1992 and 1997 general elections. In real terms, resources for health provision were set to fall up to 1997. The changes made in the health services since the late-1970s do seem to represent a qualitative shift in policy. As with the reforms made in other areas, the conventional bureaucratic structure typical of public administrative control has been replaced with a quasi-market The construction of the welfare subject in relation to health, however, continues to echo that of Victorian times referred to earlier. The welfare subject is either 'healthy' or 'unhealthy' – two distinct states – ill health requiring 'expert' intervention to restore the subject to health. Furthermore, subject lifestyles and behaviour are targeted by government because of the perceived impact on health. For example, those who smoke, or who have more than one sexual partner, have become culpable for their own ill health, whilst social and economic factors are not targeted by government for intervention, despite the extensive evidence of the impact of poverty and social inequality on the health of individuals.

New Labour, health policies and welfare discourse

New Labour has accorded a high priority to the improvement of health care in its social policy programme. Indicators of health-care standards, including life expectancy and the length of time in which people can expect to live in good health, have been covered in 13 new indicators which the government will employ as a means of measuring its overall performance. Like the neo-liberals, New Labour have embraced business and quasi-scientific approaches to health care. A key feature of the presentation of this programme is the emphasis given to 'modernisation' (DoH 1997b). A general feature of modernisation is the idea that development should not be held back by the power of existing vested interests. Modernisation also involves the idea that the most up-to-date knowledge should form the basis of health provision and that the work of doctors should be monitored to ensure that it is undertaken in line with this knowledge. A key approach adopted by New Labour is Evidence-Based Medicine (EBM), that is, 'the appropriate criterion for the provision of an intervention ... is its effectiveness' (Harrison 1998: 19). EBM is a contested concept, since it is as much a social and political construct as a scientific one, although it has been described as 'an elegant solution to the problem of health-care rationing' (p. 15). Its utility is obvious if health and ill health are conceptualised in the same individualistic way as in the health policies of the Conservatives. It is less useful if a more holistic approach to health, such as that taken by the WHO (outlined earlier), is adopted.

Improvements in the stock of social investment, including investment in health-care facilities, will also be measured as part of this process. Modernisation also appears to refer to the delivery of health care in up-to-date buildings using up-to-date equipment. This aspect of modernisation not only involves medical equipment, but also an increase in the use of information technology. The latter is aimed at improving the information available to patients, improving management, and increasing the information available to doctors in ways that will enable them to undertake treatment more effectively and economically. Like the Conservatives, New Labour have embraced the supplementary discourse of 'consumption' as critical to the formation of the welfare subject and health care. Modernisation makes reference to the idea of a 'quality' service for the clients or 'customers' of health providers. This could involve a variety of features of the service such as the removal of unnecessary delays, improved hospital food, and easier access to medical advice and medical services on the initiative of patients. It can be seen, therefore, that New Labour's approach to health remains within the positivist approach of the Conservatives, and indeed health care throughout this century, which separates the individual from their social and economic context.

However, another significant feature of the general approach of New Labour to health provision is an attempt to move away from competition towards collaboration. This is to be done by reducing the number of separate decision-making units within the service and attempting to ensure greater co-ordination between them. There will also be an attempt to ensure that the needs of patients, as viewed by primary health-care providers, are used in deciding the hospital services to be provided in any area. This will represent a move away from a system in which the needs of patients are determined by the assessment of operating units, such as the fund-holding practices. A further feature of the general approach is likely to be some shift towards emphasising health promotion as a strategy for the improvement of health standards. It would appear that there is to be a shift away from the highly individualised approach to health education towards one based more on public health, yet still based on judgements about individual lifestyles and behaviour with a strong moral impetus towards constructed normality. Whilst New Labour have announced their intention to reduce social exclusion and child poverty, they retain a distance from the impact of poverty on health:

> As Richard Wilkinson's research (1996) convincingly shows, it is the relationships between poverty and wealth, and the degree of inequality within a particular society, that are the major determinants not only of physical but also of mental ill health. Poverty is a corrosive which acts not only through the effects of malnutrition and unhealthy living and working conditions, but also through those social relationships which depict the poor as worthless. (Jones and Novak 1999: 25)

New Labour's modernisation programme does not show signs of changing power relations within the health system. Authority and power largely remains with the medical profession and central decision makers, permitting the continued dominance of the bio-medical discourse of health to set the rules that render the 'Other' dangerous, and determining who is 'deserving', or 'undeserving', of health resources. Consequently, the exclusionary tendencies within the established medical practices that we have identified are likely to continue.

The welfare subject and personal health care

New Labour has put forward plans to alter the organisation of the health service. In its consultation document *Health 2000* the Labour Party accepted the separation of the purchase, or commissioning, of health care from its provision. It proposed to replace the system of GP fund-holding with a system of Primary Care Groups (PCGs) which will be largely controlled by GPs, although other members of the health team and those engaged in social care will belong to them. In England (the arrangements for Wales and Scotland are slightly different), there will be around 500 PGCs, each serving a population of around 100 000. Initially, PGCs will operate as advisers to local health authorities. At the second stage of development they will remain part of the authority, but take responsibility for their own budget. At the third stage, they will become free-standing bodies which are accountable to the health authority. Finally, at the fourth stage, they will become primary health-care trusts, commissioning all health care and running all health services in a merger with existing NHS community trusts. Until April 2000, PCGs will be restricted to the first or second stages of development. The new system of PGCs may lead to changes in the relationship between GPs and the health service. It is likely that many GPs will become salaried employees, rather than independent self-employed contractors, answerable to the PGC board.

Each group will have a chief executive paid up to £50,000 per annum. It will normally be chaired by a GP who will get an annual fee of between £10,000 and £15,000. The board that runs the group will consist of six other GPs, two community nurses, a representative from social services and a lay member. The government believes that administrative costs will be reduced by around £100m. It also believes that these new arrangements will solve the problem of a two-tier service created by the existence of fund-holders alongside non-fund-holding GPs. However, the new arrangements may worsen conditions for some patients of former fund-holding GPs, since these will no longer be able to provide the additional services that they could under the old funding regime. These patients may now be deprived of physiotherapy, counselling, and special sessions for sufferers of particular diseases such as asthma and diabetes. It is claimed, however, that these new arrangements will improve the quality of service by giving doctors a collective interest in their success, and by providing a more integrated system of health care to the benefit of patients.

There are also moves to allow patients to obtain medical advice and treatment without consulting their own GPs. This would be a major change in the mode of operation of the NHS in terms of giving patients immediate access to non-emergency medical care. NHS Direct is a system which allows telephone or computer access to medical advice provided by nursing staff. The system has been piloted and it is planned that it will cover the whole of England by the end of the year 2000. There is also a pilot scheme of 20 walk-in centres that are to be established in a variety of environments, including railway stations and shopping centres. These will provide advice and simple forms of treatment. This innovation, along with the NHS Direct, is viewed with some suspicion by many GPs, since it breaks with the traditional pattern through which patients are attached to the doctor with whom they are registered and who acts, in effect, as a gatekeeper controlling access to other medical services. The view of the government is that these additional services are needed because there is evidence that, while many are satisfied with the current system of general practice, some patients have to wait several days for an appointment, while others think that waiting periods are too long.

In the presentation of its policies on health, New Labour committed itself to a reduction of 100 000 in the number of people recorded as waiting for treatment. This was one of the five key pledges to which Labour was committed. In the first two years in government it proved extremely difficult to achieve this target. Indeed, 18 months after being elected the number of those on waiting lists was 1.2m. The response of the government to this failure to achieve its target was to appoint a Waiting List Action Team, with a brief to reduce lists. Further difficulties in reducing these waiting lists arose from the large number of people admitted to hospital at the end of 1998, due to the flu outbreak and the lack of slack in the hospital system as a result of years with very tight control of resources. This midwinter crisis arose despite the government having arranged to increase the number of beds available by providing funds for health authorities to remove elders from hospital to care homes.

The issue of waiting lists has been the subject of considerable debate. Many people have argued that the number of people awaiting treatment is not a useful measure of the success of the health-care system; it takes no account of how long people are waiting. This issue was partly addressed by the Patients Charter which, since 1995, pledged that no patient should wait more than 18 months for treatment, although by late 1998 over 800 people were in this situation. Simply focusing on the length of the wait ignores factors such as the seriousness of the patient's condition and the damage to their health which waiting is likely to produce. In response to these considerations a variety of managerial solutions have been proposed. These generally involve some attempt to select those patients who should be treated earlier than others. One solution devised by health economists rests on the idea of QALYs (Quality Adjusted Life Years). However, the obvious objection to this solution is that it gives a much lower priority to treating the ill health of elders, since there is a lower rate of return from them in terms of additional years of healthier life. The mechanisms used by New Labour to assess all their policies, not just health care, rest largely on techniques and approaches derived from management and marketing, where human activities are defined in such a way that they can (apparently) be costed and compared to other activities. It can be argued that this whole approach is questionable for human care services and has not produced benefits to people or reduced costs.

The role of community-based nurses is also changing and is likely to involve a more important part in the provision of health care, as patients spend less time in hospital and increasingly rely on being cared for at home. Without an accompanying change in the way in which health and medicine are constructed, away from a biomedical model towards a more holistic approach, nurses may remain the handmaidens of doctors:

> GPs [adhere] to a scientific-positivist approach to health care characterised as the 'medical model of care'. This is based on the principles of correct diagnosis and appropriate medical intervention. A nursing model of care, by contrast, puts greater emphasis on factors such as the overall well-being of the patients, the social context, the prevention of ill health and the need for palliative care ... [Commentators were] wary of giving GPs too much power over nurses because of the fear that the focus on diagnosis and cure might undermine preventive and social care. (Tinsley and Luck 1998: 483)

In the 1990s, the NHS has suffered from shortages of nurses and midwives. The pay awards announced in February 1999 can be seen as an attempt to address this situation. Newly qualified nurses received a pay increase of 12 per cent; nurses on grade D, which is the basic rate for qualified staff, received 8.2 per cent; other nurses received 4.7 per cent. The government also proposed to increase the number of nurse training places by 6 000 as part of its announcement on increased funding for the health service in July 1998. Later in that year, the government announced a more comprehensive restructuring of pay for nurses in the strategy document, *Making a Difference*. There is to be a four-tier structure, made up of a basic grade health-care assistant, a main grade qualified nurse, a further grade for nurses with advanced qualifications and a 'super-nurse' grade of consultant-practitioner. The salary for the super-nurse grade will be up to £40,000 a year. The system of nurse training is also to be redesigned to enable nurses to move up the grading structure more easily. This scheme will be piloted in ten areas starting from September 2000. The concern is that this will merely increase the number of highly paid 'managers' who have little or no contact with those receiving services. This trend has been a common one within the NHS since markets were introduced, and was a frequent criticism made by New Labour of the Conservative governments. Another longstanding source of difficulty in NHS staffing concerns the position of the 30 000 junior doctors and the long hours which they are required to work. New Labour obtained exemption for junior doctors from the terms of the European Working Time Directive, which attempts to restrict working hours to 48 hours per week. The exemption allows their working hours to be phased down to the 48-hour limit over a period of 13 years. However, an agreement has been made for a maximum average working week of 56 hours for the 3 years from 1999. In addition, rates of overtime pay for junior doctors are to be increased.

The proposals for reform made by New Labour in relation to aspects of social care are detailed in the White Paper, *Modernising Social Services* (DoH 1998a). The general direction of the reforms proposed involves the establishment of national standards for care services and for care staff, and the abolition of the Central Council for Education and Training in Social Work (CCETSW). A General Social Care Council will oversee the regulation and training of care staff. Regional commissions will inspect residential provision and appoint children's rights officers to safeguard children in care. The White Paper identified a number of key problems with residential care that the reforms need to address, including protection, co-ordination, inflexibility, clarity of roles, inconsistencies and inefficiencies. The time span over which these reforms are to be introduced has not been specified and, at the time of writing, no legislation has been announced. It seems clear, however, that whilst the autonomy of health professionals is to be safeguarded, those involved in social care are to be more firmly incorporated into the surveillance aspects of state activity. Training rather than education of social care staff is the focus, and their activities are increasingly prescribed in statute, regulation and guidance.

These issues are of particular importance when aspects of care for elders, requiring a response from both health and social care services, are considered. New Labour has begun to address the problem of the provision of long-term care for elders (DSS 1999). This had become a major source of concern because of changes during the Conservative period of office which led to 40 000 elders each year having to sell their houses to pay for means-tested long-term care. The numbers of elders requiring this kind of care has increased with the ageing of the population. Around a fifth of elders will come to require long-term care at some stage. The most needy group is those over the age of 85. At present, there are about 0.8m people of this age and the number will increase to 2m by the year 2050. Every year around 160 000 elders go into a nursing or residential home at a cost of around £350 a week. At present, around three-quarters of the care for elders is provided free by family members. The annual cost to the state of direct provision is £6.5bn with individuals paying a further £3.5bn. Labour established a Royal Commission to examine this issue (Sutherland 1999). In March 1999, it proposed that for elders requiring care, nursing care should be provided free but there would still be a means-tested charge for board and lodging, although the asset test would be raised from £16,000 to £60,000. However, on the publication of the report, the government refused to accept its recommendations and instead has said that there needs to be a public debate on the issue up until the year 2000. By mid-1999 it was clear that the government rejected the proposal to provide free nursing care for elders. The approximate annual cost of implementing the Commission's recommendation would be £1bn, and the government does not seem prepared to commit this amount of money. It is worth noting that in a Court decision in December 1998, a local authority was found to be in breach of the European Convention on Human Rights when it attempted to require patients to leave hospital and enter a local authority nursing home where they would have to pay for accommodation and treatment. The case clearly established that, from the legal standpoint, nursing is a form of health care.

The government has also instituted new policies in relation to care in the community. In a number of high-profile court cases, publicity was given to incidents in which former inmates of mental hospitals had committed violent offences. While these events are actually quite unusual, it is true that a large number of former mental patients have been living in very unsatisfactory conditions, experiencing homelessness or falling into crime whilst they were supposedly the recipients of community care (Payne 1999). The Health Secretary went so far as to say that community care had failed. In July 1998, a major policy initiative on care in the community was announced. This involved increasing expenditure on mental health by £700m over three years. There will be more secure beds for mentally-ill people. These will be established in small units in line with plans initiated by the Conservative government. Those living in the community who are believed to be a risk, or at risk, will be supervised by outreach teams who will be responsible for keeping track of these patients. These outreach teams will include doctors, nurses and social workers. The social construction of the welfare subject requiring psychiatric care has not changed, and is congruent with the demonisation of madness reaching back to the Poor Laws:

> By the late 1990s we have two manifestations: the mentally disordered young man, in need of control lest the public are harmed, and the depressed neurotic woman who has always been present, but who continues to suffer in private, at home. (Payne 1999: 201)

The quality of services provided for those with learning disabilities has also deteriorated. There are about 200 000 people with learning difficulties in Britain. The introduction of markets has meant that around half of all local authorities now charge these people for attendance at day centres. While the policy of community care has led to a huge reduction of those held in long-stay hospitals for the learning-disabled in England, in Scotland large numbers of people still remain in this kind of accommodation.

One feature of the Conservative reforms that has been built upon by New Labour is the Private Finance Initiative (PFI). The PFI is a means of securing capital spending without this being recorded in the national accounts. However, there is a cost: investing companies require an annual return of around 12 to 14 per cent. Some of this money is likely to come from funds that would otherwise have been spent on treating patients. This also results in a reduction in the number of people employed in clinical jobs. It is certainly true that investment is needed in new buildings and equipment in the health service. Since the end of the long boom in the mid-1970s, capital expenditure in the health service has been relatively low. As well as a legacy of old buildings there is also a substantial maintenance backlog. However, the PFI involves a substantial decrease in current expenditure in order to finance capital investment. It is highly debatable whether or not this represents a good deal for the health service. Of 11 new hospitals announced in April 1998, 10 are to be financed privately through the scheme. In the privately-financed hospitals all non-clinical staff will be employees of the private contractors who develop and manage the building. Another aspect of the relationship between private medicine and the NHS, introduced by the Conservative government, involved partnership arrangements of various kinds between the public and private sector. The private sector usually has a much lower rate of bed occupancy than public-sector hospitals and, during periods of crisis involving heavy demand for beds, many health authorities make arrangements to purchase beds from the private sector. Some NHS trusts also encourage private provision through establishing insurance schemes that enable members to obtain fast-track treatment or enhanced conditions in hospital. Some critics view this as a further step on the road towards privatisation.

There is one area of policy where the Labour government is actually putting more emphasis on paying privately for treatment. This concerns medical care provided for victims of road accidents. Since the 1930s it has been possible for insurance companies to be charged for the care provided for accident victims. However, the majority of hospitals have not made these charges in the past for a range of reasons, mainly to do with a commitment to providing a free service, but also due to the complexity of actually claiming money from the insurance companies. The government has made it clear that it will be pursuing these charges in a rigorous fashion. A maximum payment of £2,950 per patient is involved.

Private practice has continued to have a place within NHS hospitals. The figures for 1994-95 show that the income from treating private patients was a significant source of revenue for some health trusts. While overall this revenue was below 1 per cent, for a number of trusts, usually those dominated by large and prestigious hospitals, up to 17 per cent of core income came from this source. Private practice is also an important feature of the work of many NHS consultants. The 'maximum part-time contract' allows consultants to restrict their NHS work to 10/11ths of their total time. However, the extent of their NHS work is not closely monitored, and there are indications that some consultants actually devote far more of their time to private practice than their contracts allow. The possibility of the government using DSS funds to pay for private medical care for those in receipt of sickness benefits whilst waiting for medical treatment has been raised by one government minister. This would constitute an indirect subsidy to the private sector of medicine created by the government's unwillingness to secure equality of treatment for all patients.

While New Labour has modified some operational aspects of the internal market, its approach to improving the influence of patients on the operation of the service continues along the lines instituted by the previous Conservative government (Crinson 1998). A significant contribution to the debate on democracy in the health service has recently emerged (Hutton 1999). This report argues that the NHS is the least accountable of Britain's major institutions. It also claims that accountability will deteriorate further due to changes currently being introduced, such as the establishment of PCGs. The report proposes the direct election of health authorities or control of health provision by local authorities. It also argues that Community Health Councils are not an effective means of ensuring public participation in health policy. While some are excellent, others are little more than public relations agencies for the health authorities that they are supposed to scrutinise.

There has been considerable debate about accountability in the health service. The orthodox view is that democratic accountability is ensured through the responsibility of the Minister to Parliament. Individual doctors will be held to account by their professional associations and aggrieved patients can pursue their case through legal action. These forms of accountability do not operate in a satisfactory fashion. There have been many complaints about the failure of professional organisations to deal effectively with medical incompetence. In 1997-98, there were more than 100 000 complaints and cases referred to the Ombudsman rose by 8 per cent. Legal cases brought against health authorities are increasing every year. The use of the law has proved particularly problematic for aggrieved patients. The NHS pays out around £300m a year to patients and relatives who sue for negligence by doctors. However, the average claim takes five years to be dealt with and some cases run for much longer. In March 1999, after five years of legal action, an attempt by 127 women, who received unsatisfactory treatment for breast cancer, to sue the 60 hospitals involved collapsed, leaving a legal bill of £4.5m. The government has made an attempt to improve the functioning of the legal process where claims of medical negligence are involved. From April 1999, all those involved in these claims will be required to follow a prescribed pre-action protocol. Those making a complaint will have to give precise details, and will then receive an outline response within two weeks. Medical records required will have to be handed over within 40 days of a request by a patient.

Under New Labour, the influence of patients is to be enhanced in a number of ways. A survey of 100 000 patients is to be undertaken in order to accumulate information on their experiences of medical care and their views as to the kinds of service which should be provided. However, as has been shown, access to services is problematic for many marginalised groups, so the information gathered will not reflect the wishes of those currently excluded from health services – such as the street homeless. More information is to be provided to patients to allow them to assess the quality of care and treatment provided. For some areas of treatment, data on the success rates achieved by particular medical departments or individual doctors may be made available, similar to the approach of the neo-liberals towards empowering the education 'consumer' by publishing league tables of school examination results. In June 1999, for the first time, comparative figures for surgical deaths among patients in England were published, along with a wide range of other performance indicators relating to such issues as emergency re-admissions, lengths of waiting for treatment and cancer survival rates.

The Patients Charter may be modified and given a higher profile. Research has shown that the majority of patients have little knowledge of its provisions, and that it plays little part in providing a route to improvements for those who encounter difficulties in their medical treatment. However, the proposals that were produced in late-1998 put forward the idea that local charters should replace the 'national' Patients Charter. This idea is hardly consistent with the government view that an important objective of health policy should be to reduce differences between the standards of service provided in different areas.

Public health and welfare subjects

The Labour Party manifesto for the 1997 election made a clear commitment to public-health provision, which was also outlined in the Green Paper, *Our Healthier Nation: A Contract for Health* (DoH 1998b). The government stated that the aims of its policy are to improve the health of the population and to narrow the health divide. It claimed to offer a 'third way' between an individualistic approach (which blames the victims) and what it refers to as 'nanny state social engineering'. The Green Paper proposes what appears to be a partnership approach between government, industry, local authorities and individuals. The idea seems to be that each of these partners can play a part in promoting improved health: employers can act to improve the health of their workforce; the health service can provide more equal provision across the country, as well as ensuring that the most effective treatments are universally adopted; local authorities can work to pursue local health improvement strategies; and central government can contribute to health through tackling broad social causes of ill health, such as unemployment. The document also makes it clear that the government proposes to make the improvement of the health of the most deprived people a priority.

Area-based policies in the form of 10 designated Health Action Zones are to be established. In addition, £300m from the National Lottery will be used to finance Healthy Living Centres (HLCs). HLCs may provide fitness facilities, physiotherapy services, and preventative programmes and information designed to encourage healthy living. Like the neo-liberals, however, New Labour are keen to tackle the behaviour of welfare subjects in order to improve their health, but are less eager to tackle structural issues. An example of this is their position on tobacco smoking. One of the most significant preventable causes of death and disease is tobacco smoking. In principle, New Labour wishes to reduce smoking. However, very early in its period of office it provoked considerable debate as a result of revelations that it had received a donation of £1m from the owner of the company involved in Formula One car racing, which relies heavily on tobacco sponsorship and advertising. Subsequently, the British government sought to reduce the impact of proposed EU regulations designed to reduce tobacco advertising.

Another important aspect of public-health provision involves the role of diet in personal health. Since the mid-1970s, governments have emphasised the health benefits of increasing consumption of fresh fruit and vegetables, and reducing the consumption of red meat, fat, oil and salt (DHSS 1976). Various aspects of food quality have been regulated since the late nineteenth century. However, there is plenty of evidence to show that large numbers of people are made ill as a result of eating food containing dangerous organisms or poisonous substances. Recent research has shown that around 20 per cent of all poultry sold in the shops is infected in some way. There have been well documented and publicised cases of mass poisoning resulting from infected food. For example, in 1997 twenty people died as a result of *E. coli* poisoning from meat products purchased from a butcher in Scotland. In terms of economic and social cost, the most important recent food crisis has involved BSE. The final death toll from this cannot yet be calculated, though the material cost has been estimated at £6bn or more. The Scottish *E. coli* outbreak along with the BSE crisis have played some part in stimulating the public outcry which lay behind the Labour government's commitment to establishing a Food Standards Agency (FSA). Critics of the system of food regulation argued that the Ministry of Agriculture and Fisheries, responsible for agricultural regulation, cannot be expected to deal in a dispassionate and rigorous fashion with issues of food safety because it is strongly influenced by the farming lobby. The FSA was set up in late-1999 and it has an annual budget of around £100m that will be financed by a levy on firms which sell food to the public. It will incorporate the existing Meat Hygiene Service and report to the DoH and its inspectors, who will have the power to enter premises and to take samples. Its reports will be made public and it will be constituted as an independent body.

However, some of the public health measures introduced echo elements of the social hygiene approach based on the principles of eugenics employed in the Edwardian era (Mazumdar 1991). The government has introduced measures designed to contribute to the achievement of its goal of reducing the rate of teenage pregnancies by half over the 10-year period up to 2010. This will initially target five districts with high teenage-pregnancy rates. It will involve publicity campaigns to stress the disadvantages of life as a young mother, the use of pregnancy advisers for the under-18s, the pursuit of fathers of teenage children by the Child Support Agency (CSA) and restrictions on the kind of accommodation which local councils can offer to lone mothers under the age of 18. Another public health initiative with a flavour of eugenics involves government proposals to detain people viewed as dangerous psychopaths.

This will involve using a preventive system of detention under which individuals could be held in custody, despite not having been found guilty of committing an offence. One health dimension to this issue concerns whether or not the people involved can be legitimately considered to be suffering from an illness and, if so, whether this is treatable by the medical profession. Doctors are divided on this issue. The kind of personality disorder which the government is concerned with involves severe anti-social behaviour, linked to high levels of aggression and social irresponsibility, and accompanied by a lack of sense of guilt and remorse. The number involved could be as high as 2000 people. This policy reflects continuity with the discourse of medical welfare that, as identified above, objectifies and pathologises individuals in the interests of social surveillance and control.

An important role will be played by health improvement programmes (HIMPs). These will consist of an annual plan put together by health authorities with contributions from local government, PCGs and voluntary bodies. They will combine local priorities with those nationally determined. This approach was being tested in pilot studies in 1999. One potential difficulty with the approach involves the requirement that health authorities should share funds with local government where necessary; for example, where the local priority is a health-related environmental improvement of the kind that the local council can undertake. It remains to be seen, however, how willing the agencies will be to co-operate and hand over control of some of 'their' funds.

While the public health policy of New Labour does appear to involve a more integrated approach at central government level to the formulation and implementation of policy, there is little evidence of democratic participation playing a role in policy. The targets set have been 'top down' and there is little democratic input. This continues the pattern established by the Conservative programme as announced in *Health of the Nation*. The policy does not have a clear conception of the role that might be played by more flexible target-setting processes, adjusted to local social, economic and environmental conditions.

Conclusions

While the Conservative government wished to increase the role of the private sector in the provision of social services wherever possible, they encountered considerable resistance to doing this in the case of the health service. While they were able to introduce some aspects of privatisation, especially in the ancillary services, core medical provision was largely retained within the public sector. New Labour does not have any plans to alter the overall position of the NHS. It will continue to provide free health care based on need, but clearly the mixed economy within health care will remain and, to some extent, be strengthened through funding arrangements and partnerships. The overall organisation of health policy involving both policy making and implementation is likely to continue to involve a top-down model. The relative priority accorded to different patient groups will also remain unchanged. The main priority in medical care will continue to be the acute sector.

The care provided for elders and for the disabled, especially those with learning impairments, is likely to continue to involve relatively low levels of expenditure. The provision of care by families in the community for those with enduring illnesses, or those who are aged or disabled, remains within New Labour's policies. As community care is considered humane and liberal compared to the institutional care portrayed by Goffman (1968) and Illich (1976), it is less likely to be challenged as policy. However, as Cohen suggests, such programmes can result in more insidious modes of social control:

> when ... integration and community control take place, the result is that more people get involved in the 'control problem' ... more rather than less attention has to be given to the deviance question. In order to include rather than exclude, a set of judgements has to be made which 'normalises' intervention in a greater range of human life. (Cohen 1985, cited in Sibley 1995: 85)

While at the same time as bringing more people into the process of treating and correcting the 'deviant'– for instance, housing managers and social workers, as well as the medical profession – community care diminishes public and individual awareness of its regime of discipline. Furthermore, Cohen argues:

> when there is decarceration, the community replicates the territorial divisions that occur when there is a clear policy of separation for the mentally ill, mentally disabled or criminal. Thus, while asylums removed the mentally ill from the rest of the urban population, de-institutionalisation isolates them also, particularly within inner-city areas. (Sibley 1995: 86)

Therefore, exclusion can operate in different ways, through separation in institutions and through segregation within the community – a stark example of which is street homelessness.

The relative priority given to medical services as against preventative measures, or the care of those with enduring conditions, is also likely to be maintained. New Labour has rejected the idea of returning long-term care to a system of free provision. Indeed, it has also not accepted the rather more limited proposals of its own Royal Commission on this issue. It seems likely that those in receipt of long-term care will in future be required to make some financial contribution towards it, perhaps through compulsory insurance. In line with its generally supportive attitude towards the private sector of business, New Labour is unlikely to pose the debate on rationing, access to care and waiting lists, in terms of the unfavourable impact of private medicine on the facilities and services available to NHS patients. They are more likely to continue the Conservative policy of viewing the role of the private sector of medicine as one that can operate in partnership with the NHS. Furthermore, in line with its sympathy with the private sector, it is likely that New Labour's policies on health promotion will fail to realise their full potential. It seems probable that where major business interests are concerned, significant dangers to health, such as those posed by tobacco smoking, motor vehicles and industrial emissions, will not be subject to the degree of constraint necessary to minimise their threat. It is also likely that, where the private sector is a source of services purchased by the NHS, as in the case of drugs, diagnostic and therapeutic equipment, and medical facilities financed through the private finance initiative (PFI), the funds available for patient care will be reduced as a result of the high level of payments made to private business.

The overall approach of New Labour to the health service is very much in line with its emphasis on managerialist solutions. There is a strong assumption that improvements can be made without increasing costs, simply through the widespread adoption of what can be identified as best practice in medical treatment. The emphasis on managerialism involves considerable costs in terms of increased expenditure on management, and continued downgrading of professional competence and judgement as a basis for medical care. New Labour has made some moves to support the rights of patients, but these rights are organised on an individualist basis, resting on the legal model of individual compensation where negligence has led to personal disadvantage. The notion of compensating people for disabling conditions themselves, regardless of whether or not these result from negligence (a system which is used in New Zealand), does not appear to be on the agenda. But overall, New Labour has done little to shift power in the health service away from the centre. Consequently, the biomedical model in health policy, and managerialist concerns of cost containment and value for money, are likely to continue to override notions of equity and accountability. This also means that the power of the medical scientific community will continue to assume moral responsibility for our bodies, objectifying and defining us within their discourse of 'normality'. Moreover, democratic accountability in health care is more likely to pertain to those able to express a 'consumer's voice' in service delivery by having the freedom to pay for the services they need.

A final point that needs to be made concerns the unwillingness of New Labour to mount an effective attack on the overall structure of inequality in society. While New Labour appears to aspire to the goal of the elimination of poverty, its policies for achieving this are certainly not guaranteed to succeed. Poverty as a cause of preventable ill health is likely to continue, while the maintenance of the current level of inequality in Britain will contribute further to this. New Labour has no proposals to reduce the pressures created by work. It has done little to reduce hours of work, and its embrace of globalisation and the principle of flexibility are likely, if anything, to increase pressures at work, and increase the economic insecurity of employees at all levels. As a result, work will continue to make a major contribution to the level of ill health in society.

References

Acheson, D. (1998) *Public Health in England*, The Stationery Office, London.
Ahmad, W.I. (1993) *'Race' and Health in Contemporary Britain*, Open University Press, Buckingham.
Allsop, J. (1998) *Health Policy and the NHS: Towards 2000*, 2nd ed, Harlow, Longman.
Blaxter, M. (1990) *Health and Lifestyle*, Tavistock, London.
Buck, M. (1997) 'Poverty, Gender and Mental Health', *Critical Social Policy*, Vol. 17, No. 1, pp. 79-97.
Clarke, J., Cochrane, A. and McLaughlin, E. (1994) *Managing Social Policy*, Sage, London.
Collier, J. (1989) *The health conspiracy: How doctors, the drug industry and the government undermine our health*, Century, London.

Cooper, C. and Hawtin, M. (eds.) (1998) *Resident Involvement and Community Action: Theory to Practice*, Chartered Institute of Housing/Housing Studies Association, Coventry.

Cox, D (1991) 'Health Service Management', Chap. 4 of J. Gabe, M. Calnan and M. Bury (eds.) *The Sociology of the Health Service*, Routledge, London.

Crinson, I. (1998) 'Putting patients first the continuity of the consumerist discourse in health policy, from the radical right to New Labour', *Critical Social Policy*, Vol. 18, No. 2, pp. 227-49.

Cutler, T. and Waine, B. (1997) 'The politics of quasi-markets how quasi-markets have been analysed and how they might be analysed', *Critical Social Policy*, Vol. 17, No. 2, pp. 3-26.

DHSS (Department of Health and Social Security) (1976) *Prevention and Health Everybody's Business*, HMSO, London.

DHSS (Department of Health and Social Security) (1992) *The Health of the Nation*, The Stationery Office, London.

DoH (Department of Health) (1989a) *Caring for People*, HMSO, London.

DoH (Department of Health) (1989b) *Working for Patients*, HMSO, London.

DoH (Department of Health) (1991) *Patients Charter*, HMSO, London.

DoH (Department of Health) (1992) *Health of the Nation*, HMSO, London.

DoH (Department of Health) (1997a) *A New Partnership for Care in Old Age*, The Stationery Office, London.

DoH (Department of Health) (1997b) *The New NHS – Modern and Dependable*, The Stationery Office, London.

DoH (Department of Health) (1998a) *Modernising Social Services*, The Stationery Office, London.

DoH (Department of Health) (1998b) *Our Healthier Nation: A Contract for Health,* The Stationery Office, London.

Dorling, D. (1997) *Death in Britain: How Local Mortality Rates Have Changed, 1950s to 1990s,* Joseph Rowntree Foundation, York.

Doyal, L. (1979) *The Political Economy of Health*, Pluto, London.

DSS (Department of Social Security) (1999) *With Respect to Old Age Long Term Care-Rights and Responsibilities*, Cmnd. 4192, The Stationery Office, London.

Foucault, M. (1984) *The History of Sexuality*, Peregrine, Harmondsworth.

Goffman, E. (1968) *Asylums*, Penguin, Harmondsworth.

Griffiths, R. (1988) *Community Care Agenda for Action*, London, HMSO.

Harrison, S. (1998) 'The politics of evidence-based medicine in the United Kingdom', *Policy and Politics*, Vol. 26, No. 1, pp. 15-31.

Harrison, S., Hunter, D.J., and Pollit, C. (1990) *The Dynamics of British Health Policy*, Unwin Hyman, London.

House of Commons (1995) *Breast Cancer Services, 3rd. Report*, Health Committee, HMSO, London.

Hutton, W. (1999) *Interim report of the committee on representing the public in the health service*, Association of Community Health Councils for England and Wales, London.

Illich, I. (1976) *Limits to Medicine. Medical Nemesis: the Expropriation of Health*, Marion Boyars, London.

Jones, C. and Novak, T. (1999) *Poverty, Welfare and the Disciplinary State*, Routledge, London.

Kennedy, I. and Grubb, A. (1994) *Medical Law*, Butterworths, London.

Kinnersly, P. (1973) *The Hazards of Work*, Pluto, London.

Le Grand, J., Mays, N. and Mulligan, J. (1998) *Learning from the NHS Internal Market*, King's Fund, London.

Leonard, P. (1997) *Postmodern Welfare: Reconstructing an Emancipatory Project*, Sage, London.

Mazumdar, P. (1991) *Eugenics, Human Genetics and Human Failings: The Eugenics Society, its Sources and its Critics in Britain*, Routledge, London.

McKeown, T. (1976) *The Role of Medicine*, Blackwell, Oxford.

Northway, R. (1997) 'Integration and inclusion: Illusion or progress in services for disabled people', *Social Policy and Administration*, Vol. 31, No. 2, pp. 157-72.

Payne, S. (1999) 'Dangerous and Different: Reconstructions of madness in the 1990s and the role of mental health policy', in S. Watson and L. Doyal (eds.) *Engendering Social Policy*, Open University Press, Buckingham, pp. 184-204.

Robens, A. (1972) *Report of the Committee on Health and Safety at Work*, HMSO, London.

Sibley, D. (1995) *Geographies of Exclusion*, Routledge, London.

Singer, L. (1993) *Erotic Welfare: Sexual Theory and Politics in the Age of Epidemic*, Routledge, London.

Sutherland, S. (1999) *Royal Commission on Care*, Department of Social Security, The Stationery Office, London.

Taylor, I. (1999) 'She's there for me: Caring in a rural community' in S. Watson, and L. Doyal (eds.) *Engendering Social Policy*, Open University Press, Buckingham, pp. 67-83.

Tinsley, R. and Luck, M. (1998) 'Fundholding and the Community Nurse', *Journal of Social Policy*, Vol. 27, Part 4, pp. 471-87.

Tomlinson, B. (1992) *Report of the Inquiry into London's Health Services*, HMSO, London.

Townsend, P. and Davidson, N. (eds.) with Whitehead, M. (1992) *Inequalities in Health: The Black Report and The Health Divide*, Penguin, Harmondsworth.

Webster, C. (1998) *The National Health Service: A Political History*, OUP, Oxford.

Wilkinson, R. (1997) *Unhealthy Societies: The Afflictions of Inequality*, Routledge, London.

Williams, F. (1995) *Social Policy: A Critical Introduction*, Polity Press, Cambridge.

5   Education Policies

Introduction

State education can be defined as 'the social system, or inter-organisational domain ... wherein knowledge acquisition and learning opportunities are provided for children on behalf of the state' (Hoyle 1998: 99). This definition highlights two recurring aspects of education policies. The first is the identification of knowledge that the state requires children to learn (and knowledge forbidden to children), and the second is the processes through which they acquire that knowledge. Compulsory state education for children is comparatively recent and is only one way in which knowledge is transmitted. 'Families', religious, cultural, racial and political associations have all involved themselves in knowledge identification and transmission. However, this chapter will focus on state education, beginning with an examination of the relationship between education and the state. It will then look at the New Right education policies that were consolidated by the last Conservative government. It will go on to document New Labour's policies on education, and their perceived role in the Labour government's 'modernisation' programme for Britain. It will critically assess the degree to which New Labour's approach involves continuity with the neo-liberal agenda, in particular with regard to the nature of New Labour's discourse of welfare and the degree to which its construction of the 'welfare subject' is a factor in perpetuating exclusion through education policies. In doing this, we evaluate to what extent New Labour's proposals on education will reverse the exclusionary processes of previous policies and practices.

Education policy and the state

The origins of state intervention in education are usually located around 1833 when grants of public money were first given to finance schooling, although the state had provided some education in workhouses, prisons and the armed forces before this. In earlier times the education of children was the responsibility of the family or the church. Knowledge was necessary to prepare them for their social or gender roles. Boys destined for the priesthood needed to learn Latin for example, while girls who were to be married to men of affluence acquired skills in domestic arts such as embroidery. For some children education was minimal or seen as inappropriate.

In the period from 1833, the intervention of the state aimed to encourage the adoption of a system of schooling designed largely to adapt working-class children to the requirements of capitalist wage labour. The role of the school was simply to habituate children to obedience, and provide them with the rudiments of literacy and numeracy (Salter and Tapper 1981). The Victorians believed that acquiring more knowledge than was necessary to the subject's gender and class roles might give them ideas above their station. Thus, knowledge is not only transferred through state sanctioned processes but also excluded by them too. Sibley suggests that:

> The control of knowledge has an important moral dimension. Excluded knowledge is a narrative concerning groups and individuals who have been relegated to the margins of society because the values they represent undermine the moral consensus. This knowledge becomes dangerous and threatening when it is brought to the centre and presented as a legitimate perspective on social relations. It threatens to dislodge the centre, defined ... by social knowledge which its advocates claim represents a moral consensus, and, thus, it becomes imperative to repel dissident thoughts or ... the messenger. (Sibley 1995: 132)

This highlights the significance of the exclusion of knowledge by state institutions for controlling notions of 'truth' and the construction of a legitimate moral order.

In the mid-Victorian period the state played a major role in redesigning the overall structure of education provision. Both grammar and public schools were regulated on the basis, respectively, of the proposals of the Clarendon Commission of 1864, and the Taunton Commission of 1867. The state also intervened in higher education (HE), and the universities of Oxford and Cambridge were reformed on the basis of inquiries published in 1852. Clerical influence was reduced and admissions were made more meritocratic. Several new universities and university colleges were established, alongside the ancient English and Scottish universities, particularly in the expanding industrial cities. In the Edwardian period, a rather more complex and contradictory set of influences began to operate on education policy. As part of the new Liberal approach to incorporating the working class as full citizens of a democratic society, a progressive tradition gained a place within the Board of Education. This tradition aspired to use education to create equality of opportunity, and to develop education for the working class through exposing its members to a curriculum adapted from that used in the public schools. At the same time, the desire to expand education was also partly driven by the concerns of the national efficiency movement to use state action to improve economic efficiency (discussed more fully in Chapter Two) by encouraging vocational training. As secondary education for the working class developed in the twentieth century, it never clearly adopted a vocational approach. The pursuit of a minimal competence in basic skills of literacy and numeracy, combined with a strong emphasis on moral training, existed alongside an attempt to expose the working class to a cut-down version of the full range of traditional high culture (Gordon et al. 1991).

The Education Act 1902 brought all elementary schools under the control of local education authorities (LEAs), although voluntary schools were not fully financed by the state and retained the right to give denominational instruction. The Act also, for the first time, made provision for some working-class access to secondary education, while amendments to the regulations in 1907 provided for 25 per cent of the places in secondary schools to be free. Education was to last until 13 years-of-age, although exemptions to the rule were made. The Education Act 1918 formed part of the same process, although it also owed something to the mood of radicalism created by the First World War. It made attendance from the age of 5 to 14 compulsory and enabled LEAs to abolish exemptions from education, to provide part-time continuation classes from the age of 14 to 16, and to establish nursery education. However, the permissive parts of the legislation had little impact. In the six years after its passing, there were still no LEA nursery schools, and only one LEA provided compulsory continuing education for 14- to 16-year-olds. In 1924, Labour introduced an increase in the proportion of free secondary places from 25 per cent to 40 per cent, and a few areas abolished fees for secondary education.

The Second World War led to major changes in education. The evacuation of children from threatened areas led to considerable disruption of schooling, and by 1940, about half a million children were receiving no education at all. The radicalism fostered by the war led to more support for the view of education as a right that should be available to all, rather than a privilege obtained by wealth or ability. Plans for the reform of the school system were put forward in the 1943 White Paper, *Educational Reconstruction* (Board of Education 1943). This sought to retain different kinds of secondary school, but to give them equal esteem. It recognised the strength of the forces making for reform, but sought to channel these into an extension of the form of schooling that had developed in the 1930s. Resistance to any more radical change was strong, particularly from the churches that sought, and obtained, an increased degree of state subsidy for denominational schooling (Gordon et al. 1991).

The Education Act 1944 abolished the category of elementary education, and provided for all children to receive compulsory secondary education from the age of 11 until 15 (from 1947). The Act divided education into three stages: primary, secondary and further. Education was to be child-centred and to be adjusted to the 'ages, abilities and aptitudes' of the children. It was also to include the provision of 'special schools' for those who needed them. The Ministry of Education had no direct control of the curriculum or examinations, but it was able to regulate teacher training, capital expenditure and standards through the Inspectorate. The Act did not specify how education was to be organised, but the Ministry of Education used circulars and advice to promote a system of modern, technical and grammar schools. In most cases, however, secondary education was divided between modern and grammar schools. Those independent day schools that provided 25 per cent of their places free for children who had attended LEA primary schools were given a 'direct grant'. Voluntary schools were given the opportunity to obtain state funds by adopting 'controlled' or 'aided' status. For the first time, religious education and daily worship were made compulsory in all LEA schools.

The period from 1944 to the mid-1970s was a time of expansion in education (Finch 1984). The percentage of gross domestic product (GDP) spent on education rose from 3.3 per cent in 1950 to reach a peak of 7 per cent in 1975. However, the nature of schooling continued largely unchanged. A distinctive feature of the post-war period was the dominance exercised by the progressive reformist, social democratic view, stressing equality of opportunity combined with a belief in a linkage between educational expenditure and economic growth. This consensus was indicated by the support for increases in educational provision in a succession of reports dealing with almost every area of education. During the 1960s, there was concern about a number of educational issues, many of which were linked to what was coming to be recognised as the relatively poor performance of British business compared to competing nations. There was emphasis on the inability of business to meet the challenge of advanced technology because of the relatively low level of technical education compared to some competitor countries such as Germany. Many commentators focused on the wastage of ability caused by lack of opportunity, which led many bright working-class children to achieve far less educationally than they were capable of. The relatively low educational achievement of working-class children was the subject of a number of major reports. These addressed the problems of the working-class child in terms of the need for an educated population to meet the challenge of advanced technology, and the wastage caused by lack of opportunity. Under-achievement was seen as related to living conditions and family life. The reports also evinced a strong concern to increase attachment to conventional morality as a means of dealing with the problems of 'youth'. The purpose of state education was conceptualised as preparing subjects for their roles as workers and consumers in order to contribute to social wealth. Family or personal pathologies were identified as the reason why some subjects remained 'uneducated'. There was a belief in positivist solutions and educational debates focused on finding the 'correct' system to be adopted to ensure that education could successfully counteract the 'failure' of families and communities to produce the citizens required. The solution to the problem of low levels of working-class educational achievement and 'wastage of talent' was to be improved education in the form of comprehensive schooling.

The attempt to establish a system of comprehensive schools in the state sector was begun by the Labour government with the issue of Circular 10/65 to LEAs, asking them to submit plans. However, the process was long and uneven. In 1970, the Conservative government withdrew the circular, and it was not until 1976 that legislative compulsion was established. In the 1960s, there were a number of other significant changes in the organisation of schooling. There was some increase in parent and pupil participation in the running of schools, a broadening of the curriculum, and some changes in the examination system – in particular, the introduction of the Certificate of Secondary Education (CSE), which increased the percentage of school-leavers obtaining a qualification. In primary education there was something of a move away from formal teaching methods, and some experimentation with new forms of school design, such as 'open plan'. Following the Plowden Report (Plowden 1967), there were experimental projects in positive discrimination through the designation of Educational Priority Areas. These were supposed to improve the schooling of working-class children in inner-city areas, although the project had little general impact. The Robbins Report (Robbins 1963) recommended an expansion of the universities to increase the percentage of those receiving HE from 8 per cent to 17 per cent. New universities were established and some existing colleges of advanced technology were given university status. Polytechnics were set up from 1968. Colleges of Further Education (FE) began to recruit large numbers of A-level students, while some areas established sixth-form colleges. However, part-time FE developed very unevenly, subject largely to local initiative. Partly as a result, a high percentage of working-class children left school at the earliest opportunity and received no further formal education.

Despite the post-war changes in education, there were strong elements of continuity in the curriculum, the organisation of educational institutions, the sorting function of grading and examinations, and the pedagogic principles governing the relations of teachers and learners. At the élite level, the intellectual culture of the dominant class, as indicated by the subjects studied by its children, remained influenced by the traditional high culture. At the end of the 1960s, signs of the disintegration of the post-war education consensus began to appear. The Black Papers provided a coherent New Right alternative to the prevailing viewpoint with a critique of progressive teachers, falling 'standards' and the economic irrelevance of the curriculum (Cox and Dyson 1970). The Black Papers also developed a critique of multi-cultural education and raised the issue of 'race' in an educational context. The Conservative government elected in 1970 took up some of these issues. It made a number of cuts, including the abolition of free milk to those over 7-years-old and major reductions in teacher training from 1973. These cuts led to college closures and mergers, and to reduced opportunities for women in HE. The New Right influence on education, as with other areas of policy, reconstructed the welfare subject as primarily an economic unit to be managed. Education was criticised for failing to produce the type of workers required by industry, to the detriment of the economy; much of the curriculum was criticised for being irrelevant to industry; and the culture in 'progressive' schools was criticised for failing to inculcate industriousness and socially desirable behaviour in their pupils.

The Labour government elected in 1974 at first pursued the traditional policy of improving working-class access to education. The direct grant given to independent day schools was abolished in 1974. However, this actually led to an expansion of private schooling, since few of the affected schools chose to be incorporated into LEA provided education. The Education Act 1976 gave powers to compel comprehensive reorganisation. In 1976 a major change in educational policy took place, which was related to the economic crisis of that year. Cuts in the education budget were undertaken after the financial crisis and the intervention of the International Monetary Fund (IMF). Over the period 1975-79, the proportion of gross domestic product (GDP) spent on education fell from 7 per cent to 5.8 per cent.

The Labour government also initiated a 'Great Debate' on education. This moved away from the traditional social-democratic concern with access to education, and brought to the fore issues raised in the various Black Papers, in particular the curriculum, standards, teacher competence and vocational preparation. It was also accompanied by a broader ideological campaign against progressive teaching methods and left-wing teachers. At a time when unemployment was rapidly increasing, the Great Debate served to blame economic failure on the deficiencies of schooling and to reduce resistance to additional education cuts (Wolpe and Donald 1983). 'Work' has been central to the construction of the welfare subject as pupil since the beginning of state education, but the expectation that the state system is critical to the economic performance of the UK became increasingly important as the economy declined, and unemployment rose, from the mid-1970s onwards. The subjects studied in schools were a particular concern of the critics. The curriculum was criticised for having little connection with work skills. Schools in Britain did not have an occupational training function and neither, in the main, did universities (although polytechnics and technical colleges had). Education did, however, play a major role in moral training, as the formal requirement to promote religion in schools testifies. Other subjects, such as history and geography, entered the curriculum of working-class schools in a form highly amenable to the inculcation of an uncritical and often laudatory view of existing social organisation, the ruling class, the state and Britain's imperial role.

State intervention in education in 'modern' capitalist societies largely aimed to inculcate the nation with the values, knowledge and skills deemed appropriate for the survival of the established order. The constructions of 'work', 'consumption', 'family' and 'sexuality' as part of a dominant discourse of welfare are evident at different moments in the construction of state education. From the earliest days of state education, schools have been concerned with preparing children, particularly working-class children, for the work they were expected to do. Norms of living in relation to family life and sexuality have also been evident in the school curriculum. Consequently, a key feature of any system of schooling is its impact on the experience of the pupils. The division of the system of schooling into different types of schools was clearly related to the class structure. The upper classes were educated in the fee-paying public schools that viewed their role as the creation of a leadership cadre for British society. Middle-class children, along with a sprinkling of bright working-class children, would be educated in grammar schools. Most working-class children would be educated in secondary modern, or technical schools where these existed. The level of expenditure on the education of children was also closely linked to class.

State schooling is compulsory and legal sanctions have always been available to suppress non-attendance, emphasising the custodial role of the school (Hoyle 1998). The emphasis on punctuality, subordination to hierarchical discipline and the absence of formal democratic procedures within the school habituated children to a particular form of authority that was initially based explicitly on that of the factory. There was certainly little in the way of preparation for active democratic participation. The ways in which schools varied the education provided for different children also follows long-established principles. Pupils are often distinguished on the basis of age and sex, and sometimes religion. Some subjects are confined to certain age groups, and boys and girls are not provided with a common syllabus. Pupils are also commonly classified and graded on the basis of a variety of tests and examinations which separate out an élite of high achievers whose education will be prolonged. Those from higher classes receive a prolonged and higher-quality education costing far more than the minimal provision provided for those at the bottom of the class structure. Therefore, throughout the history of modern industrial society in the UK, we can witness the increasing intrusion of the state in defining legitimate knowledge and meaning within the education curriculum, by state institutions controlling notions of 'truth' and the construction of a legitimate moral order. Such systems of control have been consistently important in the post-industrial education system in the UK.

Neo-liberals, education policies and welfare discourse

The Conservative government elected in 1979 continued with the policy initiated by Labour of attempting to place more emphasis on the occupational and vocational functions of education. The supplementary discourse of 'consumption' in the construction of the welfare subject is evident in the acceptance by both major parties that the education of children was undertaken primarily for society, and not for children. That is, the success of education was the degree to which the rest of society benefited from the education of children rather than the quality of life children experienced at school, or the contribution education made to the quality of their lives as adults. The Conservatives introduced business methods into the organisation of the educational system and promoted business values in education through a range of initiatives. These included Enterprise in HE and the reform of the research councils (aimed at placing a greater stress on the application of research to the interests of business). They also included the introduction of competition between education providers in various sectors, including schools and FE, and the increased incorporation of business interests in the control of educational provision through such institutions as the Manpower Services Commission (MSC).

In the period 1979-83, the number of teachers fell by 38 000 and 800 schools were closed. Expenditure was cut on adult education, libraries and nursery schooling. In 1979, the government repealed the 1976 legislation requiring comprehensive secondary schooling. The Education Act 1980 required LEAs to allow parents to state a preference for the school their child would attend, marking the beginning of the notion of parent as consumer in the education market place. An assisted-places scheme was established to finance attendance at independent day schools, and provision was made for parents and teachers to be represented on school governing bodies. Finally, the school-meals service was put back to the pre-1944 basis. LEAs were no longer required to provide meals, except for those receiving them free. Nutritional standards were no longer specified, and LEAs could levy whatever charge they wished for providing meals, ensuring that the adequate nutrition of school-age children, once more, became a family affair instead of a collective social responsibility.

The government also began to make changes in the school curriculum. In 1981 the Schools Council was abolished, and the government expressed support for a core curriculum and curriculum development, using the language and approach of the MSC. This involved an emphasis on transferable life skills, primarily aimed at preparing the pupil for waged work, or gender roles, through the provision of such subjects as metalwork and domestic science. The MSC also became directly involved in secondary schools through the Technical and Vocational Training Initiative, which involved a pilot four-year technical curriculum involving 14 000 children in 147 schools. The Education Act 1986 made sex education discretionary in schools, as school governors were empowered to make the curriculum decisions rather than the local authority. This reflected the increasingly dominant notion that children had no (or rather 'normal' children should have no) sexuality and that exposure to sexual knowledge was corrupting.

The Education Reform Act 1988 has been perceived as one of the most fundamental changes to the education system since 1944. Its provisions were based on New Right ideas about the best way to run state services. There was to be an emphasis on business methods and managerial skills for headteachers and other decision-makers. In addition, schools were to be forced to operate as if they were businesses competing in a market. The suppliers of education were subjected to market 'disciplines' by having their revenues determined by the 'demand' for their services from consumers. In theory, they have to 'supply' what the purchasers want or they will run short of funds and, consequently, have to reduce the scale of their operations. Since this 'market' does not involve individual private consumers and producers it is often known as a 'quasi-market' (Le Grand and Bartlett 1993). The advent of quasi-markets meant that the supplementary discourse of consumption became increasingly critical to the formation of the welfare subject, as pupil and as parent, in relation to education.

In order to encourage a more business-like approach, the 1988 Act introduced a system known as Local Management of Schools (LMS). It has been argued that the Act 'reduced children and their schooling to commodities in a futures market' (Hoyle 1998: 100). Schools were to be run by Governing Bodies that were seen as the equivalent of a board of directors of a private business. They were given new powers, including paying and employing staff. LEAs had to delegate funds to the school on an agreed formula, mainly based on numbers and ages of pupils. Governing Bodies could shop around for services, such as school meals or cleaning, which were formerly provided by the LEA. While the LEA was now a 'supplier' of services, schools could, if they chose, purchase them elsewhere. LEAs could, however, hold back a small amount of the total education budget to pay for central support staff, such as educational psychologists, which individual schools would not be able to afford.

Another aspect of this move to a market model was increased emphasis on consumer choice. Parental choice of schools was introduced to force schools to compete for pupils. However, notions of parental choice in the education system were more rhetorical than real, with overt and covert selection remaining. It can be argued that the effect was more to do with social control, with the supplementary discourses of 'family' and 'consumption' connecting within the education system to objectify the 'good parent' and the 'good consumer':

> In relation to the family, education in late modernity is both an agency of normalisation and a commodity of choice; the education market offers parents an opportunity to choose, although for some there is a significant gap between making and getting a choice. Within this market parents are interpolated and inscribed as competitive consumers (acting in the self-interest of their family and child, seeking social advantage), and the processes and skills of choice play an important part in constituting a model of 'good parenting'. (Ball 1998: 189)

The 1988 Act also meant that the income of the school was made to depend on the number of pupils recruited. Supporters of the market approach saw competition between schools as a way to increase standards. Good schools would get more pupils (and thus more income) and expand, while poor schools would contract (and thus receive less money or even close). Competition was also encouraged by allowing schools to opt out of LEA control and become 'grant maintained' (GMS), receiving their funds directly from the government. These schools were more generously funded than those run by the LEAs. The government also encouraged the establishment of schools known as City Technology Colleges (CTCs) which received business sponsorship.

The Act also contained plans for a national curriculum. The Act states the curriculum should be:

balanced and broadly based and should:

1. promote the spiritual, moral, cultural, mental, and physical development of pupils at the school and of society; and

2. prepare such pupils for the opportunities, responsibilities and experiences of adult life. (Cited in O'Hagan and Smith 1996: 173)

There was a clear intention in the legislation to use state education to instil in pupils normalised constructs of work, consumption, family and sexuality. 'Waged work' was promoted as the primary means by which pupils could achieve social status and value as adults; and the normalised 'family', a married heterosexual man and woman, was promoted as the only moral and socially desirable relationship pupils should aspire to in adulthood. These notions were promoted within an educational system that was becoming increasingly consumerised with the advent of quasi-markets and managerialism.

A National Curriculum Council was established to control what would be taught in schools. Three core compulsory subjects were specified: English, mathematics and science. Testing of children was to begin from at the age of seven. There were also seven compulsory foundation subjects: history, geography, technology, art, music, physical education and, for those in the 11 to 16 age group, a modern language. Religious education had to be provided for those pupils whose parents wished them to receive it. Three cross-curricula subjects, namely health education, personal and social education, and careers, had to be taught through other subjects. The specification of the content of the national curriculum caused considerable debate. There was major controversy about the nature of the history which was to be taught between those who preferred the traditional emphasis on the British state and those who control it, and others who wished to teach a broader curriculum with a strong element of social history. The national curriculum was designed to take up around 80 per cent of school time. Other subjects had to be fitted into the remaining time. The system was highly prescriptive, with detailed handbooks specifying what had to be taught at each stage in each subject. Its content was dominated by conventional values based upon:

a discourse which links education strongly with traditional social and political values and with social order ... It relies upon a cultural and moral naturalism, a lexicon of essential values, identities and meanings. It thus obscures and defies difference, heterogeneity and struggle. Struggles over class and race, over inequality and oppression are displaced by a discourse of common heritage and the classless society, and subsumed by cultural and legal tactics ... which carefully define who is a legitimate contributor to the performativity of the state. (Ball 1998: 189-190)

Alongside these changes in the school curriculum, 1988 also saw the advent of 'Clause 28':

a highly symbolic piece of legislation for the lesbian and gay community. Passed in 1989 [as Section 28 of the Local Government Act] ... it was intended by its creators to prevent schools dealing with lesbian and gay issues. 56 per cent of teachers believe the existence of Section 28 is damaging young lesbians and gays in schools. ('Playing it Safe', Institute of Education, 1998 cited by Stonewall, http: //www.stonewall.org.uk/news 1 November 1999)

Under Section 28 local authorities were banned from intentionally promoting homosexuality, in schools or through the publication of literature, as a pretend 'family' relationship, affirming the dominant discourse on 'sexuality' and the perceived threat to children from 'deviants' within the school system. It prevented teachers from discussing issues around homosexuality, inducing a climate of homophobia within the school system.

The new curriculum required teachers to undertake a huge body of work to adjust their teaching to its requirements. It also proved to be overloaded and overspecified and, in 1994, major amendments took place which were supposed to make it simpler to teach and to monitor, thus necessitating a further recasting of detailed programmes of work and more classroom planning. The national curriculum also specified four 'key stages', each involving a three- or four-year section of the total school career. National tests were to be used to identify attainment at the end of each key stage. Schools had to publish the results so that parents could evaluate how well the schools were performing. There is now widespread use of school 'league tables'. In a move that echoed the approach employed by the government in relation to health, a Parents Charter was published in 1991. This specified the rights of parents in a number of areas. In the Parents Charter:

> choice is powerfully promoted as a personal matter, a question of individual parents taking responsibility for their children's educational future ... This appeal to parents to 'consume' education idealises 'responsible consumerism', both typified and encouraged by the steady growth in consumer magazines and consumer programmes on TV and on the radio, all promoting the merits of being a responsible rational consumer. (Gewirtz et al. 1995, cited in Muschamp et al. 1999: 113)

Those who cannot act as responsible rational consumers will remain disadvantaged in the education system. The amended version of this Charter, published in 1994, gave parents the right to a range of sources of information about schools, including examination results and access to inspection reports. It also gave parents the right to make the choice of school and to vote for parent governors. The Charter laid down national targets for educational attainment, including a target for the numbers of young people nationally who should achieve specified GCSE grades. However, the Charter made no mention of such issues as class sizes, expenditure on books and equipment, or the quality of school buildings and grounds.

A major innovation was the replacement in 1992 of the existing system of local school inspections undertaken by Her Majesty's Inspectorate with a new system run by the Office for Standards in Education (OFSTED). OFSTED's mode of operation became immediately apparent after its first unfavourable report on a primary school was highly publicised in the press. It was instantly clear that it saw itself establishing a role in rooting out what was seen as inadequate teaching, and in pinning the label of 'failing school' where performance was judged to be below standard. OFSTED's first annual report for the year 1993-94 claimed that one quarter of lessons for 5- to 7-year-olds, and one third of those for 8- to 11-year-olds, were 'unsatisfactory'. The report also contained an attack on 'progressive' teaching methods, such as mixed-ability teaching and group work. Subsequently, OFSTED was able to expand its role by analysing the results of its inspections in order to identify what it claimed were the most effective methods of teaching. It then promoted the idea that whole-class teaching rather than group work should be employed wherever possible. OFSTED also provided evidence consonant with the New Right agenda for education. It argued that social background itself was not an explanation of low levels of educational attainment found in schools in deprived areas, since schools in these areas had differing levels of attainment. It also claimed that its results showed that class size was not a significant factor in educational attainment. The implication of all these arguments was that uniformly high levels of educational attainment could be achieved, regardless of the social conditions in which pupils lived, so long as good teachers were employed and they used the methods prescribed by OFSTED.

Throughout the period of Conservative rule ideological campaigns were run against subjects which were viewed as subversive, such as sociology and social science, and against left-wing teachers and progressive teaching methods. The government continued to promote the view that educational problems resulted from the dominance of progressive ideas and methods that had developed in the 1960s, and which had undermined the previously successful educational system. In line with this viewpoint, criticisms were levelled at the system of teacher education. Various changes were introduced which were supposed to return teacher training to a more acceptable pattern. These included a scheme to provide a cut-down training for entrants from industry, and a scheme for school-centred training in which much more of the training of the prospective teachers took place in school than in colleges.

As part of its attempt to improve the supply side of the economy, the Conservative government undertook a major reform of vocational education and training. This reform was intended to reduce the cost and transfer the burden of funding to those who would benefit from the training, especially students and employers. Courses in FE were reorganised through the establishment of the Business and Technical Education Council (BTEC). The MSC also became heavily involved, and by 1986 it financed about 25 per cent of all courses in colleges of FE. The MSC's New Training Initiative (1981) included proposals for an Open Tech, using distance-learning techniques and the provision of 'Pickup' courses (Professional, Industrial and Community Updating). The functions of the MSC in the Department of Employment were later transferred to Training and Enterprise Councils (TECs) which were led and largely controlled by employer interests. The government's strategy was to engage business at local level in the system of training and education. A key part of the strategy involved the establishment of the new system of vocational qualifications. The National Council for Vocational Qualifications (NCVQ) was set up in 1986. The idea was to bring together existing vocational qualifications and combine them into a new system. The council established the National Vocational Qualification (NVQ) for vocational awards which are organised through the NVQ system. NVQs involve five levels of vocational qualification. GNVQs were primarily designed for the post-GCSE age group of 16- to 19-year-olds as a vocational alternative to A-level examinations. This qualification was based on students providing evidence that they had acquired the competencies required for a particular job around which the qualification was based. The content of training was not specified and assessment was taken in-house rather than by external examiners. Since the government would only pay where the training was successfully completed, institutions had an incentive to pass students rather than maintain standards. The system was not immediately successful and, at first, few courses attracted more than a handful of students, generally at the lowest level (Konrad 1995).

In 1994, the government established a series of targets referring to the proportions of young people who were to achieve NVQ qualifications at various levels, by specified dates. Quasi-scientific methods, part of a positivist, rationalistic approach to state education in the UK, became the primary means by which its quality was measured. There were further targets relating to 'lifetime learning' which specified the percentages of employers who would engage in particular training or development activities. As a result of a review of the NVQ system, undertaken in 1996, the NCVQ was merged in 1997 with the School Curriculum and Assessment Authority to form the Qualifications and Curriculum Authority.

The establishment of a new system of vocational qualifications was, in part, a response to the decline of the traditional apprenticeship system, formerly a major route into employment for working-class males. Apprenticeships declined because of the fall in the size of the manufacturing sector, and prolonged periods of high unemployment that reduced industrial recruitment. In comparison with other European countries, the proportion of young people in Britain, aged 18 and in full-time education, has been very low. There is also a long history of division between vocational and academic education. Vocational education has always had a low status in terms of the dominant values of the liberal educational tradition (Weiner 1985). Various proposals have been made to move towards a more unified education system with its vocational and academic elements combined (Finegold 1998). The Dearing Report (Dearing 1996) argued for a closer linkage between schools and FE colleges for the education and training of young people in the 14- to 16-year-old age group. Many schools have developed initiatives in recent years relating to the world of work, including schemes of work experience, industrial visits, and exchanges between teachers and people working in industry.

Cuts in university education were made from 1981. The polytechnics' budgets were also cut and the National Advisory Board initiated a process of restructuring. The government undertook a rapid expansion of the numbers entering HE, although the funds provided to universities and polytechnics were not increased in proportion, leading to larger classes and a worsening of staff-student ratios. The former polytechnics were removed from the control of local authorities and, from 1992, were allowed to call themselves universities. This marked the abandonment of the binary policy in higher education which remained dominant from 1970 to 1992. One purpose of this policy had been a simple division of institutions into two sectors (universities and polytechnics) for administrative and funding purposes. The values underpinning the policy, however, had both radical and conservative elements. The left perceived the traditional universities as failing to meet the government's technological and egalitarian goals, but the policy also preserved the status quo and power interests within traditional universities by protecting them from the Labour government's agenda of change for the sector (Carr 1998). The Further and Higher Education Act 1992 established a funding council for FE, and made FE Colleges independently incorporated institutions which were no longer run by local authorities. The substantial increase in the number of students entering HE led to increased public expenditure on student grants and on course fees. Since the government was planning for a further expansion in the proportion of 18-year-olds going on to HE, the Dearing inquiry was established to consider how HE should be organised, and paid for, in the future (Dearing 1997).

Impact of the Conservative reforms

During the period of Conservative government substantial changes took place in the educational system. There were four major areas of change: a reduction in the role of local authorities; an attack on professionalism; the growing use of markets and quasi-markets; and the elevation of the role and power of management.

FE Colleges and polytechnics (later to become universities) were incorporated as independent institutions and removed from the control of local government, as has been described above. The impact of this shift in policy has been described as 'a radical challenge by the state to the intrinsic values of education which underpinned the university model' (Carr 1998: 274):

> It was not the university but the polytechnic that triumphed. The constitutional status of the British University had been shattered. In its place was Baker's concept of a work-orientated, vocational, commercial institution, run more like an externally accountable public corporation than a collegium of scholars. (Jenkins, cited in Carr 1998: 274)

The role of local authorities was reduced in other ways, through the establishment of local management of schools and the arrangements by which schools could opt out of local authority control. Other publicly financed schools, such as City Technology Colleges, were also put outside the local authority framework.

The attack on professionalism involved an increase in the power of governing bodies and the establishment of a National Curriculum, which stipulated not only what should be taught in schools but also, in some cases, how it should be taught. Further control of methods of teaching was undertaken by OFSTED. In addition, the salaries of those working in schools, colleges and universities were allowed to fall relative to the general level of white-collar incomes as a result of strong public-sector expenditure controls. There were also ideological campaigns against teachers who were held responsible for a range of social problems, including educational under-achievement and the alleged bad behaviour of young people.

The use of markets and quasi-markets was encouraged. Most importantly, schools and colleges were located in a competitive environment in which their funding depended on the number of students and pupils that they were able to attract. One of the ways government sought to empower the parental consumer was through the publication of school examination league tables. This performance criterion operates as a disciplinary system of judgement over teachers, enforced through the discourses of 'standards' and 'quality assessment' (Ball 1998) which also serve to objectify the 'enemy within' the education system – they place teachers and schools within a system of individualising self-scrutiny.

Performance 'indicators "fabricate" an organisation that is for external consumption; they provide a focus for the gaze of quality and accountability; they are there to be viewed and evaluated and compared' (p. 196). Meanwhile, there are those who believe that they also lead to the breakdown of social co-operation and wider notions of solidarity and equality:

> Teachers and head teachers are now more clearly inwardly focused upon the survival of their institutions within the education market. Budgetary devolution, 'opting out' and the removal of the powers of local authorities (together with the effects of market forces) have fragmented many local systems of education. Alongside this, the introduction of parental choice and school selection work in some circumstances to break down the relationship between schools and their localities and communities. Schools are again inwardly focused and are encouraged to have primary concern for the interests of their clients... rather than the needs of their social community. (Ball 1998: 198)

In addition, business interests and business values were given a greater place in the educational system generally.

Managerialism was strengthened in various ways. The fact that schools and colleges were now relatively independent operating units meant that the role of those who ran them contained a much greater element of managerial responsibility, and a correspondingly smaller educational component. In HE and FE the employment of professional managers increased and, in some cases, people from a business background were given the senior posts in institutions. So far as schools were concerned, management skills became more important for heads, and the rhetoric and practices of management were adopted with the encouragement of boards of governors on which management interests might well be represented. The governing boards of the new universities and those of colleges of FE also contained a strong element of management representation, which was stipulated in legislation (Clarke et al. 1994).

The ostensible aim of all these changes which took place in schooling, FE and HE was to improve standards of attainment as a means of improving the economic performance of society. There is no clear evidence that the changes had these effects. Where standards of attainment did improve it is likely that the changes took place largely because institutions concentrated on those activities that would show up on the performance indicators which they were required to use. For example, it was argued that the educational testing of young children was inherently flawed because the critical input for children is pre-school education, of which the UK has very little compared to other European countries (Hennessy et al. 1992). The differential experience of children, in this regard, will adversely affect test results and skew performance indicators:

> There has been a great deal of research on the positive effects of pre-school education and how those children who have been fortunate enough to have had this fare better when they start school. A major criticism of the National Curriculum is that it does not take into account a child's pre-school experience when carrying out the assessment tests at age seven. Thus, the results of one school may be far better than those of another because the majority of children at school with better results had had pre-school education. (O'Hagan and Smith 1996: 174)

There has been a long-term tendency for the number of pupils obtaining passes in public examinations to increase. There is no evidence that this rate of increase has risen as a result of the changes brought in. It is apparent, however, that many of the changes made have increased the administrative load on teachers and lecturers. This has been a particular problem for schools because this administrative load has largely fallen on teaching staff and heads, rather than on administrators. It is likely that in all educational institutions the proportion of the time spent teaching by those appointed as teachers has fallen as a result of the changes made.

However, a major impact of all the changes in education introduced since the mid-1970s has been to shift the debate about education. The education system generally, and schools and teachers in particular, have been held responsible for economic and social problems, which have been attributed to progressive education. This has been portrayed as having failed to provide young people with the knowledge and skills that they need, and as having failed to maintain social discipline. The 1960s, in particular, have been mythologised as a period in which effective teaching and discipline broke down, leading to a decline in school standards. However, there is evidence over the whole of the post-war period of very little change indeed in standards of educational attainment (NFER 1995). The key change is that now, whenever economic failure or social breakdown is discussed, education is always close to the top of the list of causes to which these are ascribed.

The negative depiction of state schooling within the dominant welfare discourse has created something close to a moral panic amongst many middle-class parents. Continued high levels of unemployment have made the job market more competitive for young people at all levels of educational attainment. Youth unemployment has remained high amongst young people from a working-class background. The opportunities for middle-class entrants to the labour market have also become much more restricted. Combined with the opportunity to select schools for their children, this has led to many middle-class parents, especially in London, to reject the use of their local neighbourhood schools or, indeed, moving house to live in the catchment area of a high-performing school (Jordan 1998). It has also led to a growth in private-sector provision, especially of secondary schooling. These factors are adding to the exclusionary processes inherent in Britain today.

The use of the internal market in education, and in particular the emphasis on parental choice, has certainly led to major changes in the behaviour of parents. It has also had a significant impact on many schools; some have expanded and developed, while others have declined and found it difficult to recruit pupils. Those pupils who have remained in declining schools are likely to have been adversely affected, if only by association with a school perceived to be failing. The extra resources provided for favoured sectors of publicly-financed schooling, in particular those schools which obtain their funding from the Schools Funding Agency, increased inequalities in the standards of provision within the public sector. It would appear that inequalities within the schooling system have risen and social inequality generally has not been reduced as a result of the policy changes introduced by the Conservatives during their period in office from 1979 to 1997.

New Labour, education policies and welfare discourse

The role of education

New Labour has given a high priority to its education policies. The Prime Minister famously stated that our priorities are 'education, education and education' (Muschamp et al. 1999: 101). However, New Labour have retained most of the Conservative reforms discussed above, continuing with the 'vision' of 'parental choice', blaming and shaming schools, the imposition of performance standards and curriculum guidance. Indeed, in office, 'the new Labour government ... has been even fiercer than its predecessor in its criticisms, and more decisive in its interventions, over schools and teachers judged to be failing to realize their pupils' potential achievements' (Jordan 1998: 129). The Department for Education and Employment (DfEE) White Paper, *Excellence in Schools* (DfEE 1997), talks of giving 'everyone the chance, through education, training and work, to realise their full potential, and thus build an inclusive and fair society and a competitive economy'. The DfEE also proclaims as its overriding goal the aim to build a society where everyone has 'an equal chance to achieve their full potential' (DfEE 1998b). It is worth noting that the aim is not to increase the degree of equality, but actually to provide everyone with an 'equal' chance. In the account of its overall programme to combat poverty, one of the four key objectives of government is to increase the proportion of 19-year-olds who gain two A-levels or the equivalent (DSS 1999). Education is, therefore, viewed as a central means by which the economic and social goals of the government can be achieved.

New Labour believes it can engineer a range of improvements in the current system of public-sector education that will enable its goals to be achieved. However, it is not clear how the achievement of these goals will actually be measured. The government has set targets for education, but these relate to educational achievement – in particular, improving the proportion of school pupils gaining specified scores in standard assessment tests (SATS) or public exams. These performance indicators, flawed as they are, do not even refer to recruitment to occupational roles in society, such as the extent of working-class access to senior positions in various occupational areas. If the education system is actually seen as a means of promoting social opportunity then, in line with the managerialist approach taken by the government, the policies should be evaluated with respect to improvements in social opportunity.

It can be argued that changes in the public-sector school system are unlikely to have much effect on the actual structure of social opportunity. This is because the character of social inequality in Britain is entrenched in a range of social institutions and practices that allow inequalities to be sustained, regardless of any changes made to the education system. Moreover, in examining New Labour's educational reforms, it is possible to discern a distinct continuity with the neo-liberal discourse of welfare. That is, a discourse within which state education is used to promote the work ethic, the normality of consumerism, the nuclear family and heterosexuality as the normalised condition. As a consequence, we argue that New Labour's system of education is contributing to social exclusion rather than eradicating it. These issues are discussed further in the following sections.

Education and 'difference': gender, ethnicity and class

The link between social inequality and educational inequality is a close one. The degree and nature of inequality in society both affects the education system and is affected by it. The major systems of inequality fuelled by 'difference' in society, including gender, class and 'race', all have major implications for education.

There are long-standing gender differences in education (Byrne 1978). Traditionally, boys achieved more qualifications than girls and received a longer education. This difference in qualification widens the further one moves up the hierarchy of qualifications. Moreover, from the beginning of state education, girls have generally studied subjects related to domestic labour or relevant to work that was considered suitable for women, and they have been encouraged to adopt specifically feminine attributes suited to their social reproduction responsibilities within the 'family'. In a modified and reduced form, these differences remain today; some sexual inequalities, however, have been reduced. There is no longer a sex difference in the proportions of pupils leaving at the minimum school-leaving age. Inequality in access to HE has been reduced, but major differences remain in the subjects studied, reproducing the sexual division of labour. Women are under-represented in engineering and technology, architecture, medicine and science, and over-represented in the arts and education. The post-war reduction in the differences between the education of girls and boys was related to the increasing labour market participation of women throughout the long boom. This provided favourable conditions for viewing women's under-achievement as wasteful and for attempting to improve women's educational performance.

Since the mid-1970s, more effort has been expended on understanding the differences in the educational achievement and experience of boys and girls. The levels of achievement of girls appear to be rising faster than those of boys. The performance gap between boys and girls has generally decreased in those subjects where boys previously had an advantage, such as mathematics and science. In 1999, over 53 per cent of girls achieved five or more C grades or better at GSCE, compared to 42 per cent of boys. Girls are now out-performing boys at A-level and, as a result, have substantially increased their access to HE. The falling relative achievement level of boys has been linked to the issue of masculinity, which some critics have focused on as an explanation of deviant and anti-social behaviour amongst boys (Campbell 1993). It has also been suggested that this could be linked to the changing patterns of work for men, affecting their gender role, social status and self-esteem, also linked to a rise in suicide among young men. This issue is discussed more fully in Chapter Eight.

In the HE sector, the relative difference in the rates of university entrance of members of different classes has remained remarkably constant throughout the twentieth century. There are even signs that some of the changes made in the funding of HE, especially the abolition of student maintenance grants, may be increasing these inequalities. The overall level of educational achievement is closely related to the occupational class of a child's family. So, for example, 60 per cent of daughters from manual workers' families have no qualifications, compared to 24 per cent of daughters from professional families (CSO 1997). The level of qualifications which a person achieves is correlated with their future earning power and chances of obtaining paid employment. The lifetime earnings of graduates are 76 per cent higher than those of non-graduates.

Evidence demonstrates the relatively low level of social mobility in Britain and the substantial extent to which social status is inherited from the family into which one is born. Inherited wealth plays a major role in the persistence of economic and social inequality. Data from a survey that followed all children born in a week in March 1958 highlighted the degree to which the income of one generation is related to the family income of the generation before (Johnson and Reed 1996). Where the incomes of fathers in one group are twice as high as those of fathers in another group, the incomes of the sons in the high-income group will be 40 to 60 per cent higher than those of the sons in the lower-income group. Those in the top quartile of earnings may expect over half of their sons to end up in the same grouping. Similarly, for those in the bottom quartile of earnings, over a third of their sons will end up in the same quartile. These inherited disadvantages are apparent even when educational differences are taken into account.

New Labour policy does not address the ways in which other institutions also contribute to the continued domination of leading positions by the upper-middle and upper classes in Britain. The organisations that control access to membership of various professions are important here. Access to the medical profession is strongly biased in favour of those educated in private schools or state grammar schools. These pupils made up over 50 per cent of all medical students in 1995. Over three-quarters of these came from professional families, and around 20 per cent had one or both parents who were also doctors. Two-thirds of graduates at Sandhurst in 1995 were privately educated. Recruitment to senior positions in the civil service is still heavily biased to those educated at Oxford and Cambridge, who often come from an upper-middle-class background. Recruitment to the business élite is also heavily weighted towards the upper middle class, especially in the financial sector and in older, larger and well-established manufacturing companies (Adonis and Pollard 1997).

Class inequalities in education also involve substantial differences in state expenditure. The higher classes benefit disproportionately because they receive a longer education, and because this extra education is more expensive to provide. These effects are intensified by geographical differences. LEAs with a relatively affluent population spend more on education, and middle-class suburban areas often have newer and better-equipped schools than inner-city, working-class areas. State expenditure on education also benefits those who are educated in independent schools. These children are overwhelmingly from affluent and (often) upper-class families. A wide range of subsidies and tax relief is available to parents of these children and to the schools themselves. The assisted-places scheme introduced by the Conservative government, like the free places in direct-grant schools that it replaced, mainly benefited middle-class children. Various schemes exist whereby parents or grandparents can avoid paying tax on funds used to finance private education. Some occupational groups, such as army officers and diplomats, receive subsidies for their children to obtain private education. The schools themselves benefit from charitable status, which exempts them from income, corporation and capital-gains taxes. The public schools continue to play a major role in British society. Over 80 per cent of the top 200 schools, as measured by A-level examination results, are outside the state system of schooling. The staff-student ratios in the public schools average 1 to 10 as against a figure of 1 to 17 in the state sector (Adonis and Pollard 1997). A significant role is also played by the remaining state grammar schools, of which there are over 150. Most of these are situated in relatively wealthy areas and have a largely middle-class clientele. Using the proportion of pupils receiving free school meals as an indicator of poverty, the proportion for grammar school pupils is 3.4 per cent against a national average of 18 per cent, indicating that few pupils from very poor families attend these schools (Carvel 1999). The grammar schools, along with the public schools, educate around 9 per cent of all children. They dominate entry to Oxford and Cambridge and to the old universities.

Those who still generally obtain the best education are from the higher social classes. League tables of public examination results consistently show that the highest A-level scores are achieved in the private sector of schooling and that, generally, those schools with a middle- and upper-class intake obtain the most examination passes (Financial Times 1996). Graduates from state schools earn less than those who have been privately educated, even when age, gender, subject studied and class of degree are taken into consideration. Private schooling also confers advantages in obtaining university entrance. Applicants to Oxford and Cambridge Universities who have attended private schools have a greater chance of being offered a place than those who have attended state schools. Approximately half of all entrants to Oxford and Cambridge are from private schools (Adonis and Pollard 1997). Throughout the twentieth century, class inequalities in education have remained remarkably constant despite a series of educational reforms, many of which (such as the provision of free secondary education in the Education Act 1944, and the reorganisation of secondary schooling to promote comprehensive schools in the 1960s) were justified with reference to improving equality of opportunity (Silver 1973). Studies of the impact of schooling on social mobility were carried out in 1949, 1972 and 1983 (Glass 1954, Halsey et al. 1980, Heath and Ridge 1983). These show that there has been little measurable impact resulting from educational reforms over the period covered by the research. While educational attainment, as measured by examination passes, has generally increased, educational inequalities have remained.

The education received by racial minorities shows a number of distinctive features and has been the subject of special policy measures. In the 1960s, attempts were made to assimilate members of racial minorities by special language training and through the use of 'bussing'. This involved transporting racial-minority pupils to schools some distance away in an attempt to spread them throughout the schools within an LEA. However, the general approach has now moved towards support for cultural pluralism. Surveys have demonstrated the relatively low educational achievement of members of racial minorities, especially African-Caribbeans. In the 1980s, all racial minorities had a lower chance of taking up university education, even where the qualifications for it existed, and this is likely to be as a result of racism and low-quality schooling in inner-city areas. Traveller children make up the racial group with the lowest levels of educational achievement. The material benefits of educational achievement are also lower for members of racial minorities. Of those with degrees, a far higher proportion of black people than white people are in manual jobs, due to discrimination and marginal status in the labour market. In March 1999, OFSTED produced a report on racial-minority education. This suggested that institutional racism is a feature of many schools in Britain. It claimed that while most schools have policies that stress equal opportunities, few have clear procedures for monitoring their implementation. Less than a quarter of the educational authorities in the OFSTED survey had a clear strategy for raising the attainment of racial-minority children. Some textbooks and some teachers employed racial stereotyping. The report also referred to high levels of expulsion and exclusion of black pupils; black pupils were around five times more likely to be excluded than white pupils.

Non-regular attendance and school exclusion is a problem for many children. School exclusion may be 'fixed' for a set period or 'permanent', which in effect amounts to expulsion. The number of children and young people permanently excluded from school has increased substantially in the last decade. It grew from under 3000 in 1990, to over 12 000 in 1995. However, for 1997-98 the figure is slightly down. From 1998, schools were able to exclude children for nine weeks in a term instead of the former limit of three weeks. This provision formed part of the Education Act 1996, brought in by the previous Conservative government. Many disruptive pupils have themselves experienced family breakdown. Others may have special educational needs that have not been satisfactorily met. Many children who are excluded receive very little educational assistance at home while they are out of school. Around a quarter receive some home tuition, but on average this amounts to five hours a week and many receive substantially less. A group that experiences particular educational problems is children in care. There are 50 000 children in this group. Their chance of being excluded from school is ten times greater than the average. Three quarters of these children leave school with no formal qualifications compared to 6 per cent of the general population. Only around a fifth go on to FE. Many young offenders have low levels of educational achievement. Most come from the poorer section of the working class, and many have a history of truancy. Almost two-thirds of school-age offenders had experienced a prolonged absence from school due to exclusion or truancy (Audit Commission 1996).

School exclusion represents one of the most vivid images of the growing educational divide in Britain. An estimated 100 000 children continue to be excluded temporarily from schools in Britain, with another 13 000 permanently excluded (SEU 1998). Explanations of the causes of school exclusion include both behavioural factors such as poor parenting and home environments, and structural factors such as poverty, negative racial stereotyping, the breakdown of societal discipline and educational policies (Cohen et al. 1994, Gillborn 1998, Lloyd-Smith 1993). Moreover, the organisational culture of schools and the lower expectations some teachers have of working-class pupils, both in terms of academic achievement and behaviour, appear to exacerbate the problem by intensifying psychological and behavioural problems for pupils who 'do not fit in' (Coleman 1998). While the disproportionate number of African-Caribbean children who are excluded points to a strong correlation between race and exclusion (SEU 1998, Craig et al. 1998, Cohen et al. 1994), no attention has been given to the need to reduce school exclusions for children from racial minorities within the Social Exclusion Unit's (SEU) overall reduction targets. Moreover, New Labour's support for a managerialist policy, focused on raising standards, downgrades social and racial justice, and may reinforce inequalities to the detriment of working-class and racial-minority pupils (Hatcher 1997). The rise in school exclusions appears to be associated with the quasi-market, which encourages schools to get rid of disruptive pupils who will not only require additional resources to teach them, but whose levels of attainment may reduce average scores on published test results.

Whilst truancy rates in the late-1990s are little different from those discussed by concerned educationalists in the late-1890s (Hoyle 1998), it is the purposeful exclusion of children from school by the state that has increased dramatically. It has been suggested that:

In recent years a 'blaming system' has been constructed in the domain of schooling ... [P]revailing constructions of pupil absence in the education service are based on superficial, politically convenient myths about 'deviant' and 'pathological' individuals [and]... that schooling represents a further site of what

Jones has termed a 'resurgent brutalism' ... of marginalised children and families. (Hoyle 1998: 109)

Only about one third of excluded children are quickly reintegrated back into school. The remainder generally receive what is known as 'education otherwise', arranged in most cases through special centres, home tuition or further education colleges (SEU 1998). Marginalising pupils into off-site educational provision can reinforce the message that they are unacceptable. In recognition of this, there has been an increasing lobby for inclusive education (Lloyd-Smith and Davies 1995). While the government has stated its commitment to reducing school exclusions, there is little evidence in its guidance to date (SEU 1998, DfEE 1999, DSS 1999) that the broader structural factors underpinning the school exclusion process are being acknowledged. For instance, research suggests that rising school exclusion is partly connected to selection processes in schools 'competing in the market place for the most "rewarding" pupils' (Lloyd-Smith and Davies 1995: 6). New Labour has allowed selectivity to continue. As a consequence, successful schools will continue to serve the most able pupils from wealthier families who can afford to live near these schools. In contrast, less successful schools will have the incentive to 'exclude "disruptive" children, and those with special needs, in order to improve their performance. This puts extra costs on the community, as well as contributing to injustice' (Jordan 1998: 130). Moreover, several studies have examined the interrelationship between educational experience and the influence of class, poverty, unemployment, race, poor housing conditions and disempowerment (Coleman 1998, Beynon and Glavanis 1999).

The supplementary discourse of work is evident in the new proposals aimed at pupils who are alienated from school. The government has announced that a pilot scheme will take place in which pupils from the age of 14 who are alienated from school will be sent on work experience schemes to local firms. In the scheme pupils will undertake on-the-job training for an NVQ. The scheme is designed to reduce truancy. Under the existing law, schools can only send children for work experience when they reach the age of 15. The Chief Inspector of Schools has also proposed what he refers to as a 'more flexible approach' to post-14 compulsory education in which teenagers who are not academically gifted should be allowed to train for a trade whilst still at school. This seems to be a further step away from the idea of equal education for all and a reversion towards the system of providing a minimal education for working-class children. However, the government is also introducing a scheme of means-tested grants to encourage young people to stay at home and study at sixth-form level. These will begin in 2001. The grant will be worth up to a maximum of £40 a week for those from homes with an annual income up to £30,000 a year, with the full amount being paid to families where yearly income is below £13,000. Receipt of the grant will be conditional on attendance, and on completing the required school-work in line with a learning agreement which will be made with the school or college. Part-time income from work undertaken by the student will be disregarded. The scheme was to be piloted from September 1999 in 12 towns and cities across England.

Article 12 of the UN Convention on the Rights of the Child, ratified by the British government in 1991, recognises the rights of children to participate in society. The government has also committed itself to involving children in the design and delivery of its policies on social exclusion (DSS 1999). Encouraging children's involvement in schools, however, remains a minority activity amongst the teaching profession, especially when working with pupils with special educational needs (Lloyd-Smith and Davies 1995). Moreover, there have been:

> few sociological studies based on children's accounts of their everyday lives and experiences, and sociologists and anthropologists are increasingly aware that there are large gaps in our understanding of children's perspectives ... This general lack of basic social research means it is difficult to incorporate children's perspectives in policy terms. (Morrow 1999: 297-8)

There are examples of 'alternative schools' that enable children to take charge of their own learning – such as Summerhill (Neill 1968). A key aim of these schools is to allow children and young people the 'chance to exercise democratic power [and] discover the sense of personal worth that comes from free social interaction with people of all ages' (Gribble 1999: 1). Central to the ethos of such schools is 'the notion that children are self-motivated learners' (p. 2). What is suggested here is that, given the right learning environment, children will automatically select what they need at their current stage of development. The role of the teaching team, therefore, is to be reactive rather than instructive:

> Individuals, from infants to old people, resent or fail to show any interest in anything initially presented to them through discipline, regulation or instruction which is another aspect of authority. (Report on the Peckham Health Centre in

south London in the 1930s by Dr Pearse and Dr Williamson, cited in Gribble 1999: 2)

This notion of child-centred learning is central to many pre-school programmes and is well documented in other countries. For example, the world-renowned system of pre-school education in Reggio Emilio in Northern Italy is one place where this educational philosophy has been incorporated into educational policy. The programme, implemented by state, voluntary and private provision, began 35 years ago as a way of investing in society to create new men and women who would ensure that fascism would never again become possible. The programme is not static, but takes place within a continuing process of critical debate. Young children are conceptualised as competent and full of resources and potential, who do not need to be made to learn since they are born equipped to learn. Other approaches, such as Resources for Infant Educarers (RIE), which was originally developed in Hungary, also focus on the infant and the very young child's learning potential. This approach is not just concerned with cognitive development, but with social and emotional development too (Gerber and Weaver 1998). These approaches argue that children do not need a regime to force them to learn, but rather an environment and adults that support, not suppress, their natural inclination to learn.

Pre-school programmes in the US, such as High/Scope, have been influential in the UK (Little 1999). New Labour have drawn on the results of this longitudinal research study when drafting the Sure Start programme, which is aimed at poor parents and their young children:

> Sure Start is an evidence-based policy, with its origins grounded in a thorough analysis of the research literature of 'what works'. The UK evidence on the effectiveness of early intervention is however quite limited, with evidence of many of the long-term benefits coming from the US. The programme therefore offers a unique opportunity to contribute to the knowledge base of the impact of early intervention on children and families in areas of multiple disadvantage. (Glass 1999: 262)

The High/Scope children, however, received two years pre-school education for each half day during the school term. Children spent individual time with their teacher as well as group time, and the teacher visited each child's home once-a-week. With Sure Start, New Labour have put in place a plan for the integration of pre-school services at local level, but not a child-centred educational programme that is holistic in nature and sufficiently funded to ensure each child is able to receive the same high quality and intensity of pre-school education. New Labour's expectations that Sure Start will achieve the same outcomes for children as High/Scope are therefore unlikely to be realised.

The structure of educational provision

New Labour has not attempted to reverse many of the changes made in education by the Conservatives. The enhanced role for governors, the system of LMS, the national curriculum and the place of private-sector schooling have all remained in place. The extent of structural change is limited. New Labour announced the end of the assisted-places scheme, the savings from which have been earmarked to finance the policy of reducing class sizes for 5- to 7-year-olds to below 30 by the start of the school year in 2001. New Labour did not abandon the special status of existing grant-maintained schools. Instead, they are being redesignated as 'foundation' schools, where the governors are allowed to retain aspects of autonomy as employers, owners of premises and managers of the school. Foundation schools will have to agree their admissions policy with the LEA, with any conflict resolved by an independent adjudicator. There are still around 164 grammar schools within the state system of education. These grammar schools are unevenly distributed around the country – in Kent, for example, there are 39. From late-1998, parents in an area will have the right to petition for a ballot on whether their local grammar school should switch to being a comprehensive.

However, New Labour is introducing a number of additional changes. Its first education White Paper (DfEE 1997) contained proposals on: nursery provision; baseline testing; smaller class sizes in infant schools; one hour-a-day literacy and numeracy programmes in primary schools; national English and maths tests for 9-year-olds; procedures to close failing schools and to reopen them under new management; swift dismissal procedures for incompetent teachers; reform of teacher training; home-school contracts on homework and truancy; the establishment of a new General Teaching Council; and target-setting for schools. New Labour continue the neo-liberal obsession with performance indicators as a way of educating the parental consumer. It has been suggested, however, that both the neo-liberals and New Labour have not focused on factors parents consider important:

Much research suggests that the kind of information which the government has assumed will influence parents' choice is, in reality, not prioritised by parents ... there is a relative lack of concern for examination results compared with the three most important choice factors: co-education or single sex, denomination and proximity to home ... there is a mutually supporting nexus of motivations of which the four criteria of happiness, child preference, discipline, and proximity are vital ... security or 'process' criteria (as well as the child's preference) are more important than academic success. (Thomas et al. 1997: 186).

One feature of the provision of education that may be called into question concerns the school day and the school year. In some of the City Technology Colleges (CTCs) set up under the Conservative government, a five-term year, with shorter and more even periods of holiday between the terms, has been established. The government has also introduced summer schools designed to improve the literacy and numeracy of children prior to entry into secondary education. Six hundred of these ran in 1998. It is likely that more extensive community use of school premises, resources and teachers may be made in the future. This would fit with the desire of the government to encourage parents to work by helping out with childcare. However, these programmes are not child-centred and are unlikely to make much contribution to the optimal development of the children involved.

In line with the pledge made at the election, the government has provided extra funds for new teachers and new classrooms to reduce overcrowding in infant classes. By 1999 this was being done, but at the cost of increasing class sizes for older children. New Labour has also extended the idea of a stipulated national curriculum into the pre-school age groups covering children aged from 3- to 5-years. As has been discussed above, this approach to pre-school education has little to commend it. Many 'early-years' educationalists have expressed the view that it may adversely affect the learning experience of young children because of a fundamental misconception of how children learn (O'Hagan and Smith 1996). OFSTED has been given the responsibility for regulating childcare services. This will include 100 000 childminders along with nurseries and playgroups. This was previously the responsibility of local authority social service departments. In 1999, the Qualifications and Curriculum Authority proposed a set of early learning goals which children are supposed to achieve by the end of their first year at primary school. These include a range of social skills along with learning objectives, such as being able to count up to ten, write their own names and spell simple words. These proposals have been strongly criticised by 16 of the 18 Early Excellence Centres providing nursery education that the government established as models of good practice for this sector. The critics argue that this curriculum is over-structured and wrongly downgrades the role of play for children of this age. They also fear that the process of measuring and grading will lead to the early labelling of some children as failures. After the consultation process the government has backed down on some of the more rigid aspects of the proposals and agreed to give more emphasis to the role of play. Nevertheless, this demonstrates the degree to which New Labour are failing to recognise the needs, and indeed capabilities, of young children.

From the start of 1998, baseline assessments of 5-year-olds have to be completed within seven weeks of the child entering school. These assessments constitute an extension of the testing regime. It is argued that they will be used to calculate the 'value added' which can be attributed to the work of the school, or even an individual teacher. This extension of testing is controversial, in particular because of claims that there is evidence that tests can depress self-esteem, increase anxiety of both teachers and children, and distort the teaching programme in the direction of cramming pupils in order for them to achieve high test scores. The primary school curriculum has been subject to further central control with the establishment of the literacy hour (in 1997) and the numeracy hour (in 1999). In each case, teachers are required to spend an hour-a-day on a tightly prescribed programme of work. The government has provided extensive documentation along with instructions for organising the work of the pupils, for training teachers, and for the monitoring and recording of the work undertaken. In order to ensure that time was available for the literacy and numeracy hours, the rules regarding the amount of time spent on the other compulsory subjects in the national curriculum were relaxed for a period of two years. As a result, in some schools, the amount of time spent on physical education has been reduced to as little as 15 minutes a week, with the likely result of a negative impact on health and on learning generally for those children affected. Another stipulated addition to the school curriculum from 2000 that will start in primary schools and continue throughout schooling concerns personal, health and social education. There will be a new stress on 'financial literacy' and managing money, along with moral education emphasising the importance of marriage for family life and for rearing children. As part of its policy to reduce the number of teenage pregnancies, the provision of sex education is to be modified. The training provided for teachers will be improved and OFSTED will monitor the quality of sex education.

Further amendments to the national curriculum will be introduced from September 2000. Citizenship will become a compulsory subject in secondary schools from 2002; it will take up 5 per cent of the school curriculum. There has been some relaxation in the regulations on the teaching of subjects outside the core curriculum. However, New Labour has insisted on the retention of traditional concerns in the teaching of history and geography, emphasising the importance of dates and maps. New Labour has also undertaken initiatives designed to enhance the teaching of particular subjects. Information technology is to be used to connect every school to what has been called a National Grid for Learning, allowing staff to make effective use of this computer network to improve teaching. The government also intends to 'kite-mark' educational web-sites in order to provide a resource for teachers for lesson preparation. Additional funds from the National Lottery are to be used to train teachers in the use of information technology. The government has also announced funds that can be used to enhance musical education in schools by purchasing instruments and providing free tuition.

Furthermore, the government is emphasising the responsibilities of parents through the imposition of 'home-school agreements', which schools have been obliged to send out to parents since 1998. These agreements cover attendance, discipline, homework, the information to be provided to parents and the ethos of the school. Detailed guidelines have been issued covering the number of hours of homework that children of different ages should be set. Extending the role of parents in supporting their children's education represents continuity with the supplementary discourses of 'work', 'consumption', the 'family' and 'sexuality'. According to Crozier, this new partnership between schools and parents constitutes a two-way 'surveillance' structure (of both parents and teachers), although to be successful, schools:

> need to persuade parents and through parents pupils, to adopt their value of what it means to be a 'good' parent and a 'good' pupil ... For those parents who share that agenda this may be acceptable; for others they are either left without a voice or tensions are created in the relationship. (Crozier 1998, cited in Muschamp et al. 1999: 112)

Much research attention has been given to the involvement of parents, particularly in nursery and primary education. This research generally portrays parental support in terms of the 'mother' fulfilling her natural role within the family, sitting and reading with the child, while 'father' is frequently absent (at 'work'). The old children's BBC TV programme *Watch with Mother* captured this expectation perfectly, and it is one that has endured. Mothers have been dominant figures in helping children to read at home and to settle into nursery provision. New Labour's proposal is therefore likely to exacerbate gender inequality. 'Cultural capital' – in the form of the 'consumption' of important resources, such as books and equipment, and pedagogical assistance at home – has also been shown to be an important influence on a child's educational development. However, whether it is sensible to emphasise these support mechanisms so blatantly in education policy is questionable, particularly as some parents have neither the resources nor the technical skills:

> The role of parents, while still being seen as significant in the English educational system, can also be seen as potentially divisive in these circumstances, perpetuating the social divisions that have been identified in other ways. (Burgess 1999: 87)

Such methods can do little more than create further opportunities for the state to demonise 'irresponsible parents' and 'failing families'. Moreover, David Blunkett's announcement at the Labour Party Conference 1999 that the maximum fine for parents 'condoning' truancy would rise, from £1,000 to £2,500, can only intensify hardship in families, particularly in view of the link between truancy and poverty. These measures neither add up to an education policy, nor address the education divide. Instead, they represent, as Driver and Martell argue, a 'regressiveness' consistent with other New Labour policies, and a particular brand of communitarian duties and values:

> The content of these duties and values, what Blair has called the 'new social morality', is heavily marked by conservative values, crowding out the more progressive and pluralist ethics of much recent Centre-Left thinking. On family policy, schooling and law and order, New Labour has taken policy positions which are marked by conservative values – on the role and shape of the family in society; on teaching methods; and on the causal explanatory chains for criminal acts. (Driver and Martell 1998: 119)

The centrality of the discourse of 'consumption' to education policy assumes that everyone is starting from the same position and has similar access to resources. This is a false concept, and can only serve 'to increase existing inequalities of gender, race and class' (Standing 1997, cited in Muschamp et al. 1999: 112).

The government has also announced a three-year programme aimed at renewing confidence in the comprehensive system of secondary schooling. The scheme will initially cover 450 schools in six major conurbations and is designed to provide additional specialist teaching for gifted pupils in the top 10 per cent of the ability range. These will be given extra tuition either within their own schools or in specialist schools that are being set up as 'centres of excellence' within the state system. The specialist school programme was started by the Conservative government but has been extended by Labour. More than 300 were in existence by early 1999 in England and there should be nation-wide coverage by 2001. The Secretary of State for Education and Employment also wishes to encourage more children to take GCSE examinations early. He has planned a programme of 34 summer schools for 'gifted children', and is also encouraging LEAs to offer Saturday schools for these during term time, exacerbating the advantages and privileges of high achievers.

Managing and controlling schooling

New Labour has retained the central place in educational policy occupied by OFSTED. It symbolised this by giving the Chief Inspector a substantial pay rise. It also failed to accept the findings of an inquiry by the House of Commons Select Committee on Education, which proposed a supervisory board to oversee OFSTED and recommended a less confrontational style of operation for the organisation. OFSTED has continued to fuel the debate on education by attacks on educational experts, on the in-service courses provided for teachers and on the quality of educational research carried out in the universities. The annual report for 1997-98 identified weak leadership as a problem in around 10 to 15 per cent of primary and secondary schools. The training for teachers in colleges and universities was, again, criticised. It was also claimed that there were around 15 000 incompetent teachers, 6000 in primary schools and 9000 in secondary schools, along with around 3000 incompetent heads. OFSTED has an important role in identifying and dealing with schools and local authorities which are judged to be operating at a less than acceptable level. New

Labour's education policy is to employ education 'hit-squads' – government appointed inspection teams who can go into LEAs and recommend management changes – alongside the 'naming and shaming' of persistently under-performing schools.

New Labour has extended the role of the private sector in state education. It has put forward proposals that will allow private firms to take over functions formerly undertaken by LEAs. In January 1999, the government announced that it would be advertising for private companies, non-profit organisations and other bidders to indicate their willingness to take on the education services in local authorities which were deemed to be failing. The purpose of this is to have available a pool of organisations that can take over LEA functions as and when this is required. In May 1999, the government named 10 consortiums that had been selected. The organisations selected included private-sector, profit-making companies, non-profit organisations currently involved in contracting for school inspections and public-private partnerships. It announced that one of these would be chosen to take over the school improvement service in Hackney, London, following an adverse report by OFSTED. Local authorities are also able to allow 'failing schools' to be taken over by private businesses. In early 1999, Surrey County Council invited tenders from interested organisations and firms to take over the running of King's Manor School in Guildford. The school had failed its inspection by OFSTED and the number of pupils had fallen from 1000 to 360. Parental protests stopped the council from closing the school, but the local authority then decided to seek private-sector management. Four companies were short-listed. The successful company will be able to invest funds in the school and take control of organisation and staffing. It will be able to change the school day, the salaries paid and the subjects offered.

Whether OFSTED is an effective vehicle for improving educational attainment is open to question. Independent research comparing educational attainment in schools which had been inspected and those which had not, where the educational capabilities of the school intake were comparable, found lower average scores resulted in the inspected schools compared to those which had not been inspected. The running costs of OFSTED are £130m each year. In addition, the inspection process imposes massive costs on schools. It has been calculated that the average cost to a secondary school of an inspection is around £20,000. This does not include the time and effort required to produce the necessary documentation, or the serious stress and disruption to school activities that the system involves. The issue of stress affecting teachers is now recognised as an important problem and the government has even set up a telephone helpline, 'Teacherline', for those affected. This is expected to take 15 000 calls each year.

The government also believes that the pay system is an important factor in the quality of education. The annual pay award for 1999 was set at an average of 3.5 per cent for class teachers, with 6 per cent for many heads and deputies, and larger payments for the heads of very small schools. The government also announced that there would be a system of performance-related pay (PRP) for teachers. The precise details of how this will be undertaken are still under discussion, although it is very likely that a key factor will be the results attained by pupils, as measured by public examinations and standard tests. An annual process of staff appraisal will be undertaken, based on pupils' work, classroom observation by a line manager, and feedback from pupils, parents and governors. The proposal for PRP has created considerable opposition from some of the teaching unions and its introduction will now take place in 2000, a year later than originally planned. The opposition of teachers to the scheme has focused on the damage to morale and teamwork, the extra work involved in administering the scheme, and the danger of cronyism and favouritism which the scheme may encourage. Teachers are critical of the new funding arrangements, which would mean that finance might not necessarily be available to provide all eligible teachers with these additional sums if the school budgets are unable to meet them. The government has also proposed school performance bonuses, which will be shared among staff of schools where performance has improved on a year-by-year basis. There is to be an élite cadre of advanced-skills teachers who are to act as mentors and role models for other staff members. Some entrants to the profession are also to be selected as high fliers and offered a system of accelerated promotion.

The government has proposed a range of incentives for those who are judged to be the most competent teachers. Over a two-year period, £1bn will be made available for PRP increases. PRP could add 10 per cent to the salary of a classroom teacher, and the salary could ultimately progress to a figure around 50 per cent greater than the current career grade maximum. A 'golden hello' scheme is being introduced for an élite corps of high-flying graduates, who will be given £5,000 along with extra training and an expectation that they will take on extra work. It is expected that eventually

5 per cent of teachers will be recruited in this way. There will be a special pay scale for those in receipt of these awards, along with a fast-track scheme to enable them to reach the peak levels of pay more quickly. For ordinary teachers who are not selected for any special increases, there will be little or no increase in their real income whatsoever since the government has stipulated that their pay should normally only be adjusted each year in line with the level of inflation. This means that a large number of teachers can expect to experience a worsening of their living standards relative to those in comparable occupations. This can only be divisive for the education sector.

The issue of teaching as a profession is the subject of the proposal to establish a General Teaching Council (GTC) which will oversee professional standards. The Council will have both a promotional and a regulatory role. It is supposed to help to improve the status of teaching and to draw up a code of professional conduct for teachers that it will then enforce. It will also have an advisory role for the government and for local authorities on issues connected with the recruitment, training, professional development and supply of teachers. Membership will be compulsory and teachers will be required to pay for this. At the same time the government is recognising the additional managerial requirements of those who occupy headships through its plans for a compulsory qualification for head teachers. It has proposed that there should be a National College for School Leadership and a new Professional Qualification for Headship to be implemented by 2002.

Some policies are specifically directed towards improving the education of those living in the poorest areas. The government is establishing experimental area-based programmes for education, reminiscent of the Educational Priority Areas established in 1967 by a Labour government. This time, they are to be called Education Action Zones. These zones may be established in either urban or rural areas, so long as they are deprived. The first five zones were set up in early 1998, and eventually 25 are expected to be running. Each zone will include around 20 schools: two or three secondary schools, and the primary schools that feed them. The zone will be run by a partnership forum that will include such bodies as the LEA, the local TEC, businesses, schools, community organisations and parents. The partnership may make its own decisions in relation to issues such as the curriculum, pay and conditions of employees, school holidays and the length of the school day, and the purchase of management services from private companies. Each zone will receive £0.5m of extra funding. Half of this will come from the government and half from business sponsors. The zones will also be treated favourably if any schools within them apply for specialist school status by deciding to concentrate on technology, modern languages, the arts or sport. It is likely that some of the zones selected for education may also be designated for other area-based policies under the programmes for health and employment zones. These policies are experimental, although it is suggested that the lessons learned from them may eventually be more widely applied. In themselves, even if some of the zones are extremely successful in reducing educational inequality, they will have little impact on the overall situation. The policy rests heavily on a managerialist approach along with private-sector participation. The overall picture is of a limited set of initiatives to tackle the unequal distribution of education, with little increase in the resources devoted to those who find learning most difficult.

Post-school education

The system of post-school education is extremely complex and fragmented. There are around 430 colleges and these educate around 4m students. Over half of the young people aged 16 and over study in FE and sixth-form colleges. There are now more A-level students in colleges than in school sixth-forms. FE colleges also play a major role in delivering adult education and work-related learning. Provision is uneven and there are low levels of participation by young people from the poorest families. The Kennedy Report (Kennedy 1997) stressed the need for local partnerships to bring together various interests to focus on the issue of widening participation. In response to this, in 1998, the Further Education Funding Council (FEFC) introduced a funding premium to pay colleges extra for students drawn from deprived areas. This covered about 25 per cent of existing students.

The FE sector generally has experienced considerable difficulties (Barber 1996). The FEFC has had to deal with major financial problems, including requiring one college to repay £6.4m to the local council that had been claimed incorrectly. Since becoming independent, some colleges have expanded massively using a system of franchising. This enables them to receive public funding for courses that they sell to outside bodies, such as businesses. The system of franchising allowed colleges to attract students outside of their normal catchment area. This created recruitment problems for other local colleges, who saw their potential students being signed up for courses elsewhere. It also reduced local accountability. In addition, some franchising operations involved very low quality provision. In early 1999, the FEFC introduced new rules on franchising which are likely to reduce the extent to which colleges pursue this option. The restrictions on franchising may also create problems for government attempts to encourage employers to support lifelong learning. Some colleges have made nation-wide franchised training agreements with large firms to provide for their training needs throughout the country. Whether these schemes can be retained and expanded, alongside a commitment to local control and the involvement of local 'stakeholders', remains to be seen.

New Labour is attempting to establish a stronger degree of control over standards in the FE sector. It is to employ similar tactics to those used in the school system, involving hit squads and a process of 'naming and shaming'. It also plans to require all FE lecturers to hold teaching qualifications. At present only 70 per cent have these. The administrative framework for the control of FE is to be reorganised according to a White Paper (DfEE 1999). This proposes the abolition of the FEFC and of the TECs, which currently fund most FE courses. Local authorities will no longer be responsible for funding school sixth-forms, and the whole system of post-school education outside of the universities will be subject to a common funding and inspection system.

There will be a National Learning and Skills Council (NLSC) along with 50 local Learning and Skills Councils, and Small Business Service organisations at sub-regional level. The NLSC will have a budget of around £5bn. It will be responsible for planning, funding and managing post-16 education and training. It will be established in April 2001. The sub-regional Councils will draw up plans that will have to be approved by the NLSC. OFSTED will be responsible for inspecting education and training for 16- to 19-year-olds. There will be a new independent inspectorate for post 19-year-old provision in colleges, for workplace learning, and for adult and community education courses, along with those run by the University for Industry (UfI). Work-based training for the unemployed will become the responsibility of the Employment Service. There will be a new Youth Support Service that will take over some of the work of the existing Careers Service and some aspects of youth service provision. A major aim of these changes is to reduce the number of young people aged 16 to 18 who are not undertaking any education or training.

The government also plans to employ the FE sector as a major vehicle for the expansion of both FE and HE. Recruitment is planned to increase annually, so that by the end of 2002 the number of students will be 700 000 greater than in 1997. Almost half of the planned expansion in HE will be undertaken through the FE sector in this period, with colleges taking on additional numbers of degree-level students.

The establishment of the UfI was a manifesto commitment for New Labour and has a key place in the establishment of lifelong learning. It is intended to be a public-private partnership designed to improve vocational education. The government is concerned that some 7m adults have no formal qualifications. Around 20 per cent of adults have poor literacy and numeracy skills. The aim is to improve business competitiveness and individual employability. These vocational initiatives are also taking place in an environment in which work-based training is changing substantially. Some employers are establishing major company-based training systems in which the company itself provides a wide range of customised training for employees at various levels. Rover and Unipart have established company 'universities'. The initiative to establish the UfI has been particularly associated with the Chancellor of the Exchequer rather than the DfEE. The UfI will work to make learning materials and services available for home use, workplace use and in learning centres around the country. By the year 2000 it is planned to have over 600 000 students pursuing courses through the UfI. Priority in the provision of courses is to be given to basic skills, information and communication technologies (ICT), small and medium-sized enterprises, and specified industrial sectors. It remains to be seen whether or not this new institution will fulfil the aspirations set for it, or whether it will simply become associated with the provision of low-status courses in low-level skills using a variety of delivery systems. The approach taken to improving training and increasing educational participation amongst those with the fewest qualifications involves both increasing the educational opportunities available and providing individual incentives for people to choose to take courses. There is a plan for individual learning accounts in which individuals, who open an account by depositing some of their own money, will have this topped up by £150 from the local TEC. The account will be available to finance training, and account holders will be given a package of information, advice and support, linked to the new UfI, along with a record of their personal learning achievements.

New Labour has adopted an educational rhetoric that emphasises the concept of lifelong learning (Jarvis et al. 1998). The notion of lifelong learning was developed in a report (DfEE 1998a) proposing an agenda for establishing a 'learning culture' for everyone (Hughes and Tight 1995). It put forward a utopian vision in which everyone was a learner and no citizen was excluded. However, the system is largely based on an individualistic market model in which learners have to choose to undertake learning and pay for it themselves, albeit with assistance from the state (Bentley 1998). In effect, it is a system based on vouchers of a kind which was proposed for schooling by New Right authors in the 1970s. It takes a rather instrumental view of education principally as a means to occupational advancement. There is not much emphasis on the idea that people should build upon an enthusiasm for a subject or area of knowledge, but simply that they should select a course which might improve their 'employability'.

The government has not proposed any significant structural changes in the university system. The Dearing Report (Dearing 1997) recommended the retention of student maintenance grants. However, New Labour chose instead to abolish grants and expand the system of student loans. It also instituted a major change that abolished free tuition in HE, requiring many students to contribute towards their tuition costs. Tuition fees are charged on a means-tested basis, which assumes a contribution will be made by the parents of those students who do not receive the full award. This forces most students to rely on parental contributions or loans either from banks or from the official student loan service. As a result, many students graduate with massive debts. The imposition of tuition fees represented a major shift in policy. These changes in the funding of HE have raised concerns that the government will fail to widen access to HE by creating disincentives to study, especially for those from poorer families. Indeed, it is alleged that New Labour 'deliberately ignored a survey showing that up to a third of mature higher education applicants [many of whom are from working-class backgrounds] would be deterred by the introduction of fees and the abolition of grants' (*Times Higher*, 12 November, 1999, p.1).

Other changes are taking place in HE following the proposals of the Dearing Report. One of these is an attempt to improve teaching standards in HE through the establishment of an Institute for Learning and Teaching (ILT). University academic staff may apply for membership of this Institute, although this will be voluntary. The ILT has proposed that membership will require academics to produce evidence that their teaching supports all, or almost all, of 24 specified outcomes. These refer to course design, the support of students' learning, methods of assessment, contributions to the maintenance of student-support systems, and methods of evaluation designed to improve teaching. Members will also be obliged to pay an annual fee of £50.

The financial arrangements for the university sector are very uneven. Some of the older universities, especially Oxford and Cambridge, receive very substantial sums from endowments and investments. In contrast, many of the new universities have few of their own income-yielding assets and rely almost entirely on public-sector funding. There is pressure from some more prestigious institutions to allow them to charge higher fees. The government is also attempting to encourage an increase in the number of foreign students in order to boost the UK's share of the international market in foreign students speaking English. The Prime Minister has said that he would like to see the number of foreign students increased by 75 000, by the year 2005.

Conclusion

The presuppositions on which New Labour policies are based are generally treated as self-evident by the government. It is assumed that improvements in education will lead to economic improvements. This assumption is based on the belief that human capital is a key resource in modern economies and that education will improve its quality (Jordan 1998). However, the connection between expenditure on education and economic growth has been debated for several decades and, while the two are linked, it is still not clear which way the causal process operates; whether economic growth leads to greater expenditure on education, or vice versa. A relatively new element in this debate is the belief that education needs to focus on basic skills if it is to contribute to economic success. In line with this view, particular emphasis is put on numeracy, literacy and information technology skills. However, this instrumental and utilitarian approach to education tends to down play the importance of interpersonal skills, as well as relegating many other areas of knowledge and experience to a subordinate place in the curriculum. It is by no means self-evident that an entirely utilitarian curriculum will actually contribute to economic progress. A major assumption here is the belief that modern employment requires a high level of these basic skills. However, it has been argued that a major tendency in modern employment is for a reduction in the level of skills and knowledge required of many members of the workforce (Braverman 1974). Studies have shown that two-thirds of the jobs which are undertaken by the lower occupational groups have very low skill requirements and that these can easily be met by the present workforce (Blackburn and Mann 1979, Sennett 1998). As a result, many people now find themselves in jobs for which they are over qualified.

In recent years, it has also become fashionable to argue that the success of the 'Asian Tiger' economies reflects the intensive and utilitarian character of their schooling systems. However, this view may be challenged in two ways. Firstly, the Tiger economies have proved to be less robust than previously imagined, as the economic breakdown of 1997 demonstrated. Secondly, the belief that the children in these countries invariably performed better in tests on mathematics has been shown to be erroneous. There is no clear international linkage between high scores in maths tests and economic growth (Robinson 1997). Inequalities in education, and the unequal distribution of access to formal and elaborated knowledge that this involves, closely reflect inequalities in income and wealth (Gorard 1998). Since the early 1980s, massive increases in inequalities of both income and wealth have taken place, and the economic forces that caused this are not being reduced by New Labour policies. The government proposes no effective redistribution of income or wealth from the rich to the poor, via taxation. In the present century, access to post-compulsory education has depended both on ability to pay and on the principle that those who find it most easy to learn should receive the most education. Education can be viewed substantially as a process for selecting a minority to undergo intensive teaching and study, whilst making minimal provision for the rest. As long as educational credentials remain a commodity used to enhance the value of labour power, this is likely to continue.

The evidence of the last century can be interpreted as demonstrating that simply providing educational opportunities, and perhaps subsidies for those who take them up, does not lead to a more equal distribution of education or knowledge. This has been reinforced by research recently undertaken in Wales as part of the Economic and Social Research Council Learning Society project. This showed that educational non-participation throughout a person's lifetime is overwhelmingly a function of the social circumstances into which they are born. It appears from this research that it is still true to say that it is the structure of social inequality in society which is the main cause of educational inequality, rather than the lack of opportunities for people to learn (Goodman et al. 1997). Providing learning opportunities is, therefore, not going to have the results which New Labour desires unless, at the same time, social inequality is decreased. Given the massive social apparatus that operates to exclude those outside the normalised condition from society, policies specifically designed to counter this are minimal. For example, no action at all is to be taken to restrict the privileges that accrue to those able to use the system of fee-paying schools. The policies being pursued by the government to reduce inequality do not appear to anticipate any reduction in the level of income and wealth at the top of the economic scale. New Labour's policies to raise the living standards of the poorest people are relatively modest. For example, the time period it has set itself for the abolition of child poverty is 20 years. It does not appear to have any plans to undertake a systematic attack on those features of the system of occupational recruitment which appear to work to the advantage of middle-class and upper-class people, who are also white, male and heterosexual. Simply to assume the existence of meritocratic systems of recruitment will not guarantee access to élite positions in any sphere of life for those lower down the social hierarchy. A significant example of this concerns the civil service, which was reformed on a meritocratic basis as long ago as the 1870s, but which still continues to recruit a disproportionate number of those in senior positions from white, upper-middle-class and upper-class backgrounds (Gowan 1987). From a managerialist standpoint, the government has not set itself any performance targets by which it might be possible to measure whether its policy of meritocracy was actually succeeding. The government has not specified the extent of changes it expects to see in recruitment to élite positions, although this would be a useful measure of whether or not equality of opportunity and social inclusion, as the government understands these, was being increased.

Educational institutions are not to be subject to democratic control. The changes that the government is making – to schooling, FE and HE – do not appear to rest on the idea of increased democratic control, either by the public or by the users of, or workers in, these institutions. Instead, the main emphasis in its organisational proposals appears to rest on an increased reliance on a bureaucratic regime of inspection, and methods for prescribing what is to be taught and how teaching should be undertaken. A feature of this regime is the punitive character of its operation and the way it is presented to the public through a rhetoric involving references to 'hit squads', and to the 'naming and shaming' of schools. The overall approach of the government focuses on what it views as the improvement of schooling. This is being undertaken whilst employing a managerialist agenda. This can be seen in the emphasis given to the management role of head teachers. It can also be seen in the detailed stipulation that is made concerning what ought to be taught and the methods of teaching that should be employed. Its view of learning is also mechanical rather than exploratory, and it has little space for play, recreation or cultural activities as significant aspects of learning. Managerialism of this kind represents an attempt to downgrade the importance of professional skills and professional judgement, and can be seen as involving the process of de-skilling ordinary teachers and further reducing their control over how they go about their work. Managerialism is also evident in the amount of attention that is being paid to creating a new structure for the payment of teachers. The introduction of an élite stratum of teachers, along with PRP, is evidence of this.

    This is an approach that is entirely consistent with Sibley's description of a highly-disciplined institution, designed on the principles of Jeremy Bentham's 'panopticon', a utilitarian regime for total control. The panopticon was an architectural design which allowed the controller to remain hidden (in his/her inspection tower) from the inmates (placed in their cells) who were subjected to his/her gaze and control. Bentham believed that his design could be applied to controlling a range of 'subjects' – for instance, criminals, the insane, alcoholics and school children – accommodated within it. Foucault extended the principle of panopticon as a metaphor for generalisable discipline, diffused throughout society, mediated through the dominant discourse of 'normality' and 'deviance', which we internalise to control the self (Sibley 1995). Teachers and headmasters are 'colonised' by the values and moralising strategies of the Blair project. However, as an approach to guaranteeing the elevation of school standards, or the widening of participation and inclusion, or the raising of the status and morale of the teaching professional, or improving the public perception of schooling, it remains questionable.

    There is also a strong communitarian flavour to New Labour's education policy, which sets out a vision on how we should all live our lives. All of us – parents, neighbours, teachers and pupils – are expected to live our lives in accordance with Blair's beliefs on responsibilities, standards and morality. We are all part of 'one nation, one community', sharing the same rights and obligations. Meanwhile, the processes of disadvantage in the education system, structured largely around class, gender, 'race' and disability, remain intact. Educational apartheid between the private and state sector, and within the state sector, continues, and with it the perpetuation of a poverty of resources and ambition. There is no expectation, however, within New Labour thinking that corporate responsibility for this situation – low wages, patriarchy, racism, material deprivation, and so forth – should also be harnessed within the same notion of 'sharing rights and responsibilities' thrust on the individual. The link between social inequality and educational opportunity is rejected.

While it cannot be easily quantified, it is likely that the emphasis given to an instrumental and vocational approach will further contribute to the destruction of, respect for, and interest in, knowledge and understanding for its own sake. At the same time, the attack on professionalism along with the antagonism towards the traditional ethic of public service, and the replacement of these by an individualistic, market-oriented approach, will further reinforce the cultural shift towards possessive individualism and the aggressive pursuit of self-interest.

References

Adonis, A. and Pollard, S. (1997) *A Class Act*, Hamish Hamilton, London.

Audit Commission (1996) *Misspent Youth*, Audit Commission, London.

Ball, S.J. (1998) 'Performativity and fragmentation in postmodern schooling' in J. Carter (ed.) *Postmodernity and the Fragmentation of Welfare*, Routledge, London, pp. 187-203.

Barber, M. (1996) *The Learning Game*, Victor Gollancz, London.

Bentley, T. (1998) *Learning Beyond the Classroom*, Routledge with Demos, London.

Beynon, H. and Glavanis, P. (eds.) (1999) *Patterns of Social Inequality*, Longman, Harlow.

Blackburn, R.M. and Mann, M. (1979) *The Working Class in the Labour Market*, Macmillan, London.

Board of Education (1943) *Educational Reconstruction*, Cmnd 6458, HMSO, London.

Braverman, H. (1974) *Labour and Monopoly Capital,* Monthly Review Press, London.

Burgess, R.G. (1999) 'Patterns of inequality in education' in H. Beynon, and P. Glavanis, (eds.) *Patterns of Social Inequality,* Longman, Harlow, pp. 74-96.

Byrne, E.M. (1978) *Women and Education,* Tavistock. London.

Campbell, B. (1993) *Goliath: Britain's Dangerous Places,* Methuen, London.

Carr, F. (1998) 'The Rise And Fall Of The Polytechnics: Explaining change in British higher education policy making', *Policy & Politics,* Vol. 26, No. 3, pp. 273-90.

Carvel, J. (1999) 'Grammar Schools no escape route for poorer children', *The Guardian,* 29 May, London.

Clarke, J., Cochrane, A. and McLaughlin, E. (1994) *Managing Social Policy,* Sage, London.

Cohen, R. and Hughes, M. with Ashworth, L. and Blair, M. (1994) *School's Out: The Family Perspective on School Exclusion,* Barnardo's/Family Service Units, London.

Coleman, J.W. (1998) *Social Problems: A Brief Introduction,* Longman, Harlow.

Cox, C. B. and Dyson, A. E. (eds.) (1970) *Black Paper Two,* Critical Quarterly Society, London.

Craig, G., Elliott-White, M. and Perkins, N. (1998) *Mapping Disaffected Youth,* Papers in Social Research No 10, University of Lincolnshire and Humberside, Lincoln.

CSO (1997) *General Household Survey,* CSO, London.

Dearing, R. (1996) *Review of Qualifications for 16-19 Year Olds,* School Curriculum and Assessment Authority, London.

Dearing, R. (1997) *National Committee of Inquiry into Higher Education,* The Stationery Office, London.

DfEE (Department for Education and Employment) (1997) *Excellence in Schools,* The Stationery Office, London.

DfEE (Department for Education and Employment) (1998a) *The Learning Age: A renaissance for a new Britain,* The Stationery Office, London.

DfEE (Department for Education and Employment) (1998b) *The Department's Draft Aims and Objectives,* Letter seeking comments on the Departmental research programme, 7 October 1998, DfEE, London.

DfEE (Department for Education and Employment) (1999) *Learning to Succeed,* The Stationery Office, London.

Driver, S. and Martell, L. (1998) *New Labour: Politics after Thatcherism,* Polity Press, Cambridge.

DSS (Department of Social Security) (1999) *Opportunity for All: Tackling Poverty and Social Exclusion,* The Stationery Office, London.

Financial Times (1996) *Survey of A Level Performance,* Financial Times, London.

Finch, J. (1984) *Education as Social Policy,* Longman, London.

Finegold, D. (1998) *A British Baccalaureate*, Institute of Public Policy Research, London.

Gerber, M. with Weaver, J. (eds.) (1998) *Dear Parent. Caring For Infants With Respect*, Resources for Infant Educarers, Los Angeles, California.

Gillborn, D. (1998) 'Racism, selection, poverty and parents: New Labour, old problems?', *Journal of Education Policy*, Vol. 13, No. 6, pp. 717-735.

Glass, D.V. (ed.) (1954) *Social Mobility in Britain*, Routledge and Kegan Paul, London.

Glass, N. (1999) 'Sure Start: The Development of an Early Intervention Programme for Young Children in the United Kingdom', *Children & Society*, Vol. 13, pp. 257-64.

Goodman, A., Johnson, P. and Webb, S. (1997) *Inequality in the UK*, Oxford University Press, Oxford.

Gorard, S (1998) *Patterns of participation in adult education and training*, a Cardiff and Bristol University ESRC-funded Learning Society project; Working Paper 13, Cardiff University, School of Education, Cardiff.

Gordon, P., Aldrich, R. and Dean, D. (1991) *Educational Policy in England in the Twentieth Century*, The Woburn Press, London.

Gowan, P (1987) 'The Origins of the Administrative élite', *New Left Review*, No. 162, pp. 4-34.

Gribble, D. (1999) 'Pupil power', *Red Pepper Archive*, http: //www.redpepper.org.uk/xwelfare2.html, 25 October 1999, pp. 1-3.

Halsey, A.H., Heath, A.F. and Ridge, J.M. (1980) *Origins and Destinations*, Clarendon Press, London.

Hatcher, R. (1997) 'New Labour, school improvement and racial equality', *Multicultural Teaching*, Vol. 15, No. 3, pp. 8-13.

Heath, A.F. and Ridge, J.M. (1983) 'Schools, examinations and ooccupational attainment' in J. Purvis and M. Hales et al., *Achievement and Inequality in Education*, Routledge and Kegan Paul, London.

Hennessy, E., Martin, S., Moss, P. and Melhuish, E. (1992) *Children and Day Care: Lessons From Research*, Paul Chapman, London.

Hoyle, D. (1998) 'Constructions of pupil absence in the British education service', *Child & Family Social Work*, Vol. 3, Issue 2, pp. 99-111.

Hughes, C. and Tight, M. (1995) 'The Myth of the Learning Society', *British Journal of Educational Studies*, Vol. 43, No. 3, pp. 290-304.

Jarvis, P., Griffin, C., Holford, J., Merricks, L. and Tosey, P (1998) 'Why lifelong learning is not a policy', *Times Higher,* 16 January.

Johnson, P. and Reed, H. (1996) 'Inter-generational mobility among the rich and poor: Results from the National Child Development Survey', *Oxford Review of Economic Policy*, Vol. 12, No. 4, pp. 127-42.

Jordan, B. (1998) *The New Politics of Welfare,* Sage, London.

Kennedy, H (1997) *Learning Works: Widening Participation in Further Education*, Further Education Funding Council, London.

Konrad, J. (1995) 'The Politics of Training', Chap 11 of M. Mullard (ed.) *Policy Making in Britain*, Routledge, London.

Le Grand, J. and Bartlett, W. (eds.) (1993) *Quasi-markets and Social Policy*, Macmillan, London.

Little, M. (1999) 'Prevention and Early Intervention with Children in Need: Definitions, Principles and Examples of Good Practice', *Children & Society*, Vol. 13, pp. 304-16.

Lloyd-Smith, M. (1993) 'Problem behaviour, exclusions and the policy vacuum', *Pastoral Care*, December, pp. 23-36.

Lloyd-Smith, M. and Davies J.W. (1995) *On the Margins: The Educational Experience of 'Problem' Pupils*, Trentham Books, Stoke-on-Trent.

Morrow, V. (1999) 'If you were a teacher, it would be harder to talk to you: Reflections on qualitative research with children in school', *International Journal of Social Research Methodology*, Vol. 1, No.4, pp. 297-313.

Muschamp, Y., Jamieson, I. and Lauder, H. (1999) 'Education, education, education' in M. Powell (ed.) *New Labour, New Welfare State? The 'third way' in British social policy*, The Policy Press, Bristol., pp. 101-121.

Neill, A.S. (1968) *Summerhill*, Harmondsworth, Penguin.

NFER (National Foundation for Educational Research) (1995) *Standards in Literacy and Numeracy: 1948-1994*, National Commission on Education, London.

O'Hagan, M. and Smith, M. (1996) *Special Issues in Child Care*, Balliere Tindall, London.

Plowden, B. (1967) *Children and Their Primary Schools*, Central Advisory Council for Education, London.

Robbins, L. (1963) *Higher Education*, HMSO, London.

Robinson, P. (1997) *Literacy, numeracy and economic performance*, Centre for Economic Performance, London.

Salter, B. and Tapper, T. (1981) *Education, Politics and the State*, Grant McIntyre, London.

Sennett, R (1998) *The Corrosion of Character*, W.W Norton, London.

SEU (Social Exclusion Unit) (1998) *Truancy and School Exclusion Report by the Social Exclusion Unit*, Cabinet Office, London.

Sibley, D. (1995) *Geographies of Exclusion*, Routledge, London.

Silver, H. (ed.) (1973) *Equal Opportunity in Education*, Methuen, London.

Thomas, G., Vass, P. and McClelland, R. (1997) 'Parents in a market-place: Some responses to information, diversity and power', *Educational Research*, Vol. 39, No. 2, pp. 185-94

Weiner, M. (1985) *English Culture and the Decline of the Industrial spirit 1850-1980*, Penguin, Harmondsworth.

Wolpe, A. and Donald, J. (1983) *Is There Anyone Here from Education?*, Pluto, London.

6 Housing Policies

Introduction

This chapter examines housing policy developments in the UK from their nineteenth-century origins to the present day. Rather than offer a detailed account of the history of housing policy, which has been covered sufficiently elsewhere (Malpass and Murie 1999), this exposé will highlight continuity and change in the housing debate, and the way policy developments have been framed to meet broader social, political and economic objectives of policy makers. In particular, the impact of past policies, particularly those of the neo-liberals, and the likely impact of New Labour policies, will be examined to offer an appraisal of the new Labour government's emerging housing agenda as it appears in late-1999. The tools of analysis discussed in Chapter Three will be used to show how this agenda continues to reflect particular constructions of the 'welfare subject' and the way in which unequal outcomes in the housing system are mediated, and how these affect the residential experiences of 'Other than' normalised families. The chapter concludes by suggesting that there is an inevitable gulf between New Labour's rhetoric on housing policy and what has been delivered to date, and that this is perpetuating social exclusion for many. However, the inherent contradictions within the dominant discourses shaping housing and welfare policy developments offer the potential for more inclusive policies founded on values, and mediated through processes, that seek to reduce social exclusion. We would emphasise that we are not saying that structural explanations of power relationships in the housing system are invalid – indeed, we believe that these provide a crucial source of understanding. However, we feel that placing the development of housing policy within the analytical framework suggested by Leonard (outlined in Chapter Three) offers another vantage point from which to understand the processes of social exclusion in the housing system and how these might be challenged.

Housing policy and the state

The scope of the housing policy debate in the UK has largely been concerned with the extent to which the state should intervene 'to modify the quality, quantity, price and ownership and control of housing' (Malpass and Murie 1999: 7). A particular issue in this debate has been the balance between the tenures, with home ownership increasingly seen as an important stabilising influence in society and crucial for personal well-being (Murie 1998). The dominant discourse of welfare within the housing policy debate constructs 'welfare subjects' as those unable to buy a house or maintain a mortgage, and who subsequently need to rely on 'social housing'. In no other European country is home ownership bestowed with such social significance (Kennett 1998) or used to determine the social status and value of subjects. As will be shown in this chapter, both the neo-liberal Conservatives and New Labour have based their housing policies on similar constructions of the 'welfare subject', the social value of home ownership and the moral character of those in social housing.

Housing policy has been particularly prone to 'moral debates and normative standards concerning the conduct of consumers', partly due to the fact that state housing 'has never been perceived as a universal entitlement and access is highly dependent on the discretion of local authority officers and members' (Haworth and Manzi 1999: 154). A trawl through the 'housing debate' in time reveals a range of discursive practices, mediated through policy intervention, that have sought to define and legitimate a common-sense understanding of reality – largely to maintain the material interests of dominant power holders. As Jacobs and Manzi have argued, it is the ability of key power holders to 'structure debates, to set parameters for discussion and to prevent issues from consideration' that allows the housing agenda to be manipulated and marginal interests to be excluded (Jacobs and Manzi 1996: 551). However, as history has borne out (see Grayson 1997), and as we will argue in the concluding chapter to this book, a dominant discourse can be 'reversed' to produce a different understanding and a new agenda that addresses the interests of a broader constituency.

Nineteenth century reforms

The earliest debate over housing reform in the nineteenth century reflected British society's broader preoccupation with the 'social question' – the moral and social 'health' of the working classes. 'A concern for reform and the broad project of controlling the "dangerous classes" and sustaining hegemony were often clearly expressed in the reformers' discourses and arguments' (Harloe 1995: 19). This concern has continued into the late-1990s. As Grayson observes:

> There is a cultural chasm which even in the 1990s seems unbridgeable, as academics, journalists and politicians once again seize on the dubious notion of an 'underclass'. This seething mass of humanity is seen to inhabit the council estates of urban Britain and the 'black' inner city. The conceptualization of working-class communities as 'idle, thieving bastards' is, however, simply a continuation of traditional middle-class responses characterized by Englander as 'little more than a register of revulsion suffused with a Hogarthian grotesqueness and characterized by a fixation upon the pathological, a fascination for the curious'. (Grayson 1997: 15)

Topalov demonstrates that this fascination was shared by social reformers and the state in all nations affected by the Industrial Revolution, evident in attempts 'to reshape workers' habits outside the workplace, especially through far-reaching changes in the urban environment' (quoted in Harloe 1995: 20). The worker was to become the subject of a multitude of enquiries, objectified and classified in relation to labour-market position. Artisans were defined as socially responsible and therefore 'good tenants', whose housing needs would be satisfied by private landlords or model dwelling companies, while casual labourers possessing 'bad habits', although 'not desirable tenants', could be helped by sympathetic 'lady rent collectors'. However, little could be done for the lowest order, the immoral and lazy, other than to place them in municipal lodging houses under police supervision and institutionalise their children (Harloe 1995: 21). Since the earliest stages of capitalism, therefore, the 'welfare subject' has been surveyed and defined as 'deserving' or 'undeserving', particularly by reference to their position within the labour market.

Rapid urbanisation, and the consequent concentration of overcrowded and insanitary dwellings in the new industrial centres, had 'fashioned housing into a public issue' by the middle of the nineteenth century (Lund 1996: 22). At the time, party politics was largely dominated by the Conservatives, mainly representing land-owning interests, and the Liberals, mainly representing the new industrial capitalist class. The fragile balance of power between these two dominant political groupings led to some limited state intervention in housing, although housing provision was chiefly distributed according to classical political economy and the laws of the market. The Labouring Classes' Lodging Houses Act 1851 gave local authorities powers to erect houses in certain areas for the working classes, with Treasury loans from 1866, although this legislation was rarely used. Most authorities did not consider housing provision to be a priority activity. The Artisans' and Labourers' Dwellings Improvement Act 1875 allowed local authorities to demolish slum dwellings and, with government consent, build new dwellings on these clearance sites. The new houses had to be sold within ten years of their construction.

In 1890, under the consolidating Housing of the Working Classes Act, local authorities gained powers to construct houses outside slum-clearance areas, legislation that sought to address an 'affordability problem' highlighted in the 1885 Royal Commission on the Housing of the Working Classes. While poor households needed to live in central urban locations – to be close to employment opportunities, cheaper food markets, and/or friends and relatives – rents in these areas were often too expensive:

> The Royal Commission of 1885 heard with dismay that while rents in central London were soaring, wages remained static ... [Rising rents were partly due to] pressure from immigrants [and] the removal of bad property ... Demolitions in the area of the Mint under the Torrens Act caused local rents to double ... Behind these reasons for high rents also lay the high profits which were being made from ... central area properties. (Burnett 1986: 151-152)

However, the 1890 Act never intended to promote a legitimate role for state housing provision. No direct public subsidy had been made available, the government's largely *laissez-faire* perspective being that such intervention would destroy the 'moral senses' by undermining individual responsibility, and the intention was largely to give a lead to private developers by demonstrating that model working-class dwellings could be profitably provided (Lund 1996).

By the end of the century, therefore, the housing response to the 'social question' had been largely limited to: the eradication of slums; the efforts of 'benevolent' trusts such as Peabody and the Shaftesbury Society; the 'model villages' built by employers in such places as Saltaire, Port Sunlight, Bournville and New Earswick; and working-class, self-help schemes such as friendly and co-operative building societies. These schemes, together with private lettings, would have satisfied the housing needs of the more affluent working classes in regular employment, while ensuring that market principles and property rights remained intact. However, those who failed to access reasonably-paid work would remain excluded from decent living conditions.

The development of council housing

The rise of organised Labour movements by the beginning of the twentieth century did little to change the direction of housing policy, essentially because the Labour leadership represented the interests of the more powerful trade union sections, largely concerned with the protection of employment rights rather than housing issues. It was, therefore, left to the 'masses' without regular employment or in low-paid jobs, who lived in overcrowded and insanitary housing conditions, to campaign for social change:

> Between 1900 and the outbreak of the First World War there was a mounting tide of militancy and dissatisfaction with governments and trade union leaders. (Grayson 1997: 28)

The urban poor deployed a range of tactics to improve their living conditions. Less militant action included the development of credit networks (schemes that have re-emerged as 'credit unions' in response to social exclusion in the late-1990s) and the formation of tenants' defence leagues. In contrast, conflict between the urban poor and their employers and landlords led to more radical campaigns organised around strikes, withholding rent, rioting and collective resistance against evictions (Grayson 1997). These campaigns were largely uncoordinated and short-lived (Cole and Furbey 1994), and did not pose too great a threat to the established order. What did significantly change the direction of housing policy was the First World War. According to Harloe:

> War redefined the state/economy relationship, accelerated changes in the organisation of production, altered political and social relationships between classes, and dramatically changed the politico-economic status of nations. (Harloe 1995: 75)

War required a greater degree of state control over production and services, particularly armaments, energy and transport, and greater co-operation between the state, industry, trade unions and the labour force. It also required dramatic changes in the *laissez-faire* economic order, including higher levels of public spending and massive borrowing. On the housing front, the almost complete cessation of housing investment, alongside the inward migration of populations to centres of the munitions' industry, exacerbated an already acute housing crisis. Landlords attempted to exploit the situation by rapidly inflating rent levels and, aided by the Courts Emergency Powers Act passed in the early months of the war, evicting those unwilling or unable to pay.

The Ministry of Munitions did provide wartime loans for housing key workers, albeit on a small scale. Some of these estates, largely occupied by skilled workers and their families, were constructed on the Garden City model championed by Raymond Unwin, thereby 'setting new standards for working-class housing which were later incorporated in post-war mass social housing'. However, 'unskilled and black workers, including women, were mainly housed singly in the temporary hostels located near the factories and were subjected to a high degree of supervision ... by housing managers' (Harloe 1995: 83-85). Consequently, even in wartime, housing solutions reflected distinct notions of 'deserving' and 'undeserving', based largely on class, gender and 'race'.

Exploitation and the failure of government to take adequate measures merely fuelled tenants' militancy and throughout centres of munitions production there were calls for strikes. In particular, the situation in Glasgow significantly transformed housing policy:

> In October 1915, 15 000 Glaswegians were on rent strike including five Labour councillors. By this time the women were assaulting the factors and bailiffs, pelting them with rubbish and flour ... By November 1915, 20 000 people were on strike ... The government had established the Hunter Committee in the previous October to review the situation, but the rent strikes continued to escalate – particularly around the trials of rent strikers. A General Strike was threatened after a mass demonstration on 17 November and eight days later, on 25 November 1915, a Rent and Mortgage Interest Freeze Bill was introduced, becoming law in four weeks flat, receiving the Royal Assent on 25 December. This was a famous victory. (Grayson 1997: 31)

In 1918, Britain faced the post-war reconstruction period in a situation of economic uncertainty, despite an initial short-term boom up to 1920. It had lost its pre-war status as the world's leading trade and finance centre while incurring massive debts. While the US embraced new areas of technology, throughout the 1920s the industrial base of the UK went into decline with structural unemployment setting in. Economic uncertainty was matched by political uncertainty, particularly with the continued rise of working-class militancy. Many commentators on this period agree that the British establishment held a genuine fear of social revolution, and saw the need to make concessions to working-class demands (see Grayson 1997). Certainly, there were few calls to lift the restrictions imposed under the 1915 Act. Moreover, government thinking at the time was coming round to the notion that some form of state subsidised housing was inevitable, albeit as a temporary measure until the 'normality' of the market could be restored. One reason for this was to ensure that the now organised and enfranchised (but still 'dangerous') working classes were to be incorporated into the post-war reconstruction effort.

This represents a significant shift from the historical pattern described above by Grayson, when the 'housing campaign' was largely led by elements from within the unskilled labouring classes. Now, the 'threat' to the established social order was different, coming as it did from the organised and skilled working classes. Consequently, the government's response was different, namely the provision of subsidised housing rather than intervention in the private-rented sector. As Harloe observes:

> The first mass programmes of social rented housing were, therefore, not a simple response to housing needs but a response to *strategically important* housing needs, in brief the needs of those sections of the population – the skilled, organised working class and part of the middle class – whose continuing disaffection posed the greatest threat to the re-establishment of the capitalist social order. (Harloe 1995: 101 – original emphasis)

The decline of the private-rented sector and the limited contribution of philanthropic provision meant that, when housing subsidies were first introduced in the Housing and Town Planning Act 1919 (the Addison Act), it was to local authorities that the state looked. Local authorities, who already had experience of implementing public health measures, were seen by the central state as easier to control than private or voluntary sector organisations. Moreover, local authorities and sections of the labour movement had lobbied for council housing, and there had been no significant political pressure for any alternative form of subsidised housing provision.

The new subsidy system was 'open-ended', providing central government financial assistance to cover the deficit between the cost of providing and managing the new houses, and the income from the rent plus rate-fund contributions up to the value of the product of an old penny (1d). However, this system only lasted until 1921 when it was abandoned on cost grounds. This was a time when the power of the labour movement had been considerably weakened by large-scale unemployment, assuaging any lingering fear within the governing order that the skilled working class might force a political revolution.

Throughout the 1920s, low economic growth rates and high unemployment continued in the UK. The 'normality' of market housing provision – that is, 'normal' in the sense of housing being provided universally through the market mechanism (as envisaged at the time of the Addison Act) – did not return. Owing to this, and as most voters were living in private-rented housing benefiting from rent controls, neither major party at the time, the Conservatives nor Labour, could entirely extricate themselves from state involvement in housing. The Conservatives did try to reduce state regulation of housing by legislating in 1923 for rent decontrol on change of tenancy, and directing new lower-rate subsidies towards private builders. Local authority mortgage loans were also extended, and they were given powers to guarantee building society loans. Some commentators have argued that these measures represented a clear attempt at promoting home ownership on ideological grounds (Murie 1998). Around this time, Harold Bellman, a leading building society representative, argued that:

> the man who has something to protect and improve – a stake of some sort in the country – naturally turns his thoughts in the direction of sane, ordered, and perforce economical government. The thrifty is seldom or never an extremist agitator. To him revolution is anathema; and, as in the earliest days Building Societies acted as a stabilising force, so today they stand … as 'a bulwark against Bolshevism and all that Bolshevism stands for'. (Cited in Murie 1998: 83)

Home ownership was, therefore, said to be good for the nation. In 1924, however, the first Labour Government placed the emphasis for meeting working-class housing needs back with local authorities, largely due to the influence of former Clydesider Lord Wheatley, the Minister responsible for housing. Although the Conservatives were back in power in less than a year, the Wheatley subsidy continued, albeit at a lower rate, reflecting a degree of consensus at this time around the pragmatic necessity of local authority housing, particularly in view of the government's narrow majority. By 1929-30, around a third of total housing completions were for council renting, although this programme, because of high rents, largely benefited 'the core working class and lower middle class – who would be "respectable" tenants and many of whom were … the "backbone" of the labour movement' (Harloe 1995: 112) and in decently-paid 'work'.

The 'residualisation' of council housing

Residualisation refers to the notion that council housing gradually shifted from being a housing sector catering for a range of socio-economic groups, to becoming a welfare service for those unable to afford to buy their home (Forrest and Murie 1990). As a concept, it conveys the notion that to be a 'council tenant' carries a stigma of being marginalised in the least desirable tenure, without access to other essential amenities such as quality schools, safe transport, culture and leisure, proper primary health care, a crime-free and healthy environment, and employment opportunities. The seeds of the residualisation process were laid very early in the history of council housing.

By 1931, the economic downturn of the 1920s had reached crisis point with the collapse of world trade and rising unemployment throughout the West. The Conservative-influenced National Government, who gained power from the short-lived Labour Government of 1929-31, introduced policies that were to represent a break with the consensus on general needs council housing. In 1933 they abolished the Wheatley subsidies, arguing that the affluent working class could be housed by the private sector. Subsidies for slum clearance, introduced under the previous Labour Government in 1930, were retained at a lower rate and with reduced permissible space standards. Further reductions in standards followed the Housing Act 1935, which encouraged multi-storey flats in central redevelopment areas. These developments heralded the start of council housing's transformation from general needs provision to a transient sector, or 'welfare housing', for the poorest. This is reflected in guidance circulated to local authorities in 1938 which argued that 'great social changes' had occurred through the rehousing of the 'very poorest', leading to the need for careful housing management to adapt these families to 'the modern houses where they will be given the chance to lead happier and more healthy lives' (CHAC 1938, cited in Harloe 1995: 189). This was effectively social engineering through the careful selection of tenants and social education programmes. The use of filtering systems in housing allocations, to ensure that only the 'deserving' residents acquire the better properties, has been a consistent feature of housing management practice. John Macey and Charles Baker, authors of one of the first textbooks on housing management, first published in 1965, offer the following advice to local authority officers:

> Local authorities have statutory obligations in respect of certain groups of applicants but, since the demand often far outstrips the supply there must always be discrimination in the process of selecting the fortunate few who will be offered houses each year. Personal considerations should not deprive an urgent case of an offer, though personal characteristics will affect the type of dwelling to be offered. (Macey and Baker 1973: 243-244)

In contrast, Macey and Baker suggest that the housing association is free to be influenced by personal considerations when allocating housing, although:

> On the manner in which it exercises this freedom its public repute will to some extent depend. There is, however, no general disposition to criticise a voluntary housing body for declining to offer a tenancy to a person or family on the ground that they are known or likely to be bad tenants. Indeed, apart from the avoidance of trouble to the management, it will usually accord more nearly with the popular idea of fairness that good behaviour should receive some reward. (Macey and Baker 1973: 244)

Measuring 'good behaviour' should, according to Macey and Baker, be carried out by a trained housing assistant making a home visit. Indicators of an applicant's acceptability will include 'cleanliness and tidiness', and the current rent balance. This discourse on behaviour, delineating both those 'deserving' and those 'undeserving' of housing, has remained a potent mechanism of residential exclusion throughout the century. This is a problem recognised by Certeau, who argues that cities are organised by:

> classifying operations, [where] management combines with elimination: on the one hand, we have the differentiation and redistribution of the parts and function of the city through inversions, movements, accumulations, etc., and, on the other hand, we have the rejection of whatever is not treatable and that, thus, constitutes the garbage of a functionalist administration (abnormality, deviance, sickness, death, etc.). (Certeau 1985, cited in Sibley 1995: 77)

These operations have been particularly highlighted in urban sociology since Rex and Moore's classic text, *Race, Community and Conflict*, identified the (often covert) role of urban managers in exacerbating inequalities of opportunities in Birmingham's housing system for black people and 'deviants' (Rex and Moore 1967). This research spawned a number of further important studies focusing on the distributional effects of housing allocation polices and practices (CRE 1984, 1988, 1989 and 1993; Henderson and Karn 1987).

The outbreak of war in 1939 led to a massive deterioration in the quality and quantity of the British housing stock. During the war nearly 3m dwellings were damaged and 468 000 destroyed or made uninhabitable (Cole and Furbey 1994). Due to special wartime measures – including extensive controls over the building industry and a rent freeze – only 190 000 properties were built and few were repaired. By 1945, calculations of the housing shortage ranged from 1.25m to 2m, the latter being 'the largest housing shortage ever recorded – 500 000 greater than in the period after the First World War' (Cole and Furbey 1994: 61). Not surprisingly, therefore, housing was a major political issue in the immediate post-war period:

> In 1945 public opinion polls showed that housing was the single most important issue for the majority of the electorate ... [H]ousing was the major social issue highlighted in the Conservative election manifestos in the first four post-war elections ... and again in 1970 and the October 1974 election. It figured first in the Labour manifestos of 1945 and 1955. (Harloe 1995: 282)

A Labour Government was returned to power in 1945, and a programme of mass building for 'general needs' was introduced under the Housing (Financial and Miscellaneous Provisions) Act 1946. This Act 'trebled the money value of subsidies compared with 1939' (Malpass and Murie 1999: 63) and allowed local authorities to build at a higher standard and escape the 'residual' role they were given before the war, although the crude housing shortage was not eliminated until the early 1970s. Housing still did not have its own Ministry in 1945, falling under the responsibilities of the Ministry of Health. Moreover, Aneurin Bevan, the Health Minister at the time, gave priority to the establishment of the National Health Service, and the new post-war programme of housebuilding was slow to take off.

The acute post-war shortage of housing was highlighted by squatting campaigns throughout Britain. These campaigns gained strong public sympathy, including unlikely sources of support in the *Daily Mail* and *The Economist*. The *Daily Mail* 'praised the squatters for their "robust common sense" and their ability when governments fail them "to take matters quietly but firmly into their own hands"', while *The Economist* argued that the squatters' actions were 'socially just' (cited in Grayson 1997: 43). These responses contrast with political reactions to squatting campaigns in the 1970s. For instance, when around 20 empty Bovis properties in Grosvenor Road, Twickenham, were squatted in the Autumn of 1973, George Tremlett, then Chair of the local housing committee, suggested that:

> It was clear to us that the Borough was fast developing a cancer in its midst. A cancer that could dangerously pollute the quality of our life and the moral well-being of the Borough's children. (Cited in Saunders 1976: 1)

Homeless war heroes, who squat, are to be praised; homeless 'activists', who squat, are to be pathologised as a threat to moral well-being.

Temporarily, the UK did move closer to a socialised housing system in the immediate post-war years, particularly through the nationalisation of 'betterment', instituted in the Town and Country Planning Act 1947. 'Betterment' refers to profits made from land speculation, largely brought about by increases in land value accruing from a successful planning application for development. The 1947 Act introduced a 100 per cent betterment tax on these profits which, along with measures that allowed local authorities to compulsorily purchase sites at existing land-use value, was largely designed 'to enable the assembly of land parcels in urban areas and facilitate comprehensive redevelopment by the public sector' (Atkinson and Moon 1994: 176). However, housing policy never really had a central role to play in the Labour government's post-war welfare strategy, unlike health and education. Housing policy had, as at the end of the First World War, a more pragmatic purpose:

> State housing was not a permanent monument to the virtues of public provision: it was an expedient service, intermittently making good the shortcomings of the private market. (Cole and Furbey 1994: 69)

Market conditions after the war did not favour private housebuilders. Consequently, between 1945 and 1951, 80 per cent of housing completions were in the public sector (Grayson 1997). Local authority housing starts in England and Wales were 163 518 by 1946, continuing at about this level until 1951 when they reached 170 857. In addition, 124 455 prefabricated dwellings had been built by 1948. While space standards increased, quantitatively this provision remained insufficient in relation to needs. The level of the post-war building programme had been lower than expected, falling short of the Labour government's own target by 240 000 a year (Cole and Furbey 1994). This was largely due to inadequate central government support, reflecting Labour's acceptance of a 'middle way', a form of democratic socialism between capitalism and communism (in contrast to New Labour's 'third' or 'middle way' between 'Old' Labour and the New Right [Giddens 1998]). This acceptance was partly due to the constraints forced by economic dependency on the US, and the need to demonstrate financial prudence to 'middle England'.

Meanwhile, Labour's failure to deal with the housing shortage provided the Conservative opposition with a potent campaign theme in the 1951 general election, which they won, pledging to build 300 000 houses a year. 'In the short run, this pledge could be redeemed only by increasing local authority building, which the new Housing Minister, Harold Macmillan, did, cutting space standards to reduce costs' (Harloe 1995: 284). In 1953 and 1954, council housing completions peaked at an all-time high – over 200 000. However, this initial success in alleviating the housing shortage, together with the Conservatives' ideological preference for home ownership and private sector solutions, paved the way for policies aimed at returning local authority housing to a marginal role.

In 1956, housing subsidies were restricted to slum-clearance programmes and, from the late-1950s, the increasing use of industrialised construction techniques in the production of high-rise tower blocks was encouraged. This period, more than any other in the history of council housing, was critical in bringing about its long-term decline and, despite high levels of satisfaction among the majority of council tenants living on estates (Grayson 1997), paved the way for the state to reinforce the positive ideology attached to home ownership:

> By the 1970s the image of vast, bleak high-rise estates, suffering from physical decay and vandalism, with high levels of social problems, helped to reinforce the generally negative image which council housing had obtained and the stigmatising effects of residence in some of these areas on their inhabitants. (Harloe 1995: 286)

One of the most dramatic images of the 'high-rise' problem came in May 1968 when a gas explosion at Ronan Point in West Ham caused the partial collapse of a 22-storey tower block, killing a number of residents (Grayson

1997). Jacobs and Manzi suggest that the 'tower block' image has subsequently come to symbolise the wider failings of state welfare in Britain. The tower block became the:

> great architectural symbol of the Welfare State age ... stripped of its progressive aura, the council tower block has since undergone a symbolic conversion and emerged as a monstrous emblem of the futility of all State-led social reform ... [a] tombstone not just of council housing but of the entire welfare state. (Wright 1992, cited in Jacobs and Manzi 1996: 548)

While Labour were returned to government in 1964 with a manifesto commitment to raising housing output to 500 000 completions per annum, including an increase in council housebuilding, for political expedience they had come round to the view that home ownership was the most natural tenure form, cementing the consensus on this issue between the main parties. Council housing would still be needed to meet 'exceptional needs', but 'building for owner-occupation ... is normal' (1965 White Paper on Housing, cited in Harloe 1995: 288). One reason for this change in emphasis was that the 1961 Census, the first to include details on housing tenure, showed that owner occupation had become the largest single tenure in England and Wales – 43 per cent, compared with public renting (23 per cent) and private renting (34 per cent). Moreover, in this post-war period 'home ownership ... spread from the middle class to large sections of the working class' (Saunders 1990: 15). Essentially, Labour had to adapt its housing policy to retain the support of 'middle England' home owners.

By the end of the 1960s, a widespread consensus was emerging, partly reinforced by a concern for public spending levels, that housing policy should shift emphasis towards the rehabilitation of the existing stock (Harloe 1995). Moreover, the election of 1970, won by the Conservatives, was largely fought on a political campaign in favour of assisting home owners. In an attempt to encourage the more affluent council tenants into home ownership, the Conservatives introduced a new financial regime for local authorities in the Housing Finance Act 1972. This regime involved quasi-market rents, lower subsidies and a national rent-rebate scheme. The legislation provoked a wave of militancy throughout the tenants' movement and among some Labour authorities (Grayson 1997). The resulting tension between Westminster and left-leaning Labour authorities encouraged the Conservatives to turn to housing associations to play a major role in implementing the newly-favoured housing rehabilitation programme, a scheme eventually enacted by a Labour Government in 1974.

The Housing Act 1974 provided increased funds for housing associations. There has been, on the surface, a perceptible consensus in terms of political support for housing associations. Various explanations have been given for this unanimity between the parties, largely based on the alleged benefits deriving from housing association activities – such as cost effectiveness and management efficiencies (Back and Hamnett 1985). However, Back and Hamnett dispute such explanations, and point instead at the key role of political ideology in determining the nature of state support for housing associations. So, during the 1960s, when a Conservative government introduced exchequer funds for housing associations to provide rented homes at economic rents, this support was seen as entirely 'consistent with [their] anti-collectivist principles' (Back and Hamnett 1985: 398), an attempt at stimulating a private renting movement for middle-income earners that would be 'independent of Government' (Dame Evelyn Sharp in 1961, then Permanent Secretary to the Ministry of Housing and Local Government, cited in Back and Hamnett 1985: 399).

In contrast, the way the 1974 Act was eventually implemented by a Labour government was equally consistent with its 'socialist' principles. The Act introduced housing association grant (HAG) – a generous capital grant towards acquisition and development costs – and a revenue deficit grant (RDG) to cover certain losses incurred on the running costs of the association. Throughout most of the 1970s, HAG was targeted on the acquisition and rehabilitation of privately-owned dilapidated homes largely occupied by poor tenants. This, thereby, permitted Labour to use HAG as a means of extending the social ownership of rented accommodation (Back and Hamnett 1985).

The debate on the role of housing associations in the 1970s, therefore, mirrored the then traditional party lines on the role of the state in British housing policy. Labour viewed housing associations as quasi public-sector agencies promoting 'welfare' values and complementing the housing activities of local authorities. In contrast, the Conservatives viewed them as quasi private-sector agencies promoting 'market' values and offering an alternative to local authority provision. Indeed, during the Standing Committee debate on the 1974 Housing Bill, Conservative MP Geoffrey Finsberg predicted that a future Conservative government 'may decide to legislate to compel local authorities to dispose of all properties that they have acquired, other than properties they have built themselves, to housing associations' (1974 Housing Bill, Standing committee B, col.83, cited in Back and Hamnett 1985: 404). Little did Finsberg realise at this time that, 25-years later, local authorities themselves, including many once proud to uphold the values of municipal socialism (such as Walsall and Birmingham), would be queuing up to transfer their stock to an increasingly marketised housing association movement (Curry 1999).

While housing associations have had an increasingly enhanced role in the housing system since the 1970s, the 'residualisation' of local authority provision was to continue. There are a number of reasons for the residualisation process, although many of these reflect 'the redirection of financial support away from collective provision in favour of "subsidised individualism" – whether in rent rebates to tenants, or tax concessions to owner-occupiers' (Cole and Furbey 1994: 83). This shift in housing support is mirrored throughout other areas of welfare provision, a transformation that has been characterised as 'consumption sector cleavages' (see Saunders 1981) and 'the social division of welfare thesis' (see Harrison 1998) – reflecting the increasing social divide caused by the expanding fissure between private and collective forms of welfare 'consumption'. This differentiation between areas of welfare consumption correlates with particular notions of 'work' and other elements of social status. As Harrison explains:

> Status in welfare may be linked with people's standing in relation to the world of work, and to ideas of entitlement connected with respectability, nation, gender, belonging, wealth, able-bodiedness, actuarial calculations, health, or the minimising of risk. (Harrison 1998: 800)

This underpins further processes of empowerment or disempowerment.

> Alongside provision through state-directed services and administered financial payments (council housing, housing benefit, etc.), there are extensive fiscal and occupational supports enjoyed by households. A leading example has been mortgage interest tax relief ... Through the social division of welfare, households receive assistance outside direct wages, but some are helped to maintain positions of relative advantage. Those well placed in relation to employment and wealth are frequently also leading beneficiaries via welfare systems. By contrast, those in weak positions in relation to the labour market are heavily dependent upon stigmatised services and income support. (Harrison 1998: 800)

A stark example of the differentiated experience of those who are socially and economically weak is the workings of the Housing (Homeless Persons) Act, first introduced in 1977. While providing households in certain unintentionally homeless 'priority need categories' a right to permanent rehousing, the quality of service has been poor. Research has shown that:

[S]ingle offer policies were common for homeless people ... and fewer offers were made to homeless households than to other applicants ... Homeless people could often express fewer area preferences than other applicants, and this lack of choice could result in the allocation of homeless people to estates where they did not want to live and had no contacts or support. This has been identified as a factor leading to the development of social segregation. (Mullins and Niner 1998: 184-185)

While some commentators suggest that the 1977 Act significantly eroded local government autonomy (see, for example, Malpass and Murie 1999), the homelessness legislation still allowed authorities considerable discretion over how they exercised their duty. This permitted some authorities to continue to discriminate against two categories of homeless household: those deemed 'undeserving' by virtue of their family structure or their behaviour, and who had no entitlement to housing at all; and those deemed 'less deserving' who had a right to be rehoused, but were relegated to the least desirable housing estates or bed and breakfast hostels, segregated from 'respectable' households.

Where local authorities did lose considerable autonomy in the mid-1970s was in their ability to determine their capital expenditure programmes. As Malpass and Murie observe, prior to the mid-1970s local authorities were 'substantially free to set their own capital programmes of housing expenditure. Throughout most of the period since 1919 central government has exercised only indirect influence, via the operation of the subsidy system' (Malpass and Murie 1999: 71). So long as scheme proposals met design standards and cost limits then loan approval could be expected. By the mid-1970s, declining economic growth, increased global competition, high inflation and volatile interest rates intensified government concern over public spending levels. This concern convinced the Labour government of the need to embrace 'monetarism'.

Denis Healey, Labour's Chancellor of the Exchequer in the 1974-79 government, had broken with Keynesianism by 1977 and accepted the logic of monetarism, partly due to pressure from the International

Monetary Fund. Healey cut the government's capital investment programme by 10 per cent in order to halve the Public Sector Borrowing Requirement (Barratt Brown 1987). To assist this strategy, Labour introduced the Housing Investment Programme (HIP) in their 1977 Housing Policy Review Green Paper, a system that allows central government to set the maximum amount a local authority can spend on capital works. While presented in the Green Paper as an enhancement of local discretion, HIPs effectively increase government control over local authority capital programmes, allowing substantial cuts in council housing investment (Malpass and Murie 1999). Additionally, the Green Paper reaffirmed Labour's commitment to home ownership (Kemp 1999). These shifts in emphasis were to have far-reaching implications for those most reliant on public-sector housing, amongst whom are a disproportionate number of women, older people, disabled people, black people, lone-parent families and unskilled working-class households. However, it was the election of Mrs Thatcher in 1979 that paved the way for 'a more full-blooded version' of the monetarist project to emerge (Cole and Furbey 1994: 183), with radical implications for housing.

Neo-liberals, housing policies and welfare discourse

The period of Conservative rule 1979-1997 saw home ownership in Britain expand significantly. Home-ownership policies were central to Margaret Thatcher's electoral success in 1979. The New Right rhetoric on home ownership did much to exaggerate its appeal. For example, Saunders argued that the growth of home ownership in the 1980s had meant that Britain was, for the first time in its history, 'a genuine property-owning democracy' where 'ethnic minorities as well as whites, working-class people as well as middle-class people ... have benefited financially from house purchase' (Saunders 1990: 314). Moreover:

> many people also find in home ownership a means for expressing and realizing values of autonomy, personal independence and emotional security which are deeply cherished. Home ownership enables them to personalize their surroundings and it fosters a stronger sense of belonging and personal achievement. By providing people with a secure home base which they can call their own, it also underpins a greater willingness to become involved in social affairs beyond the garden gate; for ... a sense of domestic security may well be a

necessary condition for participation in wider social and civic affairs. (Saunders 1990: 314)

By attaching such intense meaning to home ownership and, for Saunders, the concept of 'home as haven', he underplays the part 'home' plays in tensions and conflicts surrounding the use of domestic space. 'Home', regardless of tenure, also provides the context for violence and abuse against children, gays and lesbians, women, children and black people.

A nation of home owners and the 'socially excluded'

By the time Mrs Thatcher was elected in 1979, housing choice in the UK was largely polarised between owning (around 55 per cent of tenure) and public renting (29 per cent). Under Thatcherism, the political consensus on home ownership evolved more strongly, allowing this tenure to become firmly ingrained as 'natural'. In contrast, 'council housing' as a concept was disparaged, deconstructed and reconceived as 'social housing', reduced to a tenure of last resort. What had started as a concern for public expenditure control by the previous Labour administration was taken much further by the Thatcher governments in the form of an ideological project aimed at privatising state welfare.

Housing was central to the 1979 Conservative manifesto, commanding more space than social security, education and health. Its pivotal pronouncement on housing was the expansion of home ownership and the extension of the 'property owning democracy' (Kemp 1999: 126). The sale of council housing through the right-to-buy, introduced under the Housing Act 1980, was the Conservatives' most successful privatisation programme. It also significantly changed tenure patterns in the UK. Between 1981 and 1996, owner-occupation increased from 56.4 per cent to 67 per cent of all tenures, while local authority provision fell from 30.4 per cent to just 18.8 per cent (Malpass and Murie 1999).

As discussed in Chapter Two, the policy initiatives of the 1980s and 1990s drew largely on New Right notions of 'freedom of choice', allowing individual consumers to make rational choices in unfettered markets. They also reflected the rise of Public Choice theory in British politics, a view built on the critique of public-sector welfare bureaucracies (which were seen as inefficient and wasteful). This is a position that fitted in neatly with neo-liberal, New Right thinking, which not only attacked public welfare for its economic inefficiencies, but also for its moral dangers. Market liberalism was therefore seen as the solution to both the economic and social problems facing Britain in the early 1980s. However, the emergence of mass home ownership under the Conservatives was not a result of the free and unfettered operation of market forces, but the outcome of distorting the housing market through major financial incentives to own. From the early 1980s, these included not only generous right-to-buy discounts but also low interest-rate policies.

At the same time, as more households were attracted into the home-ownership sector, wider structural changes and policy reforms exacerbated the disadvantages faced by those living in council housing. Labour market deregulation and the emergence of long-term structural unemployment in areas of traditional manufacture, areas where council housing had been built largely, increased the difficulty of access to employment for council tenants. Modifications to social security entitlements under the Social Security Act 1986, removing many households from eligibility and reducing housing benefit expenditure by a further £450m (Cole and Furbey 1994), meant that council tenants had more to pay in rent. Changes to the local authority rent and subsidy system under the Local Government and Housing Act 1989 also meant higher rents. Substantial cuts in public-sector capital spending on housing meant that properties sold under the right-to-buy, generally the best quality stock in better areas (Forrest and Murie 1988), were not replaced. Between 1980 and 1996 public-sector housing completions fell from 86 027 to 863 (Kemp 1999). These policies and changes have all contributed towards the continued residualisation of council housing, making it the least favourable housing option for many households. Living in council housing increasingly became associated with an experience of multiple forms of deprivation, caused by increasing difficulties in accessing employment, education, health care, transport, leisure and, importantly, the policy-making 'community'.

Underpinning these changes has been the broader notion in British society that home ownership is the 'norm' and council renting is inferior. This process of 'normalising' home ownership has, suggests Gurney, been a significant cause of the residualisation of council housing:

> [H]ome ownership has been subject to a process of normalisation, and ... this is ... important ... in explaining the labelling of social rented housing estates... . [T]he normalisation of one form of housing consumption has been instrumental in legitimising the residualisation of social rented housing. (Gurney 1999: 163)

In British society in particular, the normalising judgement is that 'home ownership is widely desired, while council renting is preferred by few' (Saunders 1990: 314). As Gurney shows, statements contained in selected housing policy documents from the 1971 White Paper, *A Fair Deal for Housing*, to the 1995 White Paper, *Our Future Homes*, invariably discuss tenure in terms of the specific benefits derived from home ownership, such as 'independence and control'. Some commentators have fetishised home ownership, claiming that it offers people an opportunity to establish 'ontological security', a sense of 'deep' psychological well-being, generally denied to residents in other tenure forms (Saunders 1990).

By the end of the 1980s, however, there was a growing realisation that social deprivation was not confined to tenants and that the benefits of owning were not generalisable throughout that sector. With the mass growth of home ownership came increasing differentiation and fragmentation (Forrest et al. 1990) and, for many, increasing exposure to risk. This was especially true following the housing recession of 1989, which led to unprecedented levels of mortgage arrears, repossessions, negative equity and home ownership disrepair, alongside all the human misery this brings. Within its post-1989 context, the view that important social, economic and psychological benefits derive from home ownership looks less convincing.

Indeed, Ford and Burrows provide a convincing analysis of the range of costs associated with mortgage arrears and repossessions. For borrowers affected, these include the financial, social, psychological and health costs associated with debt, factors that may lead to social exclusion. In addition, these costs impinge on other housing market institutions, such as housebuilders (in terms of reduced transactions), lenders (in terms of collection costs and lost investment) and insurers (in terms of mortgage interest guarantees). They may also impact on both central government (in terms of loss of political support) and local government (in terms of the cost of meeting homelessness provision), as well as the labour market (in terms of reduced mobility) and health providers (in terms of the cost of increased treatment). This analysis has important implications for both housing policy, and the extent to which it continues to support home ownership at the cost of other tenure forms (Ford and Burrows 1999), and other areas of social policy.

Following the 1987 general election, Conservative housing policy embarked on a more stringent attack on local authority housing, alongside plans to revitalise the private-rented sector. These strategies mirrored much of the thinking coming out from the New Right think-tank, the Institute of Economic Affairs (IEA), at the time (see Minford et al. 1987, Black and Stafford 1988). Underpinning the beliefs of the IEA was the view that welfare approaches which aim to achieve greater equality in society create a 'moral hazard' by offering disincentives to people to take responsibility for their own lives. Comprehensive welfare, provided free at the point of delivery, promotes an irresponsible attitude of expecting 'something for nothing'. The most obvious ways of removing this moral hazard are, therefore, for welfare services to be transferred as far as possible into private hands, and/or to provide these services at market price to encourage efficiency, choice and value-for-money (VFM).

On housing specifically, Minford et al.'s key argument was that housing problems are largely the product of state intervention. The Rent Acts proved a disincentive to the private sector to provide rented housing, and gave an indiscriminate subsidy to tenants. Subsidising rents in the public sector, meanwhile, created an 'over-demand' for council housing and unfair competition with the private sector, again leading to the decline of the latter. The solution, therefore, lay in the deregulation of all tenancies and making council housing the tenure of last resort (Minford et al. 1987). These recommendations were reflected in the Conservative government's 1987 White Paper, *Housing: the government's proposals*, and subsequent legislation. The Housing Act 1988 introduced assured tenancies and abolished the 'fair-rent' system for new housing association tenancies. A new financial regime for housing associations was also introduced, involving the use of private finance and reduced HAG rates. The Local Government and Housing Act 1989 sought to raise council rents towards market levels by reducing council housing subsidies. Moreover, these reforms were set in the context of a changing housing role for local authorities, away from being direct providers to 'enablers', facilitating provision by other landlords (effectively housing associations).

While the broad political and financial context for council housing provision became increasingly unfavourable under the Conservatives by the late 1980s, the concept of freedom to choose was continually applied to this sector too. The freedom to choose to buy your council house (Housing Act 1980) was supposedly extended to the freedom to choose another landlord under 'Tenants' Choice' (Housing Act 1988). However, these 'choices' formed part of a broader policy agenda aimed at fragmenting and abolishing council housing and promoting 'quasi-market' solutions, where the housing service would be organised around competing, self-financed centres, similar to the operational environment in private business (Le Grand and Bartlett 1993). The intention of introducing quasi-markets was to provide the conditions for greater managerial and cost effectiveness. It also reflected a change in thinking within the Conservative government after 1987, when as much emphasis was placed on managerial efficiency as on the need to privatise state-owned services. Despite the loss of their property through the right-to-buy legislation, local authorities still owned around 4m council homes at this time. While the policy of Large Scale Voluntary Transfers (LSVTs) saw around one quarter of a million council homes transfer to housing associations by April 1997 (Kemp 1999), the estimated cost of council-housing management contracts nationally remains over £1bn per annum (Walker-Brown 1998). These contracts had to be managed more efficiently and cheaply through Housing Management Compulsory Competitive Tendering (HMCCT), introduced after 1993.

While other policies were deeply significant, it was HMCCT that brought about a visible change in the organisational shape and culture of housing authorities. HMCCT forced authorities to take a commercial view of their activities and, in doing so, organisations traditionally characterised as having 'political cultures' became 'business cultures' (Walker-Brown 1998). What emerged was a 'new managerialism' in local government:

> [M]anagerialism is the connecting thread linking markets, partnerships, an emphasis on customers and the recomposition of the labour force ... it seeks to introduce new orientations, remodels existing relations of power and affects how and where social policy choices are made. (Clarke et al. 1994, cited in Burden 1998: 83)

Managerialism introduced a range of new concepts to the management of housing, based on:

> the rhetoric of 'new wave' management involving 'quality', customer care, 'empowerment' and giving subordinates a sense of 'ownership'. (Burden 1998: 83)

Within this overall context, 'empowerment' for council tenants was largely limited to the capacity to 'exit' – either to owner occupation or housing associations (Registered Social Landlords [RSLs] since the Housing Act 1996) – or the right to be treated as a 'customer' by the housing department (with somewhat vague entitlements to 'participation'). Moreover, as Jacobs and Manzi argue:

> [T]he use of the term 'customer' within housing management ... is a deliberate endeavour on the part of policy-makers and managers to alter perceptions of staff towards consumers of services. Therefore, models of 'tenant' or 'client' are seen as no longer appropriate due to connotations with the idea of a 'dependency culture'. The new model of user choice is consciously linked to market processes. It is a calculated effort to alter attitudes towards acceptance of a competitive environment ... [illustrating] the pre-eminence of a managerial perspective in housing practice. (Jacobs and Manzi 1996: 547-548)

The acceptance of a competitive environment for housing over recent years has seen the rise in pre-eminence of RSLs, with significant ramifications for residents. RSLs do not have the same obligations as local authorities in terms of a legal duty to meet need; nor are they publicly accountable to the elected representatives of the community they serve. While throughout its history the management approach of local housing authorities has invariably given greater priority to resource control (that is, control over its properties and their occupants) than to the promotion of 'citizenship' (Spink 1998), local government does, at least, offer a greater prospect for a wider base of 'citizen control' than RSLs. Yet, as we have already mentioned above, as we enter the twenty-first century local authorities throughout the country are looking to transfer their stock to RSLs; this includes the two largest local authority landlords, Birmingham and Glasgow, who are negotiating the transfer of their entire stock of more than 90 000 homes each to RSLs (Curry 1999). This has important implications for the future accountability of 'social housing' (see Knowles 1998 for a critical analysis of the implications of LSVTs for power relationships between tenants and their landlord).

Furthermore, while managerialism may have induced a greater sense of financial accountability into the public sector, broader notions of political and civil rights have been subsumed. The UK has witnessed increasing social and economic inequality since 1979 (Howarth et al. 1998) accompanied by the 'underclass' thesis, a pathological explanation of poverty and the disintegration of moral standards (Murray 1990). Two clear examples of this can be found in recent welfare debates around the 'single-parent family' and the 'neighbour-from-hell'. For instance, Nicholas Ridley on the 'single-parent family':

There was one other category of people with which I had less than total sympathy – they called themselves 'one-parent families'. Single parents were also free-riders on the system, directly exploiting the dependency culture ... It became a way of living for some to have one or more children by unknown men, in order to qualify for a council house. (Ridley 1992, cited in Jacobs and Manzi 1996: 548)

This perception of free-riding by single parents informed the 1995 White Paper, *Our Future Homes: Opportunity, Choice, Responsibility*, which argued:

Allocation schemes should reflect the underlying values of our society. They should balance specific housing needs against the need to support married couples who take a responsible approach to family life, so that tomorrow's generation grows up in a stable environment. (DoE 1995, cited in Jacobs and Manzi 1996: 556)

More recently, the 'neighbour-from-hell' has emerged. Despite the fact that neighbour nuisance problems occur in all tenures, and that various existing powers to deal with these problems are already held by a range of agencies, reforms included in the Conservatives' Housing Act 1996 introduced new sanctions against council tenants specifically, allowing:

local authorities to reduce tenants' rights by adopting a system of introductory tenancies, under which all new tenants have to serve a 12-month probationary period. At the end of this period, the tenancy automatically converts to a secure tenancy if the standard conditions for a secure tenancy are met. However, the introductory tenancy can be terminated at any time within the 12-month period by the landlord serving a notice to quit. (Scott and Parkey 1998: 326)

These measures have echoes of the nineteenth-century style of 'professional' housing management practised by Octavia Hill and the philanthropic movement (Spink 1998). They provide further opportunities for rationing, surveillance and punishment to deal with the new 'folk devil' of our time – the 'neighbour-from-hell'. They also come close to New Labour's position on reciprocity, and the notion that rights must be balanced by obligations – underlined in New Labour's Green Paper on Welfare Reform.

Throughout its history, housing in the UK has largely been distributed as a reward for subscribing to a particular style of behaving (Cooper and Hawtin 1997). Moreover, as Somerville suggests:

mass housing provision privileged the traditional nuclear family by providing predominantly three-bedroomed housing, typically on suburban estates ... The assumption was that each home would have two adults, one of whom would go out to work while the other stayed at home and looked after the children. (Somerville, forthcoming)

This emphasis on the production of three-bedroomed council housing can be seen, in part, to be a component in a wider Malthusian strategy of controlling the breeding patterns of working-class families. It also, however, serves to exclude a range of 'Other than' 'family' forms: large families, extended families, single people, and gay and lesbian couples.

Labour's inheritance

Housing issues largely concern the supply, quality, accessibility and affordability of accommodation. According to Kemp, housing conditions in Britain, in many respects, had improved considerably since Labour was last in power:

Many more households were living in their preferred tenure of owner-occupation. Levels of satisfaction with housing had increased and hence ... standards appear to have risen in line with rising expectations. (Kemp 1999: 132)

However, at the same time, there were significant social and economic problems embedded in the British housing system. There was an estimated £10bn repair backlog in the council sector alone, whilst standards of space and amenities in the housing association sector had fallen since the introduction of the new financial regime for associations under the Housing Act 1988. Quantitatively, the shortfall between numbers of households and numbers of fit dwellings had increased, as had the number of households living in overcrowded conditions. Figures for homelessness, mortgage arrears and repossessions had reached unprecedented levels under the Conservatives, while a substantial number of home owners were living with 'negative equity' (Kemp 1999).

Housing supply in the 'affordable' public sector was in decline as a result of policies which aimed to promote home ownership. Rents in the private, public and housing association sectors increased towards market levels – putting a strain on housing benefit, creating a poverty trap and causing affordability problems for those on marginal incomes. Moreover, the quality of the housing stock and neighbourhood environment in some areas was a cause of significant dissatisfaction, particularly amongst some ethnic minorities (Lee and Murie 1997). In addition, the characteristics of those living in social housing had changed since 1979, and they were now overwhelmingly poorer households, single-parent families, women and older people (Cole and Furbey 1994).

Reviewing the situation today, it is clear that there have been significant political changes in the way the UK housing system is controlled. In the 1970s, 'social housing' was largely controlled by an expanding local authority sector. Now, authorities have lost a significant proportion of their stock through right-to-buy sales and stock transfers. Over 70 local authorities have transferred their entire stock to RSLs. In addition, the role of residents in running housing and related services is firmly entrenched in current housing policy debates. These changes raise a number of important questions about control and accountability in the housing system. In particular, there are questions about the future of council housing and, if it still has a role, what form this should take. Additionally, there is the issue to be addressed of RSLs' accountability to the 'communities' they serve, particularly if these bodies are to continue to have a central role in housing provision.

New Labour, housing policies and welfare discourse

This section offers a detailed critique of New Labour's housing policy. Kemp (1999) has followed the then Housing Minister, Hilary Armstrong, in characterising the housing policies of the new Labour government under four headings: making the market work; empowering individuals; ensuring best value in public services; and strengthening communities (Kemp 1999, Armstrong 1999). Interestingly, only the last of these can be represented as a clear discontinuity from previous Conservative policies. However, in each case, in adopting policies from its predecessor, New Labour has given them a 'spin' of its own which serves as a link with its 'Old Labour' constituency.

Making the market work

For the Conservatives, as we have seen, 'making the market work' meant privatisation wherever possible, and the adoption of quasi-market reforms wherever privatisation seemed impracticable or inappropriate. For New

Labour, however, making the market work requires state intervention in those circumstances where 'the free market cannot accommodate the needs and aspirations of all' (Hilary Armstrong, then Minister for Housing, 1998, quoted in Kemp 1999: 136). So, for example, New Labour is pledged to protect home owners with flexible mortgages and new consumer rights, and to prevent 'boom-bust' in the housing market. This sounds like Old Labour attempts to meddle with the market in order to achieve social goals, but the experience thus far has been policies designed simply to make the buying and selling of homes more efficient for the individuals concerned. In October 1999, for instance, New Labour announced plans aimed at reducing the time-lag between offer, acceptance and exchange of contracts by making the seller responsible for providing most of the necessary information about their property in advance (*Inside Housing*, 22 October 1999). Unlike under Old Labour, therefore, state intervention is designed to bolster, rather than check, the dominant forces acting in the owner-occupied housing market.

It is important to remember here that the previous Conservative government was not averse to interfering in the housing market when it suited it to do so. The best examples of this are mortgage-interest tax relief and discounts on council house sales (which New Labour is continuing). There have been many others, such as the Business Expansion Scheme, low-cost home ownership and the Rough Sleepers Initiative. Actual Conservative housing policy, therefore, typically deviated considerably from the rhetoric. Although ostensibly committed to privatisation and quasi-market reforms, in practice they found it difficult to resist the temptation of launching new initiatives in the traditional style of big governments everywhere. This raises the question of whether a similar divorce between rhetoric and actuality may have infected the practice of New Labour.

Arguably, the key issue here is whether the government actually accepts responsibility for making the housing market work. The previous Conservative government did not accept such responsibility as it went against their ideological position. Consequently, its interventions in the market were generally arbitrary and *ad hoc*, being unplanned consequences of the tax system (such as mortgage tax relief) or knee-jerk reactions to specific political crises such as street homelessness (Somerville 1999). In contrast, Old Labour believed that governments had responsibility for all aspects of the welfare of their citizens. The rhetoric of New Labour appears to echo that of the New Right, emphasising individual responsibility and the limited nature of state intervention. As with the Conservatives, however, the actuality could well turn out to be rather different because of New Labour's emphasis on the state's responsibility for social inclusion. In view of this, it seems likely that New Labour's interventions in the housing market will be more pro-active and strategic than those of the previous government.

The role of housing benefit is particularly important here. In spite of their rhetoric, the previous Conservative governments allowed low-income tenants to live rent-free on a more or less permanent basis, constituting a major distortion of the housing market and a complete removal of personal responsibility for housing costs. New Labour still has to decide whether an element of personal responsibility should be introduced and how the problem of distortions in the housing market arising from this massive state subsidy (£10bn in England alone in 1997-98) should be addressed. More than anything else, the widespread dependence of households on housing benefit shows that the market does not work, but does New Labour really want to take responsibility for this? Field (1996) has long argued for both personal and state responsibility in this policy area, but up to now these arguments do not appear to have been accepted in government. Although it is likely, therefore, that tenants will end up having to pay part of their housing costs (or at least be given the responsibility over whether or not to pay those costs out of the benefits they receive – Lawlor 1999), in line with the New Right side of New Labour rhetoric, it is not yet clear whether the government will opt for a more limited form of housing benefit or something that is even more comprehensive than the present one. If it is true, as some have argued (Bramley 1997), that housing policy as such no longer exists, then it is at least possible that housing benefit could be given a much wider social role in combating poverty and social exclusion.

Kemp argues that the crucial differences between Old Labour, the 1979-97 Conservative governments and New Labour centre on their approaches to council housing:

> Old Labour was committed to council housing and the Conservative governments of Margaret Thatcher and John Major wanted to *force* councils to get rid of it; but New Labour apparently wishes to *encourage* and incentivise councils to transfer the ownership, or at least the management, of their dwellings to other social housing landlords. (Kemp 1999: 136 – original emphases)

This statement needs to be qualified in one respect in that, although it is true that the Conservative governments talked about bringing an end to council housing (Clapham 1989), they never actually forced the issue in terms of large-scale transfers. In effect, their policy was, like that of New Labour, one of encouragement for LSVTs. In this case, therefore, the rhetoric of New Labour is different from that of the Conservatives, but the policy impact is remarkably similar, if not the same. In fact, the LSVT programme has been greatly expanded under New Labour.

This leads on to the question of how New Labour now views the so-called 'third sector' in housing (that is, RSLs). Do they regard them as quasi public-sector agencies (as with Old Labour) or quasi-private (as with the New Right)? At the present time, the answer to this question is uncertain, but the New Labour emphasis on making the market work suggests a pragmatic approach in which RSLs could be regarded as both quasi-public and quasi-private, depending upon the particular circumstances in which they are operating. The New Labour slogan, 'what matters is what works', could be interpreted as implying that New Labour has no particular ideological stance on this issue, and perhaps does not care one way or the other. New Labour's position is compatible with both the New Right emphasis on promoting markets, or quasi-markets, in housing provision, and with Old Labour's traditional commitment to 'tenure neutrality' and local autonomy in housing provision.

The policy of 'making the market work' has important implications for social inclusion and exclusion. In general, it will tend to promote the inclusion of those who can manage to access the market as 'consumers', while continuing to exclude those who cannot. If the market is subsidised at the expense of the taxpayer – for example, through mortgage-interest tax relief – then this discriminates against those outside the market. If the market is regulated at little cost this could, in principle, facilitate access for some households who would otherwise be excluded, but does nothing for the rest who require genuinely low-cost accommodation.

Empowering individuals

As with making the market work, 'empowering individuals' also sounds like a New Right slogan, but the New Labour interpretation of it is characteristically different from that of the New Right. Again, however, the practice can look surprisingly similar. New Labour shares with the New Right an antipathy towards the 'public landlordism' (Cole and Furbey

1994) associated with Old Labour, which involved paternalism and patronage by politicians, and the dominance of housing provision and management by professionals and bureaucrats. Instead, New Labour, like the New Right, wants to see the consumer placed at the heart of service delivery. Where New Labour, perhaps, parts company with the New Right is in seeing the consumer as a collectivity as well as a collection of individuals.

The Conservative government introduced major new rights such as the right-to-buy, which could be argued to be empowering of individuals. They also, however, introduced what amounted to collective rights, such as under Tenants' Choice and the right to veto stock transfers, and the right to manage under the Leasehold Reform, Housing and Urban Development Act 1993. Their stated purpose in introducing collective rights, however, was not so much to empower individual council-housing tenants as to achieve what Kemp (1999) has called 'demunicipalisation'. In other words, the collective empowerment of tenants was only a means to an end; namely, the gradual erosion and eventual destruction of local authority power. When Tenants' Choice, for example, failed to achieve this purpose, the Conservative government had no hesitation in repealing it in the Housing Act 1996. Arguably, therefore, the Conservatives were never committed to the empowerment of tenants as a whole for its own sake.

New Labour looks, or at least sounds, rather different on this. While continuing with the individual rights enacted by the previous government, they show signs of wanting to empower the collective consumer as well. The clearest example of this is in relation to Tenant Participation Compacts (TPCs), in which local authorities are expected to involve tenants collectively in the management of their homes. The right to manage is also being reviewed so as to make it less antagonistic towards local authorities while retaining the statutory collective empowerment conferred by the 1993 Act. The buzz word now is 'partnership' rather than conflict, and this again reflects New Labour's less ideological and more pragmatic stance generally. The process of developing collective involvement by tenants in decision making could also be regarded as an element in New Labour's wider programme of democratic renewal (Rouse and Smith 1999). On this issue, therefore, New Labour appears to differ significantly from both Old Labour and the New Right, and their agenda here relates to their approach on social inclusion and on strengthening communities (see below).

It should be noted, however, that there remain a number of concerns about the extent to which tenants will have meaningful influence over the way TPCs are developed. Local authorities were given a very tight timescale for TPCs to be in place (April 2000). It is unlikely, therefore, that the compacts will reflect all tenants' wishes, as they are supposed to do, because there has been insufficient time, let alone resources, for tenants to have developed a critical understanding of TPCs and all the options available to them. Landlords have admitted experiencing difficulty in obtaining widespread and 'representative' tenant consultation in designing TPCs (DETR 1999b). TPCs are not statutory, and the only sanctions the government have suggested in the event of failure to implement compacts have been possible cuts in HIPs, which would only disadvantage the very tenants whom the compacts are supposed to benefit.

A further concern, in view of the likely transfer of a large proportion of local authority property to RSLs, as discussed earlier, is the fact that New Labour has no plans to extend compacts to tenants of RSLs, nor do the latter have the right to form Tenant Management Organisations. Overall, in the RSL sector, it is the landlord who dictates the terms of tenant participation, within a regulatory framework that conceptualises tenants as 'customers', or 'service users', rather than as, say, 'citizens'. The Housing Corporation's generally *laissez-faire* approach to tenant participation is clear from the following statement:

> While local authority tenants have a statutory Right to Manage, we do not think it is appropriate to introduce a similar right for RSL tenants. We think it could, in certain circumstances, lead to confrontation between tenants and landlords. Where tenants have expressed a wish to explore the setting up of a TMO, we would expect their RSL to be supportive and work in partnership with them to achieve this. (Housing Corporation 1998: 15)

Thus, the notion of empowerment here is ambiguous, in the sense that individuals, on their own or as members of groups, could become empowered (for instance, by being better informed, consulted and taken more seriously) and yet still remain oppressed. New Labour situate empowerment within a paradigm of social inclusion that may genuinely address serious social problems, but may fall far short of social justice or real liberation. There is a risk that basic inequalities of power will not be challenged, let alone transformed, by such an approach.

Ensuring Best Value in public services

Best Value is New Labour's replacement for CCT. It is summed up by 'the four Cs': challenge, competition, comparison, consultation. It is of major importance because it sets out in detail for the first time how the government's approach differs from that of its predecessor. Although there is no space in this chapter to consider Best Value in Housing in depth (see DETR 1999a), the key relevant points are as follows: first, it incorporates, updates and substantially develops an element of the previous government's quasi-market approach through the market testing of housing (and other) services, and through processes of benchmarking with other local authorities across a number of performance indicators; second, it provides a revamp of Old Labour's approach in requiring a comprehensive, rational review of housing (and other) services, inviting comparison with the strategic management approaches of the public sector in the 1970s; third, it involves a specific New Labour dimension of consultation, not only with tenants and service users, but also with the wider local community. Here again, therefore, New Labour signals its difference from both Old Labour and the New Right through its communitarian advocacy of the collective consumer. At the same time, it again links this advocacy to its wider programme of democratic renewal.

There remains the question of whether New Labour's policies represent only a further development of the previous government's managerialism or signify a distinctively new approach. Clarke and Newman (1997) have portrayed managerialism as a new form of hegemony, that is a new set of practices through which power relations are maintained in society. A key feature of this hegemony is said to be the dispersal of state power to other agencies, in association with the promotion of values that secure the active compliance of citizens generally. Unlike previous hegemonies, compliance is not secured primarily through direct control or the threat of force, but rather through what Foucault has called 'productive subjection' (Clarke and Newman 1997: 30). The values so promoted are those that give key priority to the interests of the consumer: innovation, adaptation, performance and putting people first. Under the Conservatives, this managerialism was interpreted as putting 'customers' first, so that the stress was on giving pride of place to markets and quasi-markets. This emphasis gave rise to problems, however, in understanding the role of citizens and the responsibility of the state in relation to its citizens. In particular, this version of managerialism neglected the viewpoint of the 'collective consumer' (Lusk 1997) – effectively excluding those with little or no market power. Under New Labour, however, it can be seen that the Conservatives' managerialist discourse has been substantially reformed and extended to cover issues of collective consumption in a way which is politically more adaptable to a progressive agenda.

The new managerialism is different because it is self-consciously political, whereas the old managerialism pretended to be essentially a matter of technique. Nevertheless, it somehow incorporates within itself the old managerial values, giving them a new 'spin'. While the old managerialism denigrated the public sector and sought salvation in what it perceived as private-sector values, the new managerialism aims to break down the boundaries between public and private through the adoption of common techniques and cross-sectoral values, such as found in Best Value. So far, the new approach has been applied only to the public sector, but its application to the private sector could have far-reaching implications – for example, by increasing the power of the collective consumer, perhaps at the expense of shareholders or Board members.

A managerialist approach has major strengths, but also important weaknesses – in particular, its lack of clear democratic accountability (see Somerville, forthcoming, for a fuller discussion). However, there remains some doubt about how far managerialism has really penetrated the culture of local authorities (for example), even though it has been suggested that the New Labour version of managerialism actually originated within local authorities (Diamond 1999). Potentially, an important advantage of managerialism would be if it led to a significant dispersal of power to front-line housing staff and residents, but this does not look very likely within the Best Value regime. It is just possible that TPCs could lead to a situation where tenants offer resistance to managerialist hegemony on a more wide-ranging, more organised and systematic basis, but in the absence of more radical rights and resources such resistance is likely to prove ineffective in most cases.

The main point here is that New Labour's managerialism can be interpreted as either a continuation of that developed under the neo-liberal Conservatives or a radical new development, depending on your point of view. This ambiguity is just the same as that on empowerment. The new managerialism could herald a new, more corporate élitism, leading to deeper and more comprehensive regulation, surveillance and disciplining of the 'Other than', the 'managed'; alternatively, it could presage a more inclusive politics, where the 'Other than' are themselves constructed as active and equal citizens. Currently, however, New Labour's practice looks controlling rather than liberating, because of its failure to promote grass-roots empowerment.

Strengthening communities

The fourth slogan of New Labour's housing policy is the one that seems entirely original. 'Strengthening communities' most explicitly represents the New Labour rhetoric of empowering the collective consumer and renewing democracy at the level of housing estates and neighbourhoods. Lying behind this initiative is the wider New Labour agenda of social inclusion. Policy in this area, therefore, perhaps most clearly reflects the dilemmas and tensions within New Labour more generally.

Policies founded on notions of community are inherently problematic because of difficulties with the concept itself. For example, 'communities' can be stifling locations for some groups – such as in the case of sexually-exploited women: 'residents of a Walsall street are threatening to hose down prostitutes said to be operating from a Caldmore Area Housing Association property' (reported in *Inside Housing* 1 October 1999: 4). The notion of 'community' is invariably fashioned out of a discourse of such examples of urban breakdown and constructs of 'abnormality', serving both as the solution to urban problems and as part of the process of social exclusion. It is often an imagined concept, based on myth and constructed around a discourse of homogeneity and the 'us', effectively serving to exclude the 'Other than' who fails to conform as a result of their work ethic, consumption styles, household structure or sexual orientation. These processes of exclusion can take the form of racism – for example, targeting Asian households living in an extended family structure, or African-Caribbean households holding preferences for certain types of music and recreational drug consumption.

The idea of strengthening communities can be distinguished both from Old Labour and from the New Right. Old Labour was committed to municipal provision rather than community control, and local communities under Old Labour were typically excluded from participating in decisions that affected them deeply. The New Right was generally concerned with individual freedom rather than collective solidarity, although there is a communitarian strand within the New Right that emphasises voluntary collective action free from state interference (Murray 1984). Thus, New

Labour shows its distinctiveness from these positions by its rhetorical focus on both the collective consumer and the collective citizen. Perhaps because this is a new position, however, there is some doubt about its true significance.

Possibly the most important policy that New Labour has produced so far for strengthening communities is the New Deal for Communities, and this forms part of a wider strategy for neighbourhood renewal set out in the Social Exclusion Unit's third report (SEU 1998). The main thrust of this policy is a 'joined-up' approach involving close partnership among a variety of public and private sector agencies. The emphasis is strongly managerialist, stressing innovation, entrepreneurship, consumer-centredness and 'what works'. The development of the social exclusion policy is now being progressed by 18 cross-cutting Policy Action Teams (PATs), drawn from 10 government departments, co-ordinated by the SEU. There are action teams covering: 'getting people to work'; 'building a future for young people'; 'access to services' (mainly shops, financial services and IT); 'making government work better'; 'better information'; and, closely related to housing, 'getting the place to work'. Included within this latter theme are seven PATs covering: the promotion of effective neighbourhood management; local housing management; neighbourhood warden schemes; community self-help; the reduction of the incidence of surplus social housing; anti-social behaviour; and the maximisation of the contribution of arts and leisure to neighbourhood regeneration.

Looking at some of the early findings of these PAT reports, there is a clear managerialist emphasis appearing in some of their recommendations. For example, PAT 5, PAT 6 and PAT 7 argue for 'on-the-spot' locally-based housing management in deprived areas, including concierges, caretakers and neighbourhood wardens to reduce vandalism and increase personal security (DETR 1999c, 1999d, 1999e). The focus here is clearly on the role of housing and neighbourhood management in maintaining social control. While the PAT 5 report suggests that tenant involvement should be encouraged, using service-level agreements, there is little attention given to the possible structural causes of disadvantage, or the need to change the balance of power between residents and their landlords. The strongest impression conveyed is that neighbourhood problems can be simply 'managed away', with the role of the housing manager enlarged to embrace a range of other activities, such as helping tenants set up crèches and credit unions. The PAT 5 report also calls for lettings policies sensitive to the community and desirable for the long-term stability of an area (DETR 1999c). The danger here is that, in the interest of creating socially-homogeneous neighbourhoods, only those who fit in with the rules of the dominant culture of the area will succeed in gaining entry, exacerbating the exclusion of the 'Other than':

> This happens in places like Belle Terre, New York, or Candlelight Hills, Houston, Texas. In the 1970s, the Supreme Court ruled that the community of Belle Terre 'had a legitimate interest in excluding households whose members were not linked by "blood, adoption or marriage" in order to preserve family values, youth values, the blessings of quiet seclusion and clean air', making it a 'sanctuary for people'. (Sibley 1995: 98)

While the PAT 5 report suggests a welcome awareness of racial, religious and cultural diversity, and stresses the importance of racial-equality targets, without a stronger commitment to tackling structural racism – through education, regulating the employment market, and so forth – such target setting is likely to have minimal impact.

There is a contradiction, or at least a tension, between New Labour's neo-liberalism and its communitarianism, which echoes the tension within the New Right between its neo-liberal and neo-conservative strands. For example, while New Labour policy gives priority to getting people into paid work, which is certainly empowering of individuals, this may actually result in community decline as these newly-empowered people take advantage of opportunities elsewhere (displacement). This point has been taken up more broadly by Rouse and Smith:

> New Labour's approach to accountability owes a debt to communitarianism. For communitarianism seeks to move beyond the traditional Left-Right divide and to attach greater importance to the building of inclusive communities. The communitarian testament is predicated on three principles: co-operative inquiry, mutual responsibility and citizen participation. These three principles are evident in much of the programme of New Labour from its early days in office. However, the centralised search to improve performance throughout the welfare state, so ardently pursued by New Labour, cannot be attributed to communitarianism and appears at variance with it. (Rouse and Smith 1999: 254)

The emphasis on 'work', and the aim to make the (labour) market work, conflicts at key points with the aim to build healthy, stable communities. Moreover, there is the danger that New Labour's focus on paid work will unbalance the informal network of economic activity that has been so vital in thousands of deprived neighbourhoods:

> Informal economic activity pays better returns (despite its inherent risks) than formal employment or self-employment, when the only work available is low-paid, short-term or part-time and insecure. Above all, undeclared work for cash while claiming benefits is a way of countering the poverty trap, constituted by the combination of such work and over-loaded means-tested benefits that leave families destitute during the long delays after each claim. (Jack and Jordan 1999: 250)

Strategies to strengthen communities need to build on an understanding of the existing survival strategies and practices within these neighbourhoods:

> It must start from the experiences of poor people during the Thatcher-Major period, their interpretations of these experiences, and the framework of meanings through which they plan and conduct their lives. Simply to declare a moral war on informal economic activity, crime, drugs, and the whole cultures that have sustained such communities is unlikely to have the results that New Labour wants. (Jack and Jordan 1999: 251)

Additionally, the emphasis on partnership rather than markets or quasi-markets suggests a shift to the new, more corporatist managerialism, blurring the boundaries between public and private sector and establishing new, highly-responsive and adaptive networks, as exemplified in the multi-agency PAT approach. It could be questioned, however, how far this differs in principle from initiatives under the previous government such as City Task Forces, which were equally multi-agency and 'top down'.

New Labour's position on communities also reveals a tension between social inclusion and exclusion, which reflects the traditional dominant discourse of 'deserving' and 'undeserving'. On the one hand, there is a concern to ensure, through managerialist means, that residents are 'included' in the process affecting their communities. On the other hand, New Labour has enthusiastically signed up to an exclusionary agenda that promotes the punishment and banishment of those found guilty of breaking the community's code of conduct. The dividing line between 'deserving' and 'undeserving' is, therefore, being more rigorously drawn in terms of those who are deemed to be deserving or undeserving of inclusion in New Labour's great new corporate society. Ironically, however, the drawbacks to the state of excluding individuals from communities, in terms of increased difficulties and costs in managing and controlling the 'Other than', have not been adequately considered.

A more radical programme for social inclusion would involve a substantial redistribution of power to disadvantaged communities. Yet, New Labour has no proposals for significant new statutory rights for community groups, or for major transfers of resources to such groups, or for building democracy and accountability at the level of housing estates. One commentator, broadly sympathetic to New Labour, has complained:

> What the Social Exclusion Unit's report does not do explicitly is to see that a key ingredient in tackling social exclusion in poor neighbourhoods is to adopt policies which seek to transfer control of social housing and social housing budgets to the communities themselves. Involvement of communities will not be sustainable unless there is a radical shift of power the transfer of control to communities brings. (Rodgers 1999: 21)

In the absence of such a radical agenda, the policy seems to be not only an adoption of the previous government's policies on urban regeneration, involving a dispersal of power to a variety of market and quasi-market agencies, but also to hark back to Old Labour policies of corporatist central-local, public-private partnerships operating in an essentially 'top-down' fashion. All this tends to confirm that the change in policy is largely rhetorical. The slogan 'New Deal for Communities' is a new 'spin' to disguise what is essentially a continuation of the previous government's policies in this area.

New Labour's policy on strengthening communities is still developing, so the situation could change. The ideological 'spin', and even managerialism itself, is strongly contested. Given New Labour's emphasis on combating social exclusion, there is reason for thinking it will be responsive to proposals for developing and empowering communities, and not just individuals. Maybe it is just that the arguments in favour of such proposals need to be more cogently made. Or maybe the government has already decided that devolution of power to the people will be strictly limited and will be allowed only where it does not challenge managerial prerogatives.

This latter conclusion receives support from a consideration of other regions of New Labour policy relevant to housing, such as on 'the family', and on crime and morality more generally. For example, the Crime and Disorder Act 1998, New Labour's first major piece of housing-related legislation, has been argued to be: 'a major departure in giving [local authorities] a general undifferentiated function as agents of social control' (Hughes 1998, cited in Cowan 1999: 504). Cowan has argued that one effect of this generalised social control function may well be that traditionally reactive housing management will give way to a more proactive approach. This has already been prefigured in the harsh rhetoric aimed at 'squeegee merchants', 'neighbours from hell', unsupervised children out late, truants, drug users, 'bad mothers' and street homelessness. This latter problem, according to Louise Casey, New Labour's 'homelessness tsar', has been encouraged by the 'culture of kindness' sweeping British charities, who hand out sleeping bags and soup to 'rough sleepers' (*The Observer*, 14 November 1999, p.1). Such moral stances emerging within current policy thinking arguably represent a worsening 'lurch into authoritarianism [and an] attempt to impose a regressive morality' (cited in Driver and Martell 1998: 119) on society generally. It is a project that is in danger of enforcing particular models of social living by the application of simplistic solutions to complex human behaviour, underpinned by an award and punishment regime. Few people wish to live on the margins of their own society. What people do want is a viable alternative opportunity to act on a rational plan of life (Teles 1998). New Labour's rhetoric on 'community' and civic order is the language of coercion, punitive in the extreme, criminalising and excluding the most vulnerable members of our society, including children, young people, asylum seekers, and those who are more difficult to control or 'fit in' to mainstream social institutions, such as the labour market and the traditional nuclear family. This is counter-productive, as such measures are unlikely to encourage the changes in behaviour or collective values that characterise an inclusive society.

The shift from the previous Conservative government to the present Labour one can thus be characterised as a shift from an undeveloped and internally contested managerialism (with competing customerist and moralist agendas), to a more explicitly political and corporatist one. Corporatism was originally defined as:

> the tendencies to be found in advanced welfare societies whereby the capacity for conflict and disruption is reduced by means of the centralisation of policy, increased government intervention, and co-operation of various professional and interest groups into a collective whole with homogeneous aims and objectives. (Unger 1972, cited in Hughes 1998: 91)

Under New Labour, it is clear that in this sense each of its main types of housing policy is corporatist, in so far as they differ from the policies of the preceding government. For example, making the market work involves increased government intervention in the housing market; empowering individuals is a matter of including them in compacts, whose membership is composed of interest groups working together within frameworks laid down by central government; Best Value is seen as a way of achieving non-conflictual regulation of local authorities, in contradistinction to the conflictual regime of CCT; and strengthening communities, less clearly perhaps because of the slipperiness of communitarian rhetoric, can be portrayed as involving joined-up action at central government level (through the SEU) communicated in a top-down manner to local implementation agencies through the mediation of PATs, with the agencies being expected to deliver policy outcomes through what are essentially local forms of corporatist arrangement. This new corporatism, however, is not harking back to the old (Old Labour) corporatism of the 1970s. The latter was thoroughly bureaucratic and hopelessly ineffective, whereas the new corporatism has more or less completely absorbed the managerialist agenda – though this is no guarantee of its greater effectiveness. The problem with this new corporatism is, then, that it pretends to be democratic while being élitist. It talks the language of inclusion while at the same time being deeply exclusionary, and it gives people an illusion of influence over major decisions affecting their lives, but without any real popular control or fundamental change in the current grossly unequal system of power inequalities.

Conclusion

New Labour's housing policy shows both continuities with the neo-liberal policies of the previous Conservative governments and change. Policies continue to favour the privileged position of home ownership in the UK, despite growing differentiation and fragmentation in this sector. They continue to reward the 'deserving', those who have gained most from the 'consumption revolution' – mainly dual wage-earners in owner occupation, white and heterosexual, with few or no children. Meanwhile, the losers, largely those who remain in 'social housing' located in problem areas – mainly the poor, the old, lone parents, disabled people and racial minorities – and the homeless and rootless, continue to be subjected to experimentation and policy initiatives designed to define, objectify, police, control and exclude. For example, under New Labour, we are seeing a radical shift in the focus of housing management, away from its core activities of allocating, managing and maintaining homes, towards more holistic matters, such as the management of poverty and crime. More broadly, the thrust of government policy has shifted from a dogmatic, market-oriented managerialism under the Conservatives, to a more pragmatic, corporatist managerialism under New Labour.

In sum, we are arguing that there is an essential continuity of discourse from the New Right to New Labour, which is both managerialist and moralistic. The managerialism relates to the enthusiasm for 'technical' solutions to social problems, expressed as 'new' and 'modernisation'. The moralism is represented by the recurring theme of 'deserving'/'undeserving'. In this respect, the New Right and New Labour inhabit the same discourse of welfare, evident in the way both parties have, through housing policy interventions, privileged those in 'work' against those 'out-of-work'; those in the 'normalised housing market' (owner occupation) against those outside the market; those in the 'normalised family' against those outside the 'normalised family'' and those in 'normal sexual relationships' against those outside 'normal sexual relationships'.

At the same time, there is also a different narrative within New Labour's rhetoric, with an emphasis on combating social exclusion. This could leave New Labour's moralism vulnerable to criticism because it is divisive and, thereby, in contradiction with its agenda for social inclusion. Consequently, this opens up possibilities for the 'reversal' of New Labour's modernisation programme. In particular, we would emphasise two considerations. One, the critique of New Labour's managerialism for its technicism and authoritarianism, and ultimately its failure to deliver for the poor and needy especially; and two, the 'remoralisation' of New Labour's rhetoric by envisioning what would count as genuine social inclusion for all. We believe that to some extent the rhetoric of social inclusion can be used to promote greater equality and social justice, for example, by devolving real power to individuals and communities to control their own affairs. There is a role here for new social movements, campaigning around genuine notions of 'collective consumer rights' and 'empowerment', opening up new avenues for community involvement in housing and welfare built around the 'wants' and 'needs' articulated by local groups and individuals themselves.

There are numerous examples of successful campaigns that have demonstrated the way social exclusion is constructed around the lines of gender, 'race' and disability, leading to emancipation strategies aimed at making it possible for women to gain a greater degree of control over their lives, for black residents to voice their interests through alternative models of democracy and participation, and for disabled people to live in an 'ordinary' residential environment (see Cooper and Hawtin 1997, 1998). One example is the recent judgement ruling that homosexual couples can be defined as 'family'. The Martin Fitzpatrick case, which granted his appeal to succeed to the tenancy of his late gay partner, not only challenges homophobic tenancy laws but opens up the possibility for breaking down other areas of gay and lesbian exclusion – for instance, in family policy (such as gay parenting) and education (the repeal of Section 28 which bans local authorities from promoting positive images of homosexuality). In designing strategies for strengthening communities, we would also argue for a revival of approaches based on the radical community-development programmes abandoned in the 1970s (see Cooper and Hawtin 1997) to allow genuine 'engagement with residents as makers of their own lives, and authors of the solutions to their problems' (Jack and Jordan 1999: 252). This way, it may be possible to ensure that policies for social inclusion truly encompass the wider political agenda of comprehensive democratisation for all.

References

Armstrong, H. (1999) 'A new vision for housing in England' in T. Brown (ed.) *Stakeholder Housing*, Pluto Press, London, pp. 122-132.

Atkinson, R. and Moon, G. (1994) *Urban Policy in Britain: The City, the State and the Market*, Macmillan, Basingstoke.

Back, G. and Hamnett, C. (1985) 'State Housing Policy Formation and the Changing Role of Housing Associations in Britain', *Policy and Politics*, Vol. 13, No.4, pp. 393-411.

Barratt Brown, M. (1987) *Models in Political Economy: A Guide to the Arguments*, Pelican, Harmondsworth.

Black, J. and Stafford, D.C. (1988) *Housing Policy and Finance*, Routledge and Kegan Paul, London.

Bramley, G. (1997) 'Housing Policy: A Case of Terminal Decline?', *Policy and Politics*, Vol. 25 No.4, pp. 387-407.

Burden, T. (1998) *Social Policy and Welfare: A Clear Guide*, Pluto, London.

Burnett, J. (1986) *A Social History of Housing 1815-1985*, 2nd edn, Methuen, London.

Clapham, D. (1989) *Goodbye Council Housing?*, Unwin Hyman, London.

Clarke, J. and Newman, J. (1997) *The Managerial State*, Sage, London.

Cole, I. and Furbey, R. (1994) *The Eclipse of Council Housing*, Routledge, London.

Cooper, C. and Hawtin, M. (eds.) (1997) *Housing, Community and Conflict: Understanding Resident 'Involvement'*, Arena, Aldershot.

Cooper, C. and Hawtin, M. (eds.) (1998) *Resident Involvement and Community Action: Theory to Practice*, Chartered Institute of Housing/Housing Studies Association, Coventry.

Cowan, D. (1999) *Housing Law and Policy*, Macmillan, Basingstoke.

CRE (Commission for Racial Equality) (1984) *Race and Council Housing in Hackney: Report of a formal investigation*, CRE, London.

CRE (Commission for Racial Equality) (1988) *Homelessness and Discrimination: Report of a formal investigation into the London Borough of Tower Hamlets*, CRE, London.

CRE (Commission for Racial Equality) (1989) *Racial Discrimination in Liverpool City Council: Report of a formal investigation*, CRE, London.

CRE (Commission for Racial Equality) (1993) *Housing Allocation in Oldham: Report of a formal investigation*, CRE, London.

Curry, D. (1999) 'Death of the council house', *The Guardian*, 3 November, p.22.

DETR (Department of the Environment Transport and the Regions) (1999a) *Best Value in Housing Framework: Consultation Paper*, DETR, London.

DETR (Department of the Environment, Transport and the Regions) (1999b) *Best Value in Housing Framework: An analysis of the responses to the consultation paper*, DETR, London.

DETR (Department of the Environment Transport and the Regions) (1999c) *Report of Policy Action Team 5 on Housing Management*, DETR, London.

DETR (Department of the Environment Transport and the Regions) (1999d) *Report by the Unpopular Housing Action Team*, DETR, London.

DETR (Department of the Environment Transport and the Regions) (1999e) *Draft Report of Policy Action Team 6 on Neighbourhood Wardens*, DETR, London.

Diamond, J. (1999) 'Decentralisation: New forms of public participation or new forms of managerialism?', paper presented to Conference on Participation and Innovations in Community Governance, University of Luton, 24-26 June.

Driver, S. and Martell, L. (1998) *New Labour: Politics after Thatcherism*, Polity Press, Cambridge.

Field, F. (1996) *Stakeholder Welfare*, Institute of Economic Affairs, London.

Ford, J. and Burrows, R. (1999) 'The Costs of Unsustainable Home Ownership in Britain', *Journal of Social Policy*, Vol. 28 No.2, pp. 305-330.

Forrest, R. and Murie, A. (1988) *Selling the Welfare State: The Privatisation of Public Housing*, Routledge, London.

Forrest, R. and Murie, A. (1990) *Residualisation and Council Housing: A Statistical Update*, Working Paper 91, SAUS/University of Bristol, Bristol.

Forrest, R., Murie, A. and Williams, P. (1990) *Home Ownership: Differentiation and Fragmentation*, Allen and Unwin, London.

Giddens, A. (1998) *The Third Way: the Renewal of Social Democracy*, Polity Press, Cambridge.

Grayson, J. (1997) 'Campaigning tenants: A pre-history of tenant involvement to 1979' in C. Cooper and M. Hawtin (eds.) *Housing, Community and Conflict: Understanding Resident 'Involvement'*, Arena, Aldershot, pp. 15-65.

Gurney, C. (1999) 'Pride and Prejudice: Discourses of Normalisation in Public and Private Accounts of Home Ownership', *Housing Studies*, Vol. 14, No.2, pp. 163-183.

Harloe, M. (1995) *The People's Home: Social Rented Housing in Europe and America*, Blackwell, Oxford.

Harrison, M. (1998) 'Theorising Exclusion and Difference: Specificity, Structure and Minority Ethnic Housing Issues', *Housing Studies*, Vol. 13, No.6, pp. 793-806.

Haworth, A. and Manzi, T. (1999) 'Managing the "Underclass": Interpreting the Moral Discourse of Housing Management', *Urban Studies*, Vol. 36, No.1, pp. 153-165.

Henderson, J. and Karn, V. (1987) *Race, Class and State Housing: Inequality and the allocation of public housing in Britain*, CURS, Birmingham.

Housing Corporation (1998) *Making Consumers Count: Tenant participation – the next five years*, The Housing Corporation, London.

Howarth, C., Kenway, P., Palmer, G. and Street, C. (1998) *Monitoring poverty and social exclusion: Labour's inheritance*, Joseph Rowntree Foundation, York.

Hughes, D. (1998) 'The legitimacy of using the powers of local authority landlords as means of social control', paper presented to the Socio-Legal Studies Association Annual Conference, Manchester Metropolitan University, April.

Jack, G. and Jordan, B. (1999) 'Social Capital and Child Welfare', *Children & Society*, Vol. 13, pp. 242-256.

Jacobs, K. and Manzi, T. (1996) 'Discourse and Policy Change: The Significance of Language for Housing Research', *Housing Studies*, Vol. 11, No.4, pp. 543-560.

Kemp, P. (1999) 'Housing policy under New Labour' in M. Powell (ed.) *New Labour, New Welfare State? – The 'third way' in British social policy*, Policy Press, Bristol, pp. 123-147.

Kennett, P. (1998) 'Differentiated citizenship and housing experience' in A. Marsh and D. Mullins (eds.) *Housing and Public Policy: Citizenship, Choice and Control*, Open University Press, Buckingham, pp. 30-56.

Knowles, A. (1998) 'Large Scale Voluntary Transfer: Mythical experiences in resident involvement' in C. Cooper and M. Hawtin (eds.) *Resident Involvement and Community Action: Theory to Practice*, Chartered Institute of Housing/Housing Studies Association, Coventry, pp. 157-178.

Lawlor, S. (1999) 'Head to head: Should all tenants pay something towards their rent?', *Housing*, November, p.14.

Le Grand, J. and Bartlett, W. (eds.) (1993) *Quasi-markets and Social Policy*, Macmillan, London.

Lee, P. and Murie, A. (1997) *Poverty, Housing Tenure and Social Exclusion*, Policy Press, Bristol.

Lund, B. (1996) *Housing Problems and Housing Policy*, Longman, London.

Lusk, P. (1997) 'Tenants choice and tenant management: Who owns and who controls social housing?' in C. Cooper and M. Hawtin (eds.) *Housing, Community and Conflict: Understanding Resident 'Involvement'*, Arena, Aldershot, pp. 67-81.

Macey, J.P. and Baker, C.V. (1973) *Housing Management*, 2nd edn, Estates Gazette, London.

Malpass, P. and Murie, A. (1999) *Housing Policy and Practice*, 5th edn, Macmillan, Basingstoke.

Minford, P., Peel, M. and Ashton, P. (1987) *The Housing Morass*, Institute of Economic Affairs, London.

Mullins, D. and Niner, P. (1998) 'A prize of citizenship? Changing access to social housing' in A. Marsh and D. Mullins (eds.) *Housing and Public Policy: Citizenship, Choice and Control*, Open University Press, Buckingham, pp. 175-198.

Murie, A. (1998) 'Secure and contented citizens? Home ownership in Britain' in A. Marsh and D. Mullins (eds.) *Housing and Public Policy: Citizenship, Choice and Control*, Open University Press, Buckingham, pp. 79-98.

Murray, C. (1984) *Losing Ground: American social policy 1950-1980*, Basic Books, New York.

Murray, C. (1990) *The Emerging British Underclass*, IEA Health & Welfare Unit, London.

Rex, J. and Moore, R. (1967) *Race, Community and Conflict: A Study of Sparkbrook*, Oxford University Press, Oxford.

Rogers, D. (1999) *New Mutualism: The Third Estate*, The Co-operative Party/CDS/Labour Housing Group, London.

Rouse, J. and Smith, G. (1999) 'Accountability' in M. Powell (ed.) *New Labour, New Welfare State? The 'third way' in British social policy*, Policy Press, Bristol, pp. 235-256.

Saunders, J. (1976) 'Squat: A documentary about Grosvenor Road, Twickenham', http: //www.alt.venus.co.uk/weed/writings/squatjs.html, 1 July, 1999.

Saunders, P. (1981) *Social Theory and the Urban Question*, 2nd edn, Unwin Hyman, London.

Saunders, P. (1990) *A Nation of Home Owners*, Unwin Hyman, London.

Scott, S. and Parkey, H. (1998) 'Myths and Reality: Anti-social Behaviour in Scotland', *Housing Studies*, Vol. 13, No.3, pp. 325-345.

SEU (Social Exclusion Unit) (1998) *Bringing Britain Together: A national strategy for neighbourhood renewal*, The Stationary Office, London.

Sibley, D. (1995) *Geographies of Exclusion*, Routledge, London.

Somerville, P. (1999) 'The making and unmaking of homelessness legislation' in S. Hutson and D. Clapham (eds.) *Homelessness: Public policies and private troubles*, Cassell, London, pp. 29-57.

Somerville, P. (forthcoming) *Social Relations and Social Exclusion*, Sage, London.

Spink, B. (1998) 'Housing management 1800 to 2000: A practice in search of a policy' in C. Cooper and M. Hawtin (eds.) *Resident Involvement and Community Action: Theory to Practice*, Chartered Institute of Housing/Housing Studies Association, Coventry, pp. 38-66.

Teles, S. (1998), 'A blend of help and hassle', *New Statesman*, 6 March, pp. 17-19.

Walker-Brown, R. (1998) 'Tenant participation and the contract culture: Opportunities for resident involvement in council housing management' in C. Cooper and M. Hawtin (eds.) *Resident Involvement and Community Action: Theory to Practice*, Chartered Institute of Housing/Housing Studies Association, Coventry, pp. 127-156.

7 Income Maintenance Policies

Introduction

This chapter will examine key income maintenance discursive practices and policies under the neo-liberals, and the emerging policies of New Labour. Policies in relation to the unemployed, lone parents, elders and disabled people will be considered – areas that have been at the centre of European policy debates during the last decade (Daly 1997). The concept of a dominant discourse of welfare will be used to assess the impact of neo-liberal policies on poverty and social exclusion, and on the policy legacy inherited by New Labour. New Labour's emerging policies will then be outlined and analysed to assess the extent to which they inhabit the same discourse of welfare as the neo-liberals and, consequently, the extent to which they are likely to ameliorate or exacerbate poverty and social exclusion for particular groups in the UK.

Income maintenance and the state

As Chapter Two showed, income maintenance has been a feature of welfare provision in Britain since the Poor Law of 1601 made provision for 'outdoor relief' to be given to the impotent poor. Throughout welfare history two notions have been dominant when the discursive practices of welfare have been designed and implemented in relation to income maintenance. The first is the notion of 'family' as the resource-sharing unit for calculation purposes (under the Poor Law this was termed the household). The second is the presumption that the family's main income would be provided by a male breadwinner. As income maintenance schemes became more sophisticated and complex in the twentieth century, most western democracies drew a distinction between social insurance and social assistance. Social insurance was usually based on contributions from earnings, whilst social assistance involved means-tested benefits for those without (or with insufficient) contributions. Together these form 'social

209

security', that is all forms of public income maintenance, which aim to relieve poverty (Hill and Bramley 1986).

In the post-war period, there was a desire for a more 'inclusive' society. 'The dominant expressed public view was that the state had the economic ability, administrative capacity, and the moral duty to provide a range of services that would ensure a National Minimum' (George 1996: 2). Nevertheless, the distribution of income maintenance benefits was a discursive practice of a dominant discourse of welfare within which the supplementary discourses (of 'work', 'consumption', 'family' and 'sexuality') operated to construct the welfare subject as 'eligible' or 'ineligible' ('deserving' or 'undeserving'). The enduring constructs of family, and the breadwinner as the male head of the family, were supplemented by notions of how men and women should live together, and how women should be consumers in the domestic sphere rather than workers in the labour market. These constructs of normalised family structure and life can be summarised as follows:

(a) that marriages are for life ... until death or remarriage

(b) that sexual activity and childbirth takes place, or at least should take place only within marriage

(c) that married women normally do no paid work or negligible paid work

(d) that women not men should do housework and rear children

(e) that couples who live together with regular sexual relationships and shared expenses are always of the opposite sex. (Wickes, cited in Lavalette and Pratt 1997: 87)

The National Insurance (NI) scheme established in 1911 formed the basis for the Beveridge proposals of 1942 which were accepted during the period of wartime radicalism. Beveridge introduced flat-rate, subsistence level benefits which were paid to eligible contributors – mainly men and 'their wives'. The conditions covered were sickness, unemployment, old age, disability and maternity. The National Insurance Act 1946 enacted a scheme based largely on the Beveridge plan, coming into effect in July 1948. Means-tested National Assistance (NA) benefits were made available under the National Assistance Act 1946. Although insured workers in relatively regular work were adequately covered by the scheme, many other people were not. The self-employed were excluded from unemployment benefit while the non-employed were excluded from both unemployment and sickness benefit. Married women were not treated on the same basis as men. Those unable to enter the labour force, such as the disabled, were not able to obtain any insurance benefits and, together with those whose benefit had run out, had to undergo a means test to obtain additional funds.

Notwithstanding some criticisms from feminists and 'black' theorists (see Williams 1995), the post-war period of welfare has been characterised as one of optimism, when the ideas of the broad political left were dominant (George 1996):

> Public spending was seen in positive terms: it would not only help create a socially cohesive society and ensure a minimum standard for all but it would also encourage economic growth. (George 1996: 3)

However, the economic crisis that developed in the 1970s created the conditions in which radical critiques of the welfare state from both left and right were able to take root. The welfare state itself was increasingly portrayed as 'the problem' – the cause of the economic crisis. Support for universal benefits and generous welfare provision came under strong challenge. New Right ideas began to influence policy as a result of a financial crisis in 1976. The Labour government responded to this by introducing wide-ranging expenditure cuts. These policies were continued and intensified after the Conservatives, under Margaret Thatcher, were elected in 1979.

Neo-liberals, income maintenance policies and welfare discourse

By the time the neo-liberals came to power, the NI scheme accounted for nearly two-thirds of social security spending and the social assistance (means-tested and non-contributory benefits) for about 35 per cent (George and Taylor-Gooby 1996). The biggest spending was on pensions, even though the UK had a lower than average pension compared to the other European Union (EU) countries. As economic conditions deteriorated, in common with other EU countries and the US, the neo-liberals were concerned by what they perceived as a 'crisis' in welfare:

212 'Modernising' Social Policy

The welfare state, claimed the New Right, undermined economic growth, political legitimacy and the traditional way of community and family life. High levels of public expenditure undermined economic growth ... [A]s welfare states 'overloaded' themselves with responsibilities of all kinds, their ability to deal effectively with problems declined in equal measure ... Nothing short of a drastic reduction in both government activity and expenditure would change the situation. (George 1996: 6)

The Social Security Act 1980 abolished the Supplementary Benefits Commission (SBC) and brought supplementary benefits under the direct control of the Department of Health and Social Security (DHSS). It substantially reduced the scope for discretionary payments, leaving many claimants worse off. Cuts were instituted in November 1980, and sickness, unemployment, maternity and industrial injury benefits were increased by 5 per cent less than the current rate of inflation. Further cuts were achieved by the abolition of the Earnings Related Supplements (ERS) from the end of 1981. The benefit and tax system rules were modified to penalise those involved in strikes. The Social Security and Housing Benefits Act 1982 abolished short-term NI Sickness Benefit, and gave employers the responsibility for paying Employers Statutory Sick Pay for the first eight weeks of benefit. The Act also established a Housing Benefit (HB) to combine the previous rent rebates, rent allowances and rate rebates. Council tenants would now have their rent and rates paid direct to their council's housing department by the DHSS. The changes introduced since 1979 had, by 1982-83, reduced expenditure by about £2,000m from what it would otherwise have been.

The neo-liberal project for welfare reform had begun, an effect of which was to stiffen eligibility criteria for unpopular groups. As was argued in Chapter Three, those considered 'different' are constructed as 'deviant', 'Other than' the norm, particularly where that difference relates to 'work', 'consumption', 'family' and 'sexuality'. Welfare eligibility criteria increasingly came to serve as a moral project; a way of discouraging certain forms of behaviour and ways of living while supporting and encouraging others:

[A]s Bruce Anderson, adviser to successive Conservative prime ministers in the 1980s and 1990s, put it: 'We are in the grip of the post-modern vagabond. We have expensively constructed slums full of layabouts and sluts whose progeny are two-legged beasts. We cannot cure this by family, religion and self-help. So we will have to rely on repression'. (Jones and Novak 1999: 11)

Groups such as the unemployed and 'lone' parents became increasingly impoverished and marginalised. Meanwhile, real expenditure on social security rose by 25 per cent in the period 1979-83 due to the increase in unemployment, which accounted for 17 per cent of the social-security budget by 1983, as compared with 8 per cent in 1979. This was despite substantial cuts in the value of benefits to the unemployed. A series of reviews of different parts of the social-security system were announced in April 1984. The reviews were claimed to be the most fundamental since Beveridge. A White Paper on the reform of social security was subsequently published in 1985 (DHSS 1985), in which a familiar list of defects of the existing system were listed. These included: complexity; low take-up of benefits; high administrative costs; the size and extent of the poverty trap; the restriction on individual choice on pensions; and the heavy burden of high cost on future taxpayers of the state pension scheme. The main vehicle for reform was the Social Security Act 1988, which introduced a range of new means-tested benefits. Family Credit was used to provide regular payments to low income families with children. The Social Fund grant and loan system was employed for one-off payments for items such as furniture, clothing or a cooker. However, the government set 'cash limits' on the total amount to be paid out. In 1988, the proportion of applicants for grants who were refused was 48 per cent. In 1993-94, over 200 000 grant applications and a million loan applications were turned down solely due to lack of funds. By 1997, the proportion being refused was 79 per cent.

Clearly, those who applied for social assistance were the poor. Poverty was growing swiftly in the UK as unemployment rose, but there were other changes in social living that affected the distribution of social security. In most postmodern or late capitalist societies, there was a projected rise in the proportion of elderly and very elderly in the population (George 1996). Advances in medical technology meant that impairments that previously threatened life no longer did so and the community of disabled people grew. There was also a substantial rise in 'lone' parents (mainly 'lone' mothers). The rise in the percentage of elderly in the population was seen solely by the New Right in epidemiological terms, with no regard being given to the potential contribution of elders to society. Disabled people too were seen primarily in terms of the demands they placed on carers rather than their activities as valued citizens. As far as lone mothers were concerned, the rise in the numbers of such families was seen by the neo-liberals as a harbinger of societal breakdown rather than an inevitable consequence of women's greater empowerment. The 'Golden Age' of the 1950s and 1960s (Hobsbawm 1996) brought women increased employment opportunities (albeit briefly), and control over conception and child-bearing. As will be argued, the unemployed, lone mothers, elders and disabled people became particular targets for reductions in social-security benefits. The welfare subject was constructed as deviant because, without paid work, they had a social cost but no social value; without the ability to function as a 'consumer' in a consumerist society they had no status; without 'family' care they had no 'family' (the normalised family cared for its own); and with children but without marriage they had no morals. Moving away from benefits as of 'right' (even though these benefits marginalised women and racial minorities), and establishing a cash-limited and restricted discretionary environment for social security, effectively marginalised 'difference'. Not only did the criteria for the distribution of social security become tighter and linked to judgements about 'worth' rather than 'need', but also cash limits were a public statement of the worth of the welfare subject to society rather than an expression of collective responsibility for individual needs.

One effect of the use of social-security loans for people whose incomes were already stretched beyond the limit was to create debt. The refusal of loans by the state also created the conditions in which people would take out loans from private providers, often at extremely high rates of interest, thus further impoverishing themselves. A continuing theme in welfare discursive practices towards the social-security system under the neo-liberals involved attempts to highlight fraud, to stigmatise those who might be engaged in it, and to devise policies to reduce it. As Jones and Novak (1999) argue, however, only the 'fraud' of the poor was subject to so much scrutiny and condemnation, out of all proportion to the sums of money involved, for example, in corporate fraud. Jordan (1996) suggests that the shadow (or alternative) economy has been a rational response to the economic climate and has protected the poor from the worst effects of poverty.

The unemployed and income maintenance

The construction of the normalised family as self-reliant and self-sufficient effectively extended childhood as the state withdrew from responsibility for the effects of unemployment on the young. A key element in the approach of the neo-liberal government to youth unemployment was the withdrawal of benefits from all 16- and 17-year-olds, along with a promise that they would receive either training or a job. However, there were never sufficient training places on youth training schemes and the quality of what was offered to young people was often low. The Work Start and Project Work schemes were also established. These schemes offered a £75-a-week subsidy to employers who provided jobs for those who had been unemployed for more than six months. Therefore, the state was prepared to subsidise the socially included, the employers, but not the welfare subject to the same degree. Another important theme was the attempt to tighten up the regulations defining eligibility for unemployment benefits. In October 1996, unemployment benefit was replaced by the Job Seekers Allowance (JSA). The change in nomenclature implied there were jobs for the unemployed to find and it was the responsibility of the unemployed to find them, notwithstanding the evidence that paid work was in short supply (Gorz 1999). JSA required those claiming benefit whilst unemployed to engage in compulsory job-search activities and to participate in an interview with the Employment Service. The entitlement to a non-means-tested benefit whilst unemployed was reduced from 12 months to 6 months. In the year after the introduction of this change there was a fall in the numbers claiming benefit whilst unemployed. This was substantially greater than the fall in the numbers who were actually unemployed, according to labour force statistics. The JSA also involved a 20 per cent reduction in the level of the contributory benefit for 18- to 24-year-olds.

'Lone' mothers and income maintenance

Neo-liberal policy towards lone mothers was centred on the Child Support Agency (CSA). The Child Support Act was passed in 1991, and the CSA was set up in 1993. Its role was to take over the administration of child maintenance payments. The government believed that it would be able to make absent fathers pay for the upkeep of their children and that it would be a means of providing financial support for single mothers. It was estimated that it would save £600m of government spending each year. The decision-making of the CSA reflected the construction of 'Other than' normalised families (families composed of a heterosexual married couple with children) as undesirable. For example, in August 1995, John Redwood, Conservative MP, proposed that 'lone' mothers should consider putting up their children for adoption if their immediate family, particularly the parents of the mother, were unable to help support them (Becker 1997).

The formula used for calculating payments ignored the cost of a second family or any previous court agreements, and did not take into account ability to pay. After a year of operation the Agency had made savings of £418m. However, it had only arranged maintenance in 31.5 per cent of eligible cases against a target of 60 per cent. The perceived failure of the agency led many eligible mothers to refuse to co-operate with it. Women in receipt of income support had any maintenance money received from their former partners subtracted from their benefit. The reopening of cases previously settled by the courts imposed on many fathers economic liabilities which they had not budgeted for, and which could cause them considerable economic difficulties if they were in a new family with children. The complexity of the formula used to calculate the extent of financial liability meant that 90 per cent of the agency's staff time was taken up with assessing claims rather than with chasing up payments. In 1995 the government produced amendments to the formula used to calculate payments. Under the new regulations no absent parent was to pay more than 30 per cent of their net income in maintenance.

Elders and disabled people, and income maintenance

'Work' and 'consumption' were important aspects of the construction of the welfare subject under the neo-liberals. Those who could not undertake paid 'work' were conceptualised as social problems for whom a solution had to be found if an economically viable society was to continue. In particular, the elderly and the disabled were constructed as burdens on the shoulders of an increasingly shrinking (due to a static birthrate) workforce. Ways had to be found to ensure that income maintenance provision did not become an easy option for those too thoughtless or improvident to make proper preparation for old age or infirmity. The neo-liberals have claimed, since the early 1980s, that existing social-security provision for elders based on universal pensions could not be sustained in the future because of the projected increase in the total population and the tax burden that state provision of pensions would necessitate. The government, the private-pensions industry, right-wing think-tanks and the International Monetary Fund (IMF) approached this issue epidemiologically, contributing to something approaching a moral panic (Vincent 1996). In the mid-1980s, the government encouraged a move to a system based more on private pensions. It rescinded the requirement that employees should belong to a company pension scheme where there was one. Instead, individuals were allowed to choose to contract out. This was an attempt to encourage the growth of personal pensions (personally owned and individualised pension plans). This led to widespread 'mis-selling' in which large numbers of people were persuaded to opt out of the State Earnings Related Pension scheme (SERPS), or their occupational schemes, and purchase personal pensions which left them worse off.

Disability Living Allowance (DLA) was introduced in 1992. It replaced the Attendance Allowance and Mobility Allowance and attracted an increased number of claimants. The novel feature of this benefit was that it allowed claimants to make their own assessment of the impact of their disability on their care needs and their mobility. It has been argued (Shildrick and Price 1999) that this requirement reveals the construction of disabled bodies as 'Other than' the normal, and so the DLA 'benefit' marginalises and excludes by its own procedures:

> For the specific benefit of DLA … self-assessment plays a particularly large part in the claims procedure. Nonetheless, the limits of reliability of non-authoritative discourse are marked in that the subject's own report must be supplemented by statements from two other people who will be most usually health care professionals. In other words the gaze is multi-perspectival. What is remarkable about the claims pack … is its sheer volume, in which four pages of initial notes are followed by 28 pages of report, the vast majority of which consists of a detailed self analysis of personal behaviour. The introductory instructions are quite clear about what is expected from claimant self-surveillance … In focusing on singular behaviour, the state sponsored model of disability promotes individual failing above any attention to environmental and social factors. (Shildrick and Price 1999: 435)

Incapacity Benefit was introduced in 1995 to replace Invalidity Benefit, this benefit was available to those incapable of work. Yet again 'work' became the criterion by which the welfare subject was defined as having social value or being a social burden. Eligibility for this benefit required examination by a Benefits Agency doctor, who would decide if an individual was capable of 'work' or not (whether or not suitable paid work was available) in order to attempt to reduce the extent of entitlement. Tighter restrictions on the ability of disabled people to claim benefit meant that around 250 000 disabled people now had to claim JSA and were subjected to the tighter 'availability for work' provisions (Becker 1997).

The impact of neo-liberal income maintenance discursive practices

Under the neo-liberals there was an inexorable move towards more means-tested benefits. This was justified as a way of ensuring that public money was only given to those who 'need' it and, so, those most in 'need' were targeted. As has been shown in Chapter Three, assessments of those in 'need', and those 'not in need', were framed within a discourse of welfare that constructed 'difference' as deviance and the welfare subject as 'deserving' or 'undeserving'. As Becker argues:

> A further function of social security is to endorse the position of certain groups, by labelling them as 'vulnerable' and defining them as 'favoured', 'deserving', and as people in 'greatest need'. Policy then seeks to 'target' benefits on them, rather than on others ... The other side of this coin is the need to regulate and control the behaviour of less vulnerable, less favoured groups, by labelling them as 'less deserving' or 'undeserving' and restricting their access to benefits through means tests. (Becker 1997: 61)

This discourse of welfare held within it supplementary discourses about the worth of those without paid work (particularly unemployed 17- to 18-year-olds who were denied access to Income Support), those unable to act as 'consumers' (such as the homeless), and those 'family' types and forms of sexuality considered undesirable (particularly lone parents and gay couples). Taken together with evidence that means-tested benefits lead to lower take-up rates – many of those eligible for HB, Family Credit and free school meals do not claim (Becker 1997) – the impact of this dominant discourse of welfare is the exacerbation of social exclusion. The discursive practices of social security meant that the system which has evolved is characterised by: complexity of the procedures involved in claiming; public ignorance of the benefits available; the humiliation and invasion of privacy involved in means-testing; the stigma associated with the status of claimant; and the low level of many of the benefits (Huby and Whyley 1996).

Means-testing can also create a 'poverty trap' for those in work. A poverty trap occurs when workers receiving means-tested benefits are unable to gain much extra income from a pay increase, since this will lead to loss of benefits. Due to the low-income tax threshold, extra income is also likely to attract tax and an increased NI contribution. Additional wage income can be reduced by up to, or more than, 100 per cent. As a result, many lower-paid workers are trapped at a disposable income level only just above the poverty line. This has had the effect of supporting the socially included, the employers, by allowing them to fix wages at whatever level was profitable for the firm, with no regard for the resulting impoverishment of the employee and associated social costs.

The extent of poverty increased from the late 1970s until the mid-1990s (Becker 1997, Beresford and Green 1996), characterised by: an increase in the gap between the highest paid and the lowest paid workers; increased levels of unemployment; cuts in the value of benefits; increased numbers of lone-parent households; reduced state protection for low-paid workers (such as the abolition of Wages Councils); and greater reliance on expenditure taxes such as VAT (which hit the poor hardest since they spend a higher proportion of their incomes than the better off, who save more). The overall impact of the neo-liberal governments on inequality since 1979 was documented in a report by the Department of Social Security published in 1998 (DSS 1998a). This report showed that, since 1979, the incomes of the top 10 per cent of earners had increased by 70 per cent, the incomes of average earners had increased by 44 per cent, and the incomes of the bottom 10 per cent of earners had fallen by 9 per cent. Changes in the labour market, including the reduced demand for unskilled labour and the reduced rates that this kind of work could command in a period of relatively high unemployment, increased inequalities amongst those in receipt of incomes from work. By 1992, the pay levels of the lowest paid third of the workforce were lower in real terms than they had been in 1975 (White and Forth 1998). There was also an increasing gap between 'work-rich' and 'work-poor' households. Over this period the number of two-adult households with two working adults increased from 51 per cent to 60 per cent, while the proportion of households with no one in receipt of income from work grew from 3 per cent to 11 per cent (Barclay 1995).

Using the EU definition of an income below 50 per cent of the average, DSS figures show that, after the deduction of housing costs, just over 14m people, around 25 per cent of the population, have an income below this level (DSS 1998a). It has been suggested that the dynamic processes underlying poverty have changed over the last 20 years as a result of changes in the labour market (Falkingham and Hills 1995). Hutton has argued that we now live in a 30/30/40 society (Hutton 1995), with a bottom 30 per cent of unemployed or economically inactive people occupying a marginal position (Byrne 1997). There is also evidence that large numbers of people who would formerly have been part of the workforce are now economically inactive. This group used to consist primarily of women who had withdrawn from the labour market in order to bring up their children. However, this group is now largely made up of men of working age who have been excluded, or have excluded themselves, from the workforce, and of 'lone' parents. The middle 30 per cent are in work, although they are found in forms of employment which are insecure. Some 40 per cent of the population hold relatively secure or tenured jobs with a high expectation of a steady future income, although current trends are leading to the reduction in size of this group.

The rise in unemployment has tended to impoverish racial-minority groups. Over 40 per cent of African-Caribbeans were in the lowest 20 per cent of income recipients, while the figure for Pakistanis and Bangladeshis was over 50 per cent. There are major socio-economic differences between ethnic groups, but it is still the case that black people are more likely than white people to be living in poverty. Unemployment and concentration in low-pay occupations are more likely to be higher, particularly for the Bangladeshi community and for people of African or Caribbean descent. The earnings gap appears to be mainly the result of not being promoted, rather than being paid less for doing the same work. Women from Asian ethnic groups are more likely than others to be homeworkers or in casual employment networks (Bhavnani 1994).

It is difficult to assess the precise extent of changes in the level of unemployment in this period. During nearly two decades of neo-liberal government, 31 changes were made to the basis on which the unemployment figures were recorded. The official unemployment count was eventually defined as the number of those who were unemployed and claiming benefit. This obviously excluded many people who would take a job if one were available, but who were not eligible for the receipt of unemployment benefit. Large numbers of women fell into this category. It appears likely that if the figures for 1997 of 1.67m were recalculated on the same basis as that used before 1979, the total would increase by around 1m.

New Labour, income maintenance policies and welfare discourse

The approach of New Labour to the social-security system might appear to represent a shift away from the policies pursued by the neo-liberals in their commitment, albeit a rather muffled one, to full employment. However, the Chancellor of the Exchequer has described employment opportunity as the modern definition of full employment, shifting the focus of responsibility from the state meeting the needs of the welfare subject towards the construction of the subject's own culpability for their predicament. As has been argued in Chapter Three, the neo-liberals and New Labour inhabit the same discourse of welfare and thus policy, the discursive practices of welfare, under New Labour represents continuity with the neo-liberals. Of particular importance is the emphasis given to paid 'work' as the basic means through which income should normally be acquired (Walker 1998). Under New Labour, the foundation of a modern welfare state is 'work for those who can; security for those who cannot' (DSS 1998b: iii). Other forms of work which may be equally socially important (such as a range of caring responsibilities or voluntary work) are given much less value. As Gorz suggests:

> The imperative need for a sufficient, regular income is one thing. The need to act, to strive, to test oneself against others and be appreciated by them is quite another. Capitalism systematically links the two, conflates them, and upon that conflation establishes capital's power and ideological hold on people's minds. It admits no activity which is not 'work', done to order and paid for by those ordering it. It admits no regular income that is not earned from 'work'. (Gorz 1999: 72)

According to Bauman, the work ethic has served two purposes throughout modernity: to ensure a ready supply of labour; and to justify making life less attractive for those relying on relief instead of wages (the principle of 'less eligibility'):

> It was hoped that the more the life of the non-working poor were degraded and the deeper they descended into destitution, the more tempting or at least the less unendurable would appear to them the lot of those working poor who had sold their labour in exchange for the most miserable of wages. (Bauman 1998: 12)

Just as those unable to adapt to the changing circumstances of post-industrial nineteenth-century Britain – mainly 'invalids, the weak, sick and old' (Bauman 1998: 11) – were perceived as a social problem to be got rid of, so too are those unable to adapt to the changing circumstances of today, brought about by 'globalisation', seen as a problem to be managed:

> In general, the design of New Labour's welfare reforms is shaped by its perception of the problems faced by the poor, and especially by lone parents, the unemployed, people with disability and pensioners – the fastest growing groups of poor whose growth has contributed to the rising cost of social security. Apart from the concern expressed ... about means-testing and its contribution to benefit fraud and ... concern about the growth in social security spending, the case for welfare reform is made largely in terms of the intrinsic problems presented by these social groups. (Hewitt 1999: 153)

Welfare spending was linked to social breakdown and the emergence of an 'underclass' and the growth of 'lone' mother households, constructed as sexually irresponsible and improvident consumers of society's scarce resources. New Labour came to office with these concerns in mind, soon appointing Frank Field as Minister of Welfare Reform. Field was told to think the 'unthinkable'. Central to New Labour's approach to welfare reform has been increasing 'opportunities' for 'work', for those capable of it.

The Prime Minister, Tony Blair, undertook to raise the issue of welfare reform around the country in a series of speeches, accompanied by a welfare reform road show. It was apparent that there were considerable divisions within the government, and even within the DSS, on how to proceed. The approach favoured by Field was to reduce benefits where, in his view, they created a disincentive to people making provision for themselves. He also opposed means tests because he viewed them as tending to create a residual stratum of around 20 per cent of the population. The people would be maintained on stigmatised benefits at the bottom of the social hierarchy in a way which would guarantee their social exclusion. His preference was for a revival of the principles of social insurance along with greater emphasis on the welfare role of voluntary organisations, such as friendly societies, as an alternative to provision made exclusively by the state. His Green Paper on welfare reform was published in March 1998 (DSS 1998b). A series of seven focus files were published by the Department in order to show the central problems in social security policy. These adopted modernist, positivistic and epidemiological terms, conceptualising the welfare subject solely within a deficit model, a problem to be solved by the application of the 'correct' quasi-scientific solutions. Areas such as pensions, families and the disabled were covered.

The government also identified what it viewed as key elements in the failure of the system. These included the concern that despite high levels of expenditure, inequality and poverty had increased, incentives to work had been reduced and fraud was high. The Green Paper proposed that the welfare state should be rebuilt with a stronger emphasis on the work ethic. People should have a duty to provide for themselves and their families. The availability of some benefits which were believed to be subject to widespread abuse, such as Disability Benefit, was to be means-tested. In addition, there should be a massive attack on benefit fraud which was believed to be very high, costing around £4bn each year. The divisions and conflicts within the government eventually led to the resignation of Frank Field and the sacking of the responsible minister, Harriet Harman.

Clear proposals for legislation were included in the Welfare Reform and Pensions Bill, published in February 1999. The major proposal included in the Bill was for a new 'single work focused gateway' for all claimants. New Labour's legislation rests on the same notion that the benefit system is more attractive than paid 'work' for many claimants. It is therefore designed to put a stop to this by requiring that people of working age who are not in full-time work, but who are claiming benefits, should be required to attend an interview to discuss their options for employment. They will be assigned a personal adviser and they will receive a 'balanced package' of financial support along with help and advice on obtaining work. Claimants will normally be required to attend within three days of making a claim. Claimants who refuse three interview requests will not have their claims processed or will have their benefits cut. Legislation covers all those on income support and housing benefit, as well as disabled people and 'lone' parents, although those on DLA will not be required to attend for interview. These proposals were to be implemented in a pilot project in 12 areas, beginning mid-1999. A nation-wide system is likely to be implemented in the year 2000.

Like the neo-liberals, New Labour have put particular emphasis on social-security fraud. In September of 1997 it was revealed that the government had asked security agents of MI5 to play a part in the investigation of benefit fraud, estimated at £4bn at the time of the Green Paper on welfare reform in early 1998. By the time of the Green Paper of July 1998, *Beating fraud is every one's business* (DSS 1998c), the estimate had been increased to £7bn. The volume of resources committed to combating fraud is substantial. The Benefit Fraud Inspectorate has around 5 000 staff and there are probably around another 5 000 local authority staff involved in anti-fraud activities, particularly in relation to HB. The actual levels of fraud are a matter of controversy, yet government ministers continue to legitimate the construction of the welfare subject as work-shy, consuming common resources that are 'undeserved'. Frank Field wrote in 1996 that the benefit system is 'steadily recruiting a nation of cheats and liars' (cited in Jones and Novak 1999: 95). The neo-liberal government planned a major investigation into fraud in relation to recipients of the DLA. After New Labour's election victory in 1997, civil servants in the DSS went ahead with this investigation without informing the minister. The investigation created a great deal of opposition from disability rights groups. The report by the House of Commons Public Accounts Committee in March 1998 suggested that the value of HB fraud was just over £900m per annum. In total there are 4.7m HB recipients and around £11.5bn is paid out each year. According to the report, only around 1 per cent of those undertaking HB fraud who are detected are then prosecuted.

A major difficulty facing the government in attempting to reform the benefits system involves HB. Large numbers of poor people are tenants in receipt of HB and if their income from work increases they will end up paying an effective marginal tax rate of up to 95p in the pound. The whole area of housing costs has always been a source of difficulty for the social-security system because they vary so widely from place to place. The rents charged for council housing are not based on a national scale and differences between areas are substantial. Most tenants on benefit pay no rent at all from their own resources. Under the current system tenants have no economic incentive to seek cheaper housing. They could only do this if the level of income support was increased substantially. In addition, substantial numbers of tenants in local authority housing have rent arrears. Around 6m homes do not have a current bank account – what has been referred to as 'financial exclusion', where people lack access to basic financial services such as banking and credit. In many inner-city areas, bank branch closures have made access to banking difficult for many, especially poorer people. At the same time, because poor people find credit difficult to obtain, they are often forced to take on loans at very high rates of interest from various loan merchants. Since the Consumer Credit Act 1974 abolished the 48 per cent ceiling on annual interest rates, there is no limit to what consumers can be charged. Many poor people find themselves paying rates much higher than this for credit. The Office of Fair Trading report, *Financial Services to Vulnerable Consumers* (OFT 1998), did not recommend any radical action in the form of setting limits to interest rates or outlawing the various kinds of credit offered on a door-to-door basis. However, the report did recommend that banks should offer simple accounts to vulnerable customers such as the elderly, disabled people, racial minorities, and those with fluctuating or low earnings. The government has also shown some interest in what is called 'community banking'. In the US, this is secured by a legal requirement that banks should meet the credit needs of the entire community.

It is not yet clear what policy the government will pursue with respect to financial exclusion. However, it has shown some interest in the promotion of credit unions. In Britain there are currently 447 credit unions covering 108 000 members. Two-thirds are only open for six or less hours a week while many are struggling. Around 80 per cent were established by local authorities rather than as the result of community initiatives. A task force has been established to explore how the banks might work more effectively with credit unions. In some countries, such as Ireland and the US, these have proved an extremely successful way of providing credit for poorer people.

The unemployed and income maintenance

New Labour was elected with a commitment to tackle unemployment through a scheme designed to get 250 000 young people aged 18 to 24 off the dole, and to put more than half the long-term unemployed into subsidised jobs or training. It was claimed that this would be done with a New Deal programme costing £3.5bn, introduced nation-wide in April 1998. This policy certainly does have some distinctive features. In contrast to the situation facing many other areas of policy, New Deal is not restricted by expenditure levels set by the previous government. The scheme is also being financed in a unique way, by a one-off windfall tax on the profits of the public utilities. This tax has yielded around £5.2bn of which £4bn has been set aside for New Deal. The bulk of the funding, £2.62bn, is earmarked for the programme for 18- to 24-year-old unemployed people. Another £450m is to be used for a scheme for the long-term adult unemployed. The sum of £190m will be used for lone parents seeking employment (DfEE 1999a).

Another distinctive feature of the scheme is that it does leave some room for local initiative since it is not being imposed in a uniform fashion across the country. The Employment Service is administered by 136 districts across the country. In ten of these districts New Deal is run by private-sector agencies, although only three of these have a rate of success in getting clients into work which is above the national average. In the others, a variety of approaches based on partnerships involving local authorities, local businesses, Training and Enterprise Councils (TECS) and voluntary organisations are being used. From the spring of 1999 each district was required to publish performance indicators covering the number of young people in the schemes who had obtained jobs, the number who had remained in work for at least six months after leaving the scheme, and the level of satisfaction with the scheme amongst employers and participants. The government hopes to use the results to identify best practice.

The whole approach to New Deal is forged within the dominant discourse of welfare, constructing the young unemployed welfare subject as someone different from the 'norm', likely to engage in criminal activity in order to acquire the goods they wish to consume without 'working' for them. The twin approach of the government generally in relation to the young, evident in both their employment and youth offending policies (discussed in Chapter Eight) involves both compulsion and repression, reflecting New Labour's suspicion of young people. The rise in suicides amongst very young men (Watson and Doyal 1999) is surely an indication of their social construction as 'worth little', as well as their experience of exclusion. Many young people feel they have failed in school, and may be unwilling or unable to get involved again in education or to undertake a training course. There is also evidence to suggest that young men can differentiate between 'real work' and 'work' manufactured to stop them being 'idle', seeing the latter as being of little value (Lloyd 1999, Stafford et al. 1999). The government, therefore, faces serious difficulties in dealing effectively with youth unemployment. According to recent research, up to 500 000 young people who might be eligible for the New Deal programme are not currently involved with it (Bentley and Gurumurthy 1999). This is the number of those aged 16- to 24-years who are not on the unemployment register and who are also not in work, full-time training or education. Around a third of these have no qualifications, 40 per cent have never worked at all and half live in a workless household. This group includes 130 000 young people aged 16- to 17-years who have left education but are not in work, and who have been denied benefits since 1998 (Bentley and Oakley 1999). The programme for the young unemployed will cover all young people aged 18- to 24-years who have been claiming JSA for six months or more.

New Deal involves a considerable shift in the mode of operation of the Employment Service. This is supposed to take a less punitive approach to those who are unemployed, and to focus more on improving their chances of employment and on helping them to obtain jobs. The scheme began with 12 pathfinder or pilot projects that started in January 1998. The key aspect of the operation of the scheme, which is designed to make it more 'user-friendly' for the unemployed, is the 'Gateway' programme, which will last for one month for each participant. In this period, the participants will be interviewed by a personal adviser who will counsel them to assess their employment potential. People are then supposed to consider the various options open to them in terms of employment training, education and work experience. Like the DLA, the policy focus is on reconstructing the welfare subject rather than addressing the structural causes of unemployment such as the unavailability of paid 'work' in a locality, or the valuing of, and 'paying' for, non-waged 'work'. If participants are still unemployed after the Gateway programme they will be offered one of four options.

The first is a job with an employer, including at least one day per week or its equivalent in education or training designed to reach an accredited qualification. The employer will receive £60 a week for up to 26 weeks, and £750 per person has been allocated to finance the associated training. Yet again, benefits are to be distributed to the socially included, the employer, rather than the welfare subject directly, signifying his or her ineligibility for support without 'work'.

The second option is a job for six months with the Environment Task Force (ETF), which will include day-release education or training towards an accredited qualification. The ETF will engage young people on projects which benefit the whole 'community', including projects to help meet the government's targets for heat conservation and efficiency. Participants will receive an allowance equivalent to that of benefit and will remain entitled to passported benefits. In addition, they will receive a grant of up to £400 paid in instalments. This is an example of 'joined-up' thinking and tackling two 'problems' together – the problem of the young 'underclass' and the problem of environmental degradation. However, the outcome is likely to be unsatisfactory for all concerned. The early planning for the ETF has involved several difficulties, and its success rests heavily on the local availability of environmentally-oriented voluntary organisations, and these are not found everywhere. Additionally, some environmental groups claim that the criteria for these projects are too vague, and that they do not guarantee a benefit to the environment.

The third option is a job for six months with a voluntary sector employer, again including day-release education or training towards an accredited qualification. As with the ETF option, participants will receive an allowance equivalent to that of benefit and will remain entitled to passported benefits. In addition, they will receive a grant of up to £400 paid in instalments. There will be a particular emphasis on voluntary-sector placements to provide 50 000 new trained childcarers. The 'joined-up' thinking behind this programme is unbelievably crude, reflecting a complete disregard for young children and the quality of care to which they are entitled. Pressure on 'lone' parents to enter the labour market has been accompanied by assurances that sufficient childcare places will be available. New Labour propose that this can be easily delivered by young people with little or no training, working within organisations which are often characterised by low levels of training support, low wages and poor working conditions (SCCSSD 1998). Consequently, the combination of these policies is likely to prove disastrous for many young children and, indeed, the young 'childcarers' themselves.

The fourth option is full-time education or training in skills up to NVQ level 2. The '16 hour rule', which currently prevents people receiving JSA while in full-time education and training, will be changed to accommodate this. For up to twelve months, young people on this option will receive an allowance equivalent to that of benefit and remain entitled to passported benefits. They will also have access to a discretionary grant to help with travel and other costs. It is necessary to consider the quality of the learning experience offered to young people by this route in the context of a further and higher education sector starved of resources, and facing declining standards (see Chapter Five).

Each of the first three options include one day per week of education or training. During their time in the New Deal options, young people will continue to receive intensive support from Employment Service advisers designed to help them get a job in the regular labour market. Intensive help will continue for those who return to claim unemployment after their option finishes. Help with childcare is available on all options although, as has been argued, the quality of this care is likely to be variable at best and questionable in some instances. Young people who fail to take up an option will be required to take a place identified for them by the Employment Service. If they do not, benefit sanctions will be applied. The standard sanction for failing to go on a compulsory programme or failing to obey a Jobseeker's Direction is a loss of the JSA personal allowance for two weeks, or for four weeks if a similar sanction has been imposed in the previous 12 months.

Following New Labour's election in 1997, employment conditions for young people apparently improved and the numbers of young unemployed recorded in the official statistics fell to 118 000, far below the expected numbers that the scheme was designed for. This helped to persuade the government to extend the scheme, earlier than they had anticipated, to older workers. However, the way in which unemployment is measured has again been changed, with the government publishing unemployment figures on a new basis. These are now taken from the Labour Force Survey, which records all those who are unemployed, actively seeking work, and available for work within a two-week period. This figure is published alongside the existing figure of those out of work and claiming benefit. While this figure shows a higher level of unemployment, adding over 400 000 people to the figure of about 1.4m calculated on the existing basis in mid-1997, it does not include the 2m people, the majority of whom are women, who do not have a job and would like to work (Campbell 2000).

The New Deal for the long-term unemployed also forms part of the government's Welfare to Work programme which started in June 1998. There are two components to the New Deal: firstly, payments of £75 per week for 26 weeks will be made to employers who recruit people aged 25 and over who have been unemployed for two years or more; and secondly, there will be opportunities for those unemployed for two years or more to study for up to twelve months in full-time, employment-related courses designed to reach an accredited qualification. This will be achieved by relaxing the '16 hour' rule which prevents unemployed people from receiving benefit while studying full-time. New Labour claims that a side effect of this scheme will be to encourage young people to be more optimistic in their assessment of future employment prospects, encouraging more economically inactive people to enter the labour force. There is evidence that this has been happening in 1997 and 1998, since the numbers of people in 'work' have been increasing more rapidly than the reduction in the numbers unemployed. This may be explained by the return to the labour market of people who were not in work and not claiming benefit, some people who had retired early and possibly some people who were in receipt of disability benefits. However, it may also reflect 'a constant recycling of claimants through short-lived and low-paid jobs' (Jones and Novak 1999: 198), furthering the pauperisation of labour by forcing people into low paid, exploitative 'work'.

New Labour has also established a minimum wage, set at £3.60 per hour for workers over 21-years-of-age (£3 for 18- to 21-year-olds), and criminal sanctions to enforce it. Given that the level of wages offered for many unskilled jobs can be as low as £1.50 an hour, this legislation is likely to have an important effect. While there are various categories of workers under 26 who will not be eligible for the £3.60 rate in their first year at work, around 2m workers – particularly those in security jobs, catering, hotel work, cleaning, portering, retailing, textiles and childcare – are likely to benefit from the minimum wage. The longer-term impact of the minimum wage will depend, however, on the level at which governments decide to set it. Data for April 1999 (ONS 1999a) shows that some low-paid groups have obtained relatively large wage increases (hairdressers 11.7 per cent, waiters and waitresses 9.7 per cent). Overall, it has been estimated that 1.9m workers received an increase of up to 30 per cent as a result of the minimum wage. Some economists have argued strongly that a minimum wage will cause employers to reduce the size of their workforce because of the subsequent increase in their direct costs (Low Pay Commission 1998). Others, however, argue that employers are likely to benefit from the minimum wage in a number of ways. Firstly, the minimum wage will have a knock-on effect in the local economy since it is likely that much of the increased income will be spent locally rather than be saved. Secondly, employers may benefit from reduced indirect costs on, for example, training and recruitment by increasing the retention of workers and making vacancies easier to fill. Thirdly, the minimum wage may boost productivity by increasing worker motivation.

'Lone' mothers and income maintenance

The post-war benefit system, founded on the Beveridge proposals, was based on the assumption that women would normally be maintained by their husbands. This was reflected in the provision that allowed women to opt out of the full NI contribution and in lower rates of benefit for women. It was also reflected in the assumption that, within the family, women were responsible for controlling the money to be spent on children. While the benefit system has moved towards a situation of greater equality for men and women since the mid-1980s, partly as a result of the need to conform to European regulations on sex equality, the special needs of women are still not properly recognised (Lister 1998). The distinctive position of women rests in part on their role in the labour force. The majority of women are now in paid work. However, their participation in the labour force is more uneven than that of men because of periods of child-bearing and child-rearing, and a lack of available, affordable, good-quality childcare. Around two-thirds of working women return to work before a year has passed after the birth of their baby. Around 360 000 employees become pregnant every year, but 50 000 of these have incomes which are too low for them to pay NI contributions and, therefore, they are not entitled to NI maternity benefits. Over half of all mothers with children under five are in paid employment. Women are also more likely to work in low-paid jobs and in part-time employment. The wages received by women are substantially less than those received by men. This situation is, in part, perpetuated by the areas within which women work. These continue to reflect traditional gender stereotypes (Crompton 1997).

The pay gap between men and women is apparent very early on in their working lives. By the age of 20, women's incomes are around £40 a week less than those of males. In addition, the way in which earned income is distributed throughout the lifetime of women differs from the pattern characteristic of men. Women's earnings generally begin to dip in their 40s, and they do not benefit from the age and skill premium which many men obtain (Andersen and Larsen 1998). Probably the lowest paid and the least protected section of the workforce are the million or so home workers, mostly women, who work long hours with few benefit entitlements. Little is known about this group, although some people receive rates of pay as low as 30p an hour (Bhavnani 1994). While the Equal Pay Act 1970 was an attempt to promote equality, the hourly wages of women were still 20 per cent below those of men in 1997. Women not only receive less from work than men, but their pension entitlements are also less. The increase in divorce and the expansion of the number of lone-parent households has further disadvantaged women.

Against this backdrop it is illuminating to examine New Deal for Lone Parents, where entry into the labour market is promoted as the path out of poverty for these 'Other than' 'families'. Around a quarter of all families in Britain are now headed by lone parents, primarily women. This is a very high level in comparison with other EU member states. It is also a relatively recent situation which mainly emerged in the 1980s and 1990s. Lone parents in Britain are very likely to be economically inactive, to have low levels of educational attainment, and to experience a high risk of unemployment (Bryson et al. 1997). There would appear to be a strong connection between lone parenthood, unemployment and poverty. Despite the moral panic over teenage mothers, only 4 per cent of lone parents fall into this category. However, it is evident that marriage is less popular than it once was and 38 per cent of lone parents have never been married (Rodgers and Pryor 1998). The intention of New Labour is to increase the proportion of lone parents who are in work. In July 1997 the new government established eight pilot schemes designed to encourage lone parents to seek work. The participation of lone mothers in the New Deal pilot schemes was initially voluntary. Lone parents on income support were invited to an interview with a personal adviser when the youngest child reached the age of five years and three months. The DSS has reported that around 20 per cent of those interviewed did find a job, although less than a quarter of those invited to interview attended (DSS 1997a). The scheme was introduced nation-wide in April 1998, forming an integral part of the government's Welfare to Work programme. Under this programme lone parents with school-age children are invited to the local Job Centre for help and advice on jobs, benefits, training and childcare. After an initial interview each lone parent will develop an individual plan of action with the help of their personal caseworker. This will cover job search skills, training and finding childcare in order to help them into work.

It is clear, however, that both childcare and 'work' are in short supply. Yet the government's approach here, as with DLA and New Deal for Young People, is to focus on the welfare subject rather than the broader structural context of their lived experience. While at present there are no sanctions proposed for those who choose not to take part, in the case of the US workfare programmes, upon which New Labour base their approach, sanctions are an integral part of the scheme. However, if those called to attend an interview do not attend then an adviser will call on them at home. There may be a hidden agenda here in that the government, appearing to believe that some lone parents are drawing benefit fraudulently, subject them to public scrutiny by inviting them to discuss their financial circumstances. This way, the government hope that lone parents may stop claiming income support and meet their obligations as a responsible member of society. In reality, of course, a great deal of public expenditure benefits the middle classes – health and education services, law and order, employment subsidies, and so forth – without bestowing the same obligations on them to show reciprocity:

> Instead, these obligations are more strongly enforced upon minorities, with little political clout, or capacity to resist through democratic processes. The Blair government chose lone parents and disabled people as the first targets for its welfare reform programme. It is difficult not to suppose that this was because they were in a bad position to oppose these cuts. By the same token, young people from minority ethnic groups are particularly likely to be required to participate in welfare-to-work programmes. (Jordan 1998: 107)

The marginal position of lone parents is illustrated by the difficulties which they have if they wish to undertake full-time education. If they take this option they will lose their income support and be forced to take out a student loan. They will also be ineligible for childcare tax credits, and they will lose other means-tested benefits (such as housing benefit or free school meals). Under the New Deal, financial support for education and training is only available up to NVQ level 2.

As part of their strategy to reduce child poverty, New Labour announced in July 1998 that it was to simplify the operation of the CSA. These changes reflected the government's concern about inefficiencies within the CSA, rather than the principles underpinning its functions (Jordan 1998). Only around 13 per cent of CSA cases resulted in the collection of the full amount from the father (Smith 1997). In future, a fixed percentage of net income would be paid by the father depending on the number of children who were being supported – 15 per cent for one, 20 per cent for two and 25 per cent for three or more, where the net weekly income was above £200. Where the net income was less, then less would be paid. Non co-operation with the CSA would be made a criminal offence. These changes are to take effect in 2001. The principles behind the CSA reflect the dominant welfare discourse and its construction of the normalised 'family' and, thereby, allowing the lone-parent household to be reconstructed as the 'Other' – 'families' who are designated socially undesirable and even dangerous. The CSA reflected the desire to privilege:

> biological parenthood over social parenthood, ignoring the realities of income and poverty in lone parenthood and second marriages and the negotiated nature

of family obligation. It attempted to change behaviour by coercion without regard for popularly constructed notions of social justice. (Jordan 1998: 194)

New Labour's reforms to the CSA demonstrate the extent to which they remain firmly within this discourse of the 'family', despite individuals defecting from their 'obligations', and the strong collective dissent against this policy instrument (Jordan 1998).

Family Credit (FC), which is currently claimed by 0.85m people, is to be replaced by a new benefit called Working Families Tax Credit (WFTC). The basic weekly credit will be £48.80 with additional payments for children, depending on their age, rising to £25.40 for 16- to 18-year-olds. Claimants have to work a minimum of 16 hours a week, while those working over 30 hours receive £10.80 extra. Where weekly pay exceeds £90 the credit is progressively clawed back. WFTC should benefit up to 1.5m recipients. To be eligible families must have savings of less than £8,000. WFTC is designed to improve work incentives for the poorest households by reducing or eliminating the poverty trap. However, tax credits also do three other things:

> They give a selective advantage over their competitors to employers who pay low wages; they give disincentives to increased earnings for those who receive them, because they have their benefits or tax credits withdrawn if their wages rise; and they discriminate against others who earn just above the prescribed levels, who do not qualify for supplements. (Jordan 1998: 141)

WFTC also aims to remove 0.8m children from poverty. However, where FC was paid directly to mothers, WFTC can be included as a tax allowance in the main earners pay packets (usually male), or it can be given to a non-working spouse as a cash benefit. Evidence suggests that policies which do not take account of power differentials within 'families' are likely to disadvantage women. Moreover, by changing the benefit from one that was usually received directly by the woman in the 'family' and spent on the welfare of children, to a tax credit, is likely to reduce, not increase, the income available for children (Goode et al. 1998). In relation to social justice and economic efficiency, therefore, these tax credit policies appear fundamentally flawed.

Another important new policy designed to support the family is the Children's Tax Credit (CTC) which replaces the married couple's allowance and will be worth over £416 per year, from April 2001, to families with children. This will replace the Family Credit Childcare

Disregard which was received by only 40 000 families. It will cover up to 70 per cent of childcare costs for single working parents or for couples where both parents work for at least 16 hours per week. It will only be payable for registered childcare. In reality, however, CTC is unlikely to cover these costs for many households. In many regions, childcare is in short supply, and is of variable quality, expensive, and often incurs additional costs such as transport, particularly in rural areas, which are not included for calculation purposes.

Elders and disabled people, and income maintenance

A central difficulty facing British governments in their attempts to reduce expenditure on social security since the end of the long boom has been the fact that the biggest area of expenditure involves people above the age of retirement. Retired people in all classes normally have lower incomes than their working counterparts. Poverty in old age is closely related to class. The experience of old age under capitalism involves an intensification of the patterns of inequality that exist amongst the working population. Many working-class elders suffer extreme deprivation, often involving social isolation and a sense of uselessness resulting from exclusion from the labour market and from social life generally (Harding 1997). The impact of poverty on elders has important health implications. During winter cold spells the numbers dying increases substantially as many suffer from what has been termed 'fuel poverty'. This affects around 4m households in England. It is defined as occurring when heating costs amount to more than 10 per cent of the household income. People aged 60 and over account for more than half of those in this category. In May 1999, the government announced that it would be offering grants of up to £1,800 to elders and disabled people to allow them to install central heating and insulate their homes in an attempt to eliminate fuel poverty. As elders and disabled people are usually without paid 'work', they are constructed as 'social burdens' rather than 'social assets' within the neo-liberal welfare discourse, and this is continuing under New Labour.

The elderly have been increasingly excluded from work in recent decades. About a third of people over 50, but below pensionable age, are neither working nor registered as unemployed (ONS 1999b). In 1979, 95 per cent of men aged 55 to 65 were employed. The figure in 1999 was around 60 per cent. Many older people would like to work, but have a struggle to find employment. They constitute a large pool of people experiencing social exclusion, often under the apparently benign label of 'early retirement'. Many of these people are victims of discrimination taking the form of ageism. A survey commissioned by Age Concern (1998) found strong evidence of age discrimination amongst workers aged over 50. Although the New Labour government initially appeared committed to outlawing this form of discrimination, it subsequently decided to rely instead on a voluntary code of practice covering various aspects of employment, such as recruitment, promotion, training, redundancy and retirement.

Elderly women are particularly disadvantaged by the UK's income maintenance system, not only as a result of ageism, but also due to the normalised concept of 'family' constructed by the dominant welfare discourse. The heterosexual family norm has provided the basis upon which households' entitlement to income support has been calculated since the Poor Law. This disadvantages elderly women, particularly in relation to pensions (Arber and Ginn 1991, 1995). Half of all women aged over 65 are widowed, but only a third of elderly women have any pension of their own, apart from that provided by the state. Where women do have a pension of their own it is normally around a third of the value of the average male pension. Of those pensioners who receive means-tested income support, three-quarters are women and many more female than male pensioners live on incomes around the poverty level. The occupational pension system provides few benefits for women. As a consequence, the majority of women rely on the pensions of their husbands for financial security in retirement (Boaz et al. 1999).

It has been argued that pensions form part of 'a generational contract', based on the reciprocal care provided between the generations (Walker 1996). At a personal level, this reciprocity is expected to occur within normalised family structures through the care parents provide for their children, and through the care children may provide later in life for their parents. However, this expectation is outside the lived experience of many, particularly as the period of dependency in old age has increased and the number of younger relatives available to provide care has fallen. It is an expectation that also excludes the lived experience of 'Other than' families, such as gay and lesbian couples. Moreover, it is an expectation that fails to reflect social values in British society, where caring is not valued, either in monetary or cultural terms, as much as paid 'work'. As a result, at the societal level, this generational contract depends largely on the willingness and good will of the current working population to support the current retired population. However, this willingness has largely been undermined by the decreasing adequacy of state provision and funding support for long-term care for elders, and the individualisation of pension arrangements through the growth of private, personal schemes which remove the pooling of risks found in the state pension and many occupational schemes.

In the last 20 years Britain has moved increasingly towards maintaining the incomes of the elderly through the use of means tests. The basic flat-rate pension has been allowed to fall in value through a failure to uprate it in line with increases in economic growth. The extent to which the basic state pension fails to provide an adequate living standard is illustrated by the fact that it is set at £6 below the level at which income support is payable. NatWest Bank published a report in February 1998 on the adequacy of existing pension arrangements (NatWest Bank 1998). It found that only 21 per cent of those in work are on course to receive a pension of £179 a week, calculated as the minimum which elderly people require today for a comfortable retirement. About 7m people rely entirely on the basic state pension. However, only around half of these qualify for the full basic pension, itself worth only 16 per cent of average earnings. The other half, who are mainly women, qualify for a lesser sum. Not only do many pensioners have inadequate incomes, but they also lack savings. The Annual Family Resources Survey (DSS 1997b) shows that 20 per cent of pensioner couples, and 34 per cent of pensioners living alone, have no savings.

An issue under debate in 1997 was whether to revert to universalist principles by reinstating the system by which the flat-rate pension increased in value in line with average earnings. This would provide recipients with a standard of living that improves over time. If this change is not carried out it has been estimated that, by 2030, the flat-rate pension will be worth just 9 per cent of average earnings (Boaz et al. 1999). After a long period of disagreement within the government, New Labour finally came up with a proposed minimum retirement income, to be set at 20 per cent of average earnings. This proposal was implemented in the March budget of 1999 as a minimum income guarantee of £78 for single pensioners and £121 for couples. The existing state pension is to be retained, although its value will not be increased. This will be backed up by means-tested income support. A major problem with this is that up to

0.75m pensioners do not claim the income support to which they are entitled. The government claimed that it would attempt to rectify this situation by trawling through its computer records to identify eligible pensioners. A trial scheme designed to test out ways of doing this was announced in March 1998, although no results were available by June 1999.

The State Earnings Related Pension Scheme (SERPS) is to be abolished and replaced by a new second state pension. Incentives are to be provided through a government subsidy to encourage people to take out 'stakeholder' pensions. Companies will once again be allowed to require employees to join their pension scheme. The stakeholder pension is aimed at people earning between £9,000 and £18,500 a year. An important feature of the stakeholder pension is that the companies providing it will not be allowed to charge more than 1 per cent per annum to recipients. People will also be able to stop and start contributions in line with their own requirements, and there will be no charges for transferring between stakeholder schemes. At the time of writing, the numbers of people taking out stakeholder pensions has been far lower than the government's plans require.

In September 1999, the government announced the end of the link between paid employment and pension contributions. In the future those who are not in work will be allowed to contribute to a pension and obtain tax relief. This could benefit some people who were taking a break from paid work to continue to make contributions to a pension. The most radical element of the proposals involved providing Pension Tax Credits for 4m carers and disabled ex-workers in order to provide them with the pension they would otherwise not have received. Occupational pensions and personal pensions will still remain available. This can hardly be described as a simple system and whether or not it provides adequate incomes will depend on the stakeholder pension proving sufficiently attractive for large numbers of people in the mid-range of earnings to take them up. Under current proposals they will not be compelled to do so, although it is possible to imagine compulsion being brought in later if the incentives do not work as hoped.

The debate in relation to income maintenance for disabled people centres on the division between what has been called a 'benefits approach' and a 'rights approach'. The benefits approach has traditionally dominated policy and implies a system of benefits tailored to the individual needs of disabled people, based on their category of impairment. It is sometimes called the 'individual' model. Critics view this approach as one that tends to neglect the wider social context within which disabled people can secure full citizenship (the 'social model' of disability). This social model also believes that current practices supporting disabled people encourage a 'victim culture' in which provision is sponsored and controlled by able-bodied people, with the disabled themselves seen as passive victims who need to be helped. '[I]t is not us it is non-disabled people's embodiment which is the issue: disabled people remind non-disabled people of their own vulnerability' (Shakespeare, cited in Price and Shildrick 1999: 433). Those who take a social view of disability highlight society's failure to adjust to the different impairments experienced by people. In this view, for example, disabled people do not need a mobility allowance, but society needs a transport system free of the barriers which restrict those with a mobility impairment. The social model, or 'rights approach', to disability is more amenable to the emphasis on supporting disabled people into paid work than the benefits approach (Northway 1997).

There is a complex array of benefits for disabled people. Incapacity Benefit (IB), which was formerly known as Invalidity Benefit, was claimed by 2.4m people at a cost of £7.7bn in 1997. The benefit is payable to those incapable of work on a sliding scale according to the assessed level of incapacity. Attendance Allowance is received by 1.2m people aged 65 plus, and cost £2.4bn a year in 1997. Disability Living Allowance (DLA) is paid to those under 65 who need care or who have restricted mobility. This benefit is not means-tested and so it is received in addition to any other income from benefits or other earnings. It is paid on a sliding scale according to the level of disability. In 1997, it was paid to 1.8m people and cost £4.4bn a year. New Labour has set up a Disability Rights Commission with an annual budget of £11m which will replace the existing National Disability Council. Its mode of operation will be analogous to that of the Equal Opportunities and Racial Equality Commissions who, while both failing to challenge the structural causes of discrimination and exclusion, have had some success in relation to individual cases. New Labour has also established a Disability Working Tax Credit which is designed to encourage disabled people to find work. This will guarantee an income of at least £150 a week for a disabled person working full-time. The purpose of this benefit is to top up the incomes of poorly paid disabled workers. It will operate along the lines of the WFTC which, as we saw above, has inherent problems.

In December 1997 a leaked government document indicated New Labour's intention to restrict disability benefits. Justification for this centred on the government's concern that payments to the disabled accounted for around a quarter of all benefits spending. This concern reflects the close proximity between the neo-liberal and New Labour's discourse of welfare, and the construction of the welfare subject as a consumer of resources to which they were not entitled. It also highlights continuity with the neo-liberal welfare narrative of over-generous benefits encouraging 'welfare dependency' and welfare fraud. It is certainly true that spending on the disabled has increased substantially, from £4.1bn in 1982 to £23.5bn in 1997. The estimated number of disabled adults in Britain, in 1998, was 8.6m, nearly 3m more than had been estimated a decade earlier (Barnes et al. 1998). While it is possible that this increase reflects the ageing of the population, the reason for the growth in the numbers of people claiming long-term sickness and disability benefits is mainly due to the rising numbers of women leaving work through ill health. By comparison, in the 1980s the main contributors to the growing numbers of disabled and long-term sick came from male workers previously employed in traditional heavy industry. The number of female claimants is now almost the same as the number of male claimants – 2.9m women in a total of 6.1m claimants in August 1998.

The leak of the government document led to a major mobilisation of disability groups in protest and opposition to the cuts under consideration. Many disabled people at this time were already being subjected to investigation under the Benefit Integrity Project (BIP), which had been established in 1996 by the Conservative government. Proposals in the Welfare Reform and Pensions Bill, published in November 1998, included a comprehensive plan for the reform of benefits for the disabled. The government believed that many of those currently in receipt of IB were not actually incapable of work, and were in receipt of benefit as a means of subsidising what is, in effect, an early retirement. The reforms are aimed at eliminating the abuse of IB, along with more generous benefits for those who really are severely disabled and 'deserving'. Only those who have worked recently and have paid NI contributions will, in future, be inclined to be entitled to claim IB. The 'all work test' (whose emphasis was on proving an inability to work) is to be replaced by a 'capacity test' which will assess what work the person is capable of doing. In addition, the benefit will be reduced for those claimants in receipt of private pensions or private-health insurance payments, by half the value of these payments. Those who are judged to be severely disabled will receive higher levels of benefit – £129 week for a single person, and £169 per week for a couple. There will also be extra assistance for severely disabled children. The BIP is to be abolished.

The economic disadvantage of disabled people as a group is well established (Knight and Brent 1998. There is a consensus that disabled people – including those with physical and learning impairments, and those with a severe mental illness – are over-represented among the poor, and that strikingly high levels of this group are not in employment (Beresford 1996). However, a system that focuses solely on the welfare subject as 'deserving victims', or 'undeserving fraudsters', rather than the structural and institutional barriers to employment and social inclusion, as New Labour is continuing to do, is unlikely to address this disadvantage.

Conclusion

New Labour remains within a discourse of welfare that has emerged and re-emerged since the Poor Law. In particular, through analysing New Labour's income maintenance policies, we can see how its construction of the welfare subject as 'eligible' or 'ineligible' is largely founded on the supplementary discourses of 'work', but also the 'family', 'consumption' and 'sexuality'. The idea that recipients of state support should have to show their willingness to work in order to obtain benefits goes back to the principles of the workhouse. New Labour has pursued policies designed to link 'eligibility' for benefit with the requirement that recipients should co-operate with attempts to place them in 'work', training or education. What is now referred to as 'conditionality' has been a long-standing feature of state welfare provision (Dwyer 1998). Income support policies have normally reinforced obligations to work, with benefits kept well below wage levels. In addition, throughout the history of the social-security system, recipients of unemployment benefit have, on occasions, had to demonstrate that they were seeking work. Those who could not do this were often excluded from benefit under various 'not genuinely seeking work' rules. The deficiencies of the benefit system are identified, therefore, in terms of their failure to encourage paid labour.

New Labour has placed considerable emphasis on 'paid work' as the solution to poverty. Paid work constructs social identity, as those without 'work' are constructed as 'Other than' the desirable social norm. This fails to acknowledge the importance of unpaid labour activities – for example, in the form of childcare, care for other dependants, voluntary work or community involvement. As these are neither paid for nor valued in British society, their importance to the local community is often overlooked. Moreover, the classification of benefit recipients as 'Other than' the norm allows 'difference' to be identified as 'deviant' and, thereby, their unequal treatment. This process reinforces social divisions and the exclusion of particular groups. Lone parent 'families', for example, are not classified as 'real families', but as deviant groups unable to rear children as useful social animals. They are blamed for contributing to the apparent social breakdown (Levitas 1998). Furthermore, the expectation is that those without paid 'work', and their children, will learn to accept that they cannot be 'consumers' in a consumerist society – otherwise they will be criminalised.

The emphasis on paid 'work' as a way out of poverty also fails to take account of the structural and institutional barriers to employment. As Jordan argues, national labour markets in developed nations do not offer people comparable opportunities for employment. This is because they are clearly divided between 'insiders' already in the system (chiefly, white middle-class men with regular employment paying high salaries, and offering promotion prospects and occupational perks such as pensions), and 'outsiders' without such advantages (often women and black people). The rewards bestowed by labour markets are not due to merit and do not deliver any kind of social justice. Differential earnings reflect differential power-relationships within the labour market and the ability of the 'insiders' to negotiate collective agreements which both exclude 'outsiders' and distort market allocations in favour of their own organised interests (Jordan 1998). The New Deal, therefore, is unlikely to help young people from racial minorities, particularly when employer resistance to the recruitment of black people is still a major barrier, and when referral organisations collude in 'anticipatory discrimination' by failing to refer these clients on. Black Jobseekers on the New Deal were less likely to find work than their white counterparts: 43 per cent of black entrants of African-Caribbean origin were still at the Gateway (training and consultation) stage compared with 33 per cent of all entrants (Berthoud

1999, DfEE 1999b). The proportion of racial minority Jobseekers obtaining jobs was 39 per cent, compared to a figure of 52 per cent for white Jobseekers. Similarly, a range of barriers, including employer resistance, inflexibility of work patterns and lack of access to work environments, currently prevent many disabled people from working. Unless these barriers are dismantled, employment opportunities for disabled people will not increase.

New Labour's welfare discourse also assumes the notion of the normalised 'family', an emphasis which allows the government to pursue policies that seek to reduce reliance on state assistance by imposing the obligation to maintain those without resources on liable relatives. In doing this, the government is helping to maintain existing sexual relationships and gender roles in society, thereby reinforcing the unequal treatment of women, lesbians and gay men, in the public and private sphere.

Where changes are being made by New Labour, as with the minimum wage and the use of tax credits to raise the income of various groups, the new target levels of income are low. Where more significant commitments are made, as in the case of the abolition of child poverty, the timescale is substantial, in this case 20 years. The restrictions which Labour has placed upon itself in relation to avoiding policies which have explicit redistributive aims, and of broadly maintaining current levels of public expenditure, are, therefore, likely to pose problems for its attempts to alleviate poverty and increase social inclusion.

Finally, it may be asked, what sort of society does New Labour intend to create through the pursuit of its polices to alleviate poverty? Certainly, a central role in this will be played by the process of welfare reform. It is becoming clear that, like the neo-liberals, New Labour's 'modernisation' project is one in which welfare has a role in moral reconstruction, and in shaping a particular society in which certain ways of living will be encouraged and others discouraged:

> One of welfare's roles is to reward and to punish ... As Christian morality becomes unsustainable without being recharged in each generation by waves of new Christian believers, so societies must seek different ways of affirming right and wrong conduct. Welfare has such a role. (Frank Field, cited in Jones and Novak 1999: 180)

The benefit system continues to mark the boundaries separating those who are 'included' in the national community and those who are not. The unemployed, 'lone' mothers, elders and disabled people are all constructed as 'Other than' the norm by the dominant discourse of welfare. Some people are excluded from benefit because officials consider that Britain is not their habitual place of residence. This has affected up to 100 000 people annually. Three quarters of these are British nationals and many are black people or Asian. The European Court of Justice ruled in February 1999 that this was a breach of European law.

New Labour claims that welfare has failed. The precise character of this failure is not always clear, although what appears to be meant is that despite the widespread provision made by the welfare state many people are still poor. In addition, New Labour claims that many of the benefits which are dispensed go to those who do not really 'need' them. It is also occasionally claimed, though by no means as frequently as it was by neo-liberals, that expenditure on social security is excessively high, even though the actual level of benefits in the UK is extremely low by EU standards. In view of these claims, New Labour appears determined to do little to modify the existing level of inequality in Britain (Townsend 1998). However, it is this level of inequality that has always formed the main barrier to the success of schemes designed to reduce poverty (Howarth and Street 1998). There is clear evidence from the area of health that the extent of inequality is itself a major cause of social deprivation, resulting in illness and premature death amongst the poor (Wilkinson 1996). The government appears to believe that the existing level of inequality has to be maintained as the basis for economic efficiency. It can be argued, however, that economic advance would be encouraged by shifting the control of social resources so that poor people had more access to them. It is certainly the case, as the experience of the Second World War showed, that egalitarian policies are an essential element in strategies designed to secure social inclusion (Calder 1969).

References

Age Concern (1998) *Age discrimination: Make it a thing of the past,* Age Concern, London.
Andersen, J. and Larsen, J.E. (1998) 'Gender, poverty and empowerment', *Critical Social Policy*, Vol. 18, No.2, pp. 241-58.
Arber, S. and Ginn, J. (1991) *Gender and later life*, Sage, London.

Arber, S. and Ginn, J. (1995) *Connecting Gender and Ageing*, Open University Press, London.

Barclay, P. (1995) *Inquiry into income and wealth*, Joseph Rowntree Foundation, York.

Barnes, H. Thornton, P. and Campbell, S.M. (1998) *Disabled people and employment: A review of research and development work*, Policy Press, London.

Bauman, Z. (1998) *Work, consumerism and the new poor*, Open University Press, Buckingham.

Becker, S. (1997) *Responding to Poverty: The Politics of Cash and Care*, Longman, Harlow.

Bentley, T. and Gurumurthy, R. (1999) *Destination Unknown*, Demos, London.

Bentley, T. and Oakley, K. (1999) *The Real Deal*, Demos, London.

Beresford, P. (1996) 'Poverty and disabled people: Challenging dominant debates and policies', *Disability and Society*, Vol. 11, No. 4, pp. 553-67.

Beresford, P. and Green, D.I. (1996) 'Income and wealth: An opportunity to reassess the UK poverty debate', *Critical Social Policy*, Vol. 16, No. 1, pp. 95-110.

Berthoud, R. (1999) *Young Caribbean men and the labour market: A comparison with other ethnic groups*, Joseph Rowntree Foundation, York.

Bhavnani, R. (1994) *Black women in the labour market: A research review*, Equal Opportunities Commission, Manchester.

Boaz, A., Hayden, C. and Bernard, M. (1999) 'Attitudes and Aspirations of Older People – A review of the literature', *Department of Social Security Research Report Series, Report No. 101*, The Stationery Office, London.

Bryson, A., Ford, R. and White, M. (1997) *Making Work Pay: Lone mothers, employment and well-being*, Joseph Rowntree Foundation, York.

Byrne, D. (1997) 'Social exclusion and capitalism: The reserve army across time and space', *Critical Social Policy*, Vol. 17, No. 1, pp. 27-51.

Calder, A. (1969) *The People's War*, Cape, London.

Campbell, M. (2000) 'Labour Market Exclusion' in Chap 3, J. Percy-Smith (ed.) *Policy Responses to Social Exclusion*, Open University Press, Milton Keynes.

Crompton, R. (1997) *Women and work in modern Britain*, Oxford University Press, Oxford.

Daly, M. (1997) 'Welfare States Under Pressure: Cash Benefits in European Welfare States Over the Last Ten Years', *Journal of European Social Policy*, Vol. 7, No.2, pp. 129-146.

DfEE (1999a) (Department for Education and Employment) *New Deal For Young People And long-term Unemployed People Aged 25+: Statistics*, http://www.dfee.gov.uk/news/sfr/sfr9.doc, 27 May 1999.

DfEE (1999b) (Department for Education and Employment) *Unemployment and Jobseeking: The Experience of Ethnic Minorities*, DfEE Publications, London.

246 'Modernising' Social Policy

DHSS (Department of Health and Social Security) (1985) *Reform of Social Security*, HMSO, London.
DSS (Department of Social Security) (1997a) *A New Deal for Lone Parents: Moving Forward*, DSS, London.
DSS (Department of Social Security) (1997b) *Family Resources Survey*, The Stationery Office, London.
DSS (Department of Social Security) (1998a) *Households below average income*, The Stationery Office, London.
DSS (Department of Social Security) (1998b) *New ambitions for our country: A new contract for welfare*, The Stationery Office, London.
DSS (Department of Social Security) (1998c), *Beating fraud is every one's business*, The Stationery Office, London.
Dwyer, P. (1998) 'Conditional citizens? Welfare rights and responsibilities in the late 1990s', *Critical Social Policy*, Vol. 18, No.4, pp. 493-518.
Falkingham, J. and Hills, J. (1995) *The dynamics of welfare: The welfare state and the life cycle*, Harvester Wheatsheaf, Hemel Hempstead.
George, V (1996) 'The Future of the Welfare State' in V. George and P. Taylor-Gooby (eds.) *European Welfare Policy: Squaring the Welfare Circle*, Macmillan. Basingstoke.
George, V. and Taylor-Gooby, P. (eds.) (1996) *European Welfare Policy: Squaring the Welfare Circle*, Macmillan, Basingstoke.
Goode, J., Callendar, C. and Lister, R. (1998) *Purse or wallet? Gender inequalities and income distribution within families on benefits*, Policy Studies Institute, London.
Gorz, A. (1999) *Reclaiming Work: Beyond the Wage-Based Society*, Polity Press, Cambridge.
Harding, T. (1997) *A life worth living: The independence and inclusion of older people*, Help the Aged, London.
Hewitt, M. (1999) 'New Labour and social security' in M. Powell (ed.) *New Labour, New Welfare State? The 'third way' in British social policy*, The Policy Press, Bristol, pp. 149-170.
Hill, M. and Bramley, G. (1986) *Analysing Social Policy*, Blackwell, Oxford.
Hobsbawm, E. (1996) *Age of Extremes: The short twentieth century*, Abacus, London.
Howarth, C. and Street, C. (1998) *Monitoring poverty and social exclusion: Labour's inheritance*, New Policy Institute and Joseph Rowntree Foundation, York.
Huby, M. and Whyley, C. (1996) 'Take-up and the social fund', *Journal of Social Policy*, Vol. 25, No. 1, pp.1-18.
Hutton, W. (1995) *The State We're In*, Jonathan Cape, London.
Jones, C. and Novak, T. (1999) *Poverty, Welfare and The Disciplinary State*, Routledge, London.

Jordan, B. (1996) *A Theory of Poverty and Social Exclusion*, Polity Press, Cambridge.

Jordan, B. (1998) *The New Politics of Welfare*, Sage, London.

Knight, J. and Brent, M. (1998) *Access denied: Disabled people's experience of social exclusion*, Leonard Cheshire, London.

Lavalette, M. and Pratt, A. (1997) *Social Policy: A Conceptual and Theoretical Introduction*, Sage, London.

Levitas, R. (1998) *The Inclusive Society? Social Exclusion and New Labour*, Macmillan, Basingstoke.

Lister, R (1998) *Citizenship: Feminist perspectives*, Macmillian, London.

Lloyd, T. (1999) *Young men, the job market and gendered work*, Joseph Rowntree Foundation, York.

Low Pay Commission (1998) *The National Minimum Wage*, The Stationery Office, London.

Natwest Bank (1998) *Natwest Pensions Index*, National Westminster Bank, London.

Northway, R. (1997) 'Integration and inclusion: Illusion or progress in services for disabled people', *Social Policy and Administration*, Vol. 31, No. 2, pp. 157-72.

OFT (Office of Fair Trading) (1998) *Financial Services to Vulnerable Consumers*, The Stationery Office, London

ONS (Office of National Statistics) (1999a) *New Earnings Survey*, The Stationery Office, London.

ONS (Office for National Statistics) (1999b) *Social Focus on Older People*, The Stationery Office, London.

Price, J. and Shildrick, M. (eds.) (1999) *Feminist Theory and the Body*, Edinburgh University Press, Edinburgh.

Rodgers, B. and Pryor, J (1998) *Divorce and separation: The outcomes for children*, Joseph Rowntree Foundation, York.

SCCSSD (Suffolk County Council Social Services Department) (1998) *The HERA Project: Suffolk 1995-1997*, Suffolk County Council, Ipswich.

Shildrick, M. and Price, J. (1999) 'Breaking the Boundaries of the Broken Body', in J. Price and M. Shildrick (eds.) *Feminist Theory and the Body,* Edinburgh University Press, Edinburgh, pp. 433-44.

Smith, R. (1997) 'Paying the penalty: The impact of the Child Support Act', *Critical Social Policy*, Vol. 17, No. 4, pp. 111-20.

Stafford, B., Heaver, C., Ashworth, K., Bates, C., Walker, R., McKay, S. and Trickley, H. (1999) *Work and young men*, Joseph Rowntree Foundation, York.

Townsend, P. (1998) *Will poverty get worse under Labour?*, University of Edinburgh Press, Edinburgh.

Vincent, J. (1996) 'Who's afraid of an ageing population? Nationalism, the free market and the construction of old age as an issue', *Critical Social Policy*, Vol. 16, No.2, pp. 3-26.

Walker, A. (1996) *The New Generational Contract*, UCL Press, London.

Walker, R. (1998) 'Does work work?', *Journal of Social Policy*, Vol. 27, No.4, pp. 533-42.

Watson, S. and Doyal, L. (1999) *Engendering Social Policy*, Open University Press, Buckingham.

White, M. and Forth, J. (1998) *Pathways through unemployment: The effects of a flexible labour market*, Joseph Rowntree Foundation, York.

Wilkinson, R. (1996) *Unhealthy Societies: The Afflictions of Inequality*, Routledge, London.

Williams, F. (1995) *Social Policy: A critical introduction; issues of race, gender and class*, Polity Press, Cambridge.

8 'Family' Policies

Introduction

The 'family' has been central to social policy and welfare issues since the development of the centralised state. Much of the policy debate in the UK has concerned itself with 'family life', often in reaction to media attention given to 'lone' parents, teenage mothers, absent fathers, rising divorce rates, truancy and 'problem' youth. There has been a political consensus between the major parties about the need to implement policies that support the 'family'. However, as has been argued in Chapter Three, the notion of 'family' itself is problematic, largely because it is an idealised concept or social construct, based on a particular model of social living rather than reflecting the way most of us live. However, as an idealised model of living, the normalised family – in which men are breadwinners and women are carers – formed the base upon which the post-war welfare state in the UK was built. Moreover, the normalised family has been increasingly targeted by social policy developments over the past two decades, not only in the UK, but elsewhere in Europe and the US (Daly 1997).

It is with the failure of the neo-liberal and New Labour governments to recognise diversity and change in 'family' formation that this chapter is concerned. Meanings and contradictions inherent in the construction of normalised family life have clearly affected the discursive practices and welfare policies targeted at the 'family'. Uncovering these meanings and contradictions enables the consequences of welfare practices and policies to be identified. In particular, this will show who are being included by practices and policies, who are being excluded, and why. Using Leonard's (1997) four supplementary discourses, or narratives, of 'family', 'work', 'consumption' and 'sexuality' (explained in Chapter Three), the impact of the neo-liberal Conservative governments' policies on 'Other than' normalised families, and the likely outcomes of New Labour's welfare reforms, will be examined. We argue that both the Conservatives and New Labour base 'family' welfare policy on a construction of 'difference' – that is, on ways of living together that are defined as 'Other than' the norm. By constructing the 'abnormal' – in effect, any alternative to the normalised family – we construct the 'normal'. Lone parents, gay couples and teenage mothers are constructed as 'Other than' 'normal' families, which infers that a heterosexual man and woman living together in a marital relationship in order to rear children is the most desirable and 'natural' family form. We argue that this construction of the normalised family is an inherent part of the dominant discourse of welfare inhabited by both the neo-liberals and New Labour. This discourse of welfare became the means by which millions of children and their parents were impoverished under the neo-liberals. Furthermore, as New Labour's stance on welfare continues to construct difference as deviance, it is likely that their policies will serve to prolong, rather than alleviate, poverty and social exclusion for many.

'Family' policies and the state

The successive Conservative governments, from 1979 to 1997, proclaimed a central interest in the welfare of families. Margaret Thatcher, the first neo-liberal Prime Minister, set up the Family Policy Group (FPG) to advise government on welfare policy shortly after taking up office in 1979. The public remained largely unaware of this group until its existence was leaked to the media in 1983. Concerns were voiced by the FPG about 'declining morality and family values' (Coppock 1997: 64). By 1994, right-wing attacks on welfare as a cause of 'family' decline and the rise in the social instability were ferocious. A report issued by the Adam Smith Institute called for a phased withdrawal of state responsibility for welfare on the grounds that it was undermining the 'family' (Bell et al. 1994). Dr David Marsland, one of the authors of the report, argued that state welfare 'is rapidly destroying the family – the main arena of genuine welfare in a free society – and thereby crippling children for life more reliably than "dark satanic mills"' (*The Guardian*, 28 February 1994: 10). New Labour have also proclaimed a central interest in the 'family' and, from their arrival to power in 1997, aspects of 'family' life (such as childcare for working parents) were targeted for priority. The Green Paper, *Supporting Families*, began '[F]amilies [are] at the heart of our society and the basis of our future as a country' (Home Office Ministerial Group on the Family 1998: 4). This emphasis on the 'family' was evident not only in policy, but also in cross-departmental planning fora which considered the impact of a number of policy initiatives on the lives of families, such as the review of children's services undertaken by the Treasury in 1998.

Peter Mandelson, as primary spokesperson for the new Labour government, was clear that 'New Labour's mission is to move forward from where Margaret Thatcher left off, rather than dismantle every single thing she did' (cited in Jones and Novak 1999: 178). Thatcher's governments embarked on a programme to dismantle and de-regulate state provision. Although welfare provided by voluntary and commercial organisations alongside state provision has had a long history (Mooney 1997), it was the balance between these sectors, and the role of the state as service provider, the neo-liberals sought to change. However, the administrative burden and cost of welfare provision, despite Thatcher's vow to 'roll back the state', did not decrease under the Conservatives. Increased resources were required to manage the market, and these came directly from savings in actual service provision. The state did not roll back, but merely transferred resources from providing services to managing bureaucracy, as statistics released by the Labour party in opposition revealed:

> Between 1989 and 1994 the number of NHS managers in Scotland alone multiplied by five, while there was a 29 per cent decrease on the number of nurses employed ... This is a pattern reproduced across Britain. (Mooney 1997: 239)

However, New Labour's proposals for welfare reform (DSS 1998) unequivocally accepted the necessity of a market economy, even in welfare:

> Not only is the privatisation of former state industries and services left unchanged, and the encroachment of market forces and values into remaining state provision unchallenged, but these things are actively encouraged. (Jones and Novak 1999: 181)

New Labour's stated intent has been to reduce poverty and social exclusion. In a speech at the launch of the Social Exclusion Unit (SEU), in December 1997, Tony Blair called social exclusion 'a modern problem' (cited in Jones and Novak 1999: 200) and vowed his government would bring about a more inclusive society. Yet, if the mechanics of welfare distribution are to remain the same, can the discursive practices of welfare, including policies, reduce social exclusion for children and their families?

Neo-liberals, 'family' policies and welfare discourse

Neo-liberal policies aimed at encouraging the normalised family and discouraging other family forms were strongly influenced by the theories of the American social scientist, Charles Murray. He laid the blame for the growth of what he called the 'underclass' in the UK (poor families and individuals 'choosing' to live outside social norms and values) on liberal welfare (Jones and Novak 1999). He identified three primary phenomena as threats to the social order: illegitimacy, violent crime and drop-out from the labour market (Scraton 1997). Immediately, the constructs of 'sexuality', 'consumption' and 'work' can be seen to be part of this construction of deviance out of difference in 'family' living.

The supplementary discourse or narrative of 'sexuality' is a strong element in the construction of 'Other than' normalised families. Illegitimacy was identified as the most pernicious of these threats. Unmarried mothers were portrayed as lustful, greedy and idle, having babies to acquire resources such as houses, and escape work by receiving income from social-security benefits. Black lone parents were even more vilified than their white counterparts:

> As in the US, links were made between black lone motherhood and the welfare benefits issue in the British tabloid press. For instance, a *Sunday Express* front page article, headlined 'The Ethnic Timebomb' (13 August 1995) placed the statistics on lone motherhood alongside the welfare bill figures, with an implicit causal relationship between the two. (Song and Edwards 1997: 237-238)

Lone mothers' sexuality was constructed as rapacious and uncontrollable – married mothers, by inference, being more nurturing and less sexual. Lone mothers, unmarried or divorced, were accused of rearing children who would inevitably form part of the underclass, outside 'normal' social values. Lone mothers were also responsible for 'warrior' males (Morgan 1995) who formed part of the underclass because they were not 'civilised' by marriage and fatherhood:

> Murray's thesis is that children become 'responsible parents and neighbours and workers' because they copy the role models in their communities. Given that 'responsible' community is one of 'appropriately' formed nuclear families with functioning parental roles, Murray's identification of dysfunction is as predictable as it is simplistic and crudely reductionist. It begins with an easily recognised

stereotype, the 'lone mother', and quickly shifts to the pathologization of entire communities. (Scraton 1997: 174)

Policy was directed at young and poor women in order to prevent them conceiving and rearing children outside a marital relationship. It was made increasingly difficult to rear children outside the normalised family. For instance, the Child Support Agency, which resulted from the White Paper, *Children Come First* (DoH 1990), was promoted as a way of tackling child poverty and supporting women abandoned by men. However, the Agency was plunged into controversy almost from its inception because of its punitive approach. Apart from the fact that it was administratively chaotic, with prolonged delays and bureaucratic mistakes, the construct of the normalised family was used as a basis for decision-making (see Chapter Seven). Both lone mothers and 'second families' complained of insensitive and inappropriate responses to the different life situations they were now facing. Lone mothers were pressurised to name the father of their child on threat of losing benefit, even when they wished no further contact. 'Separated fathers' complained they were made to feel like criminals, even when they wanted to support their child.

Other narratives of lone motherhood, such as those described by Beatrix Campbell (1984) in *Wigan Pier Revisited*, were not heard in policies aimed at these women and their children. Narratives of women choosing to be on their own with their child because they were responsible and loving, seeking a more stable, and perhaps, less violent and abusive life than they had experienced with their child's father, were silenced. As Campbell points out, these women should have been supported rather than criticised for rearing children in such adverse circumstances. Whilst the state was empowered to withhold financial support from 'Other than' families (if women were suspected of 'cohabiting' for example), there was a marked reluctance to intervene in 'family' inequalities. 'As a result, power within families will lie where it falls' (Farmer and Boushel 1999: 85). Many of the 19 child abuse inquiries, held between 1980 and 1989, highlight not only the reluctance of the state to support women and children against violent men, but also the expectation that vulnerable women should be able to protect their children from such men without support. If unable to do so, mothers were often held as accountable as the perpetrators (DoH 1991a). 'The child protection system is characterised by an over-focus on the regulation of mothers and too little attention to fathers and male partners' (Farmer and Bushel 1999: 91).

Not only were lone mothers constructed as deviant, but poor and troubled children were either victimised or demonised – as has been vividly documented by Pilcher and Wragg (1996) and Scraton (1997). The media debates after the killing of Jamie Bulger in 1993, and the subsequent trial and conviction of his 10-year-old murderers, revealed the degree to which British society polarised children into 'victims' or 'demons'. Much interest centred on the role of 'video nasties' and the sexual behaviour of the children's mothers during the trial. On the one hand, children raised in normalised families were expected to be non-aggressive, high achievers, without sexual identity, and who related well to their parents and observed all social mores; on the other hand, children raised in 'Other than' families were scrutinised for signs of 'Other than' humanity:

> We seem to be speeding ever faster to a nightmarish world where children rarely go to school, roam the streets 'til midnight, know how to roll a joint, gloat over sick videos and think fun is tying a firework to the tail of a cat and setting it alight … We have a world where children are growing up virtually as savages. (Lynda Lee Potter, *Daily Mail,* 26 November 1995: 22)

If children from 'Other than' families were not demons then they were victims, not of poverty and its effects, but of some form of child abuse – particularly sexual. Hudson (1994) points to the similarities between the Victorian preoccupation with 'incest' and the lower classes, and the growth of the child protection industry in the 1980s, which was predominantly concerned with sexual issues. Both were manifestations of pathologising a range of behaviours as 'sexual' rather than considering how constructs of masculinity and childhood interacted to disempower children. For example, children were sometimes held wholly or partially responsible for inciting sexually-abusive behaviour against them by adults, usually men. Moreover, sexual activity between youthful peers was often categorised as abusive, even when coercion was not present. On the one hand, children were regarded as asexual beings, to be kept uninformed and unaware of sexuality issues; on the other hand, the child image in advertising was often sexualised and the sexual exploitation of poor children tacitly condoned (Corteen and Scraton 1997). Child protection legislation, policy, social work practice and resource allocation became increasingly focused on identifying and assessing child sexual abuse, and the more extreme manifestations of physical abuse. The majority of children and their carers referred to the personal social services, however, received little attention and few resources from state welfare, perhaps because the adverse consequences for children's well-being were caused by poverty and not parental action (DoH 1995).

Disabled children and young people have also been affected by the supplementary discourse of sexuality. This has occurred in a number of ways. First, disabled children and young people were not commonly recognised by child protection systems as being vulnerable to sexual abuse and exploitation. Second, few child protection workers had the skills necessary to communicate with children with language and sensory impairments. Consequently, these children's voices went unheard, with appalling consequences for some in out-of-family care (Kennedy 1995). Last, disabled young people were also denied sexual identity because their opportunities to form couple relationships were restricted. Their lack of access to social activities, peer groups, adequate sexual-health information and assistance, and the fact that many were 'warehoused' in residential accommodation segregated by gender, did not give them the opportunity to share the same lifestyle as other young people (Morris 1999).

'Other than' 'normal' sexuality was pronounced a threat to the normalised family in a number of ways, and policy sought to isolate and pathologise sexual difference. The AIDS epidemic was firmly linked to gay men (indeed, it was initially identified as the Gay-Related Immune Deficiency or GRID) and, as such, received little attention from the government. It was not until 1985, four years after the first reported case, that Department of Health (DoH) funds were made available for treatment (Wilson 1997):

> Undoubtedly, if AIDS had initially affected a different social group to gay men then the situation would have been different. As long as the disease was confined to gay men the British Government did very little. (Richardson, cited in Cooper 1987: 12)

Health advice and information was only belatedly aimed at those involved in heterosexual activity, leaving many women and their unborn children at risk of infection.

When television advertising was finally undertaken, images of cliffs crumbling into the sea and pneumatic drills chiselling gravestones were chosen, implying catastrophic retribution for immorality, lack of self-control and 'abnormal' behaviour. As the *Daily Express* argued:

AIDS is not a threat to *normal* men and women who do not have sexual relations with drug users, homosexuals and bisexuals. For officialdom to suggest otherwise is to promote needless general anxiety, and even panic. Worse, it is to remove attention from the actual focus of the problem. And by doing so to lessen the claims of moderating the behaviour and practices of those most at risk. (*Daily Express*, 11 August 1987, cited in Cooper 1987: 14 – our emphasis)

The same constructs of sexuality fuelled the right-wing lobby to remove sex education from schools. The Education Act 1986 removed the power from local authorities for curriculum decisions in this area and placed it with school governors, giving them the authority to allow schools to abandon teaching and advice on this issue. At the very time when the consequences of unprotected sex were potentially lethal, and when there was an increase in pregnancies among very young girls, young people were denied the knowledge they needed to make informed choices. Notwithstanding the eventual resolution of the Gillick hearing in 1986, upholding the right of 16-year-olds to contraceptive information and treatment, Department of Education and Science (DES) advice to teachers on this matter was ambiguous. This led to a form of self-censorship by teachers choosing to remain silent on matters of sexuality and sexual identity (Corteen and Scraton 1997).

The fear of 'Other than' sexuality reached its height with Section 28 of the Local Government Act 1988, Part 1 (b), which states that local authorities must not 'Promote the teaching in any maintained school of the acceptability of homosexuality as a pretended "family" relationship'. These constructs impacted on 'Other than' families in a number of ways. Guidance to the Children Act 1989, issued by the DoH, warned local authorities against equal-opportunities policies that implied gay or lesbian couples had a 'right' to be considered as foster-carers or adopters. They advised that children would be disadvantaged growing up in an 'abnormal' 'family'. Pressure to equalise the age of consent for 'homosexual' and 'heterosexual' sex (criminal under the age of 21 for gay man as compared to 16 for 'heterosexual' men and women) resulted in the Criminal Justice and Public Order Act 1994. Fierce opposition meant that only the decriminalisation of homosexual activity in private, for those men aged 18 or over, was secured. Older gay and lesbian couples also suffered because their unions were not recognised by law. Surviving partners could not be regarded as next of kin following the death of their loved one, and so were denied access to such things as pensions and property. Non-UK partners were not eligible, under immigration law, to live permanently in the UK (Wilson 1997).

The divorce law was eventually changed, after prolonged debate, in response to two main issues, both reflecting the construct of the normalised family. It was argued that fathers had a right to equal participation in parenting and, furthermore, that children's well-being was impaired without their father's involvement. Whilst both perspectives may represent a 'truth', they are clearly not 'true' in all circumstances, for all children. Nevertheless, these truths were manifested in statute when the Family Law Act 1996 was implemented. The process of divorce became more protracted and intrusive, with the emphasis on 'thinking time' and mediation:

> Making this process more public is not necessarily problematic in itself, but the political context in which this trend takes place will determine the meaning of the process. Unfortunately, this political context is the one in which those who divorce are increasingly defined as defective. (Smart and Neale 1997: 24)

Couple relationships are changing throughout postmodern and late capitalist societies, and so it could be argued that policies need to take account of this by focusing on how people are actually living together to rear children, rather than enforcing a mythical model of normalised family life which is, as evidence suggests, doomed to fail (Smart 1997). Even though forms of 'family' structure in the UK continue to change, those constructed as 'Other than' the normalised family, in the dominant welfare discourse, remain marginalised and excluded.

The supplementary narrative of 'consumption' is vividly evident in the neo-liberal concern with crime, another issue identified as a social problem springing from the failure of the 'family'. The 1980s was a decade of increasing polarity between the rich and the poor. 'From Margaret Thatcher's arrival in power to her departure, the average income rose by 36 per cent but the bottom tenth fell by 14 per cent and that of the top tenth rose by 64 per cent' (Barry Hugill, *The Observer*, 13 April 1997: 29). The emphasis on conspicuous consumption pervaded society throughout this period as advertising and marketing became more aggressive and sophisticated. Yet, as Novak (1997) points out, only the desire and effectiveness of the poor to acquire money and goods was constituted as 'criminal':

> The crimes of the rich receive very different attention, although both in scale and in terms of cost to the community corporate fraud and other crimes committed by the economically and politically powerful far outweigh the activities of petty burglars or those who cheat the social security system. (Novak 1999: 224)

Jack and Jordan argue that activities constructed as deviant, such as prostitution, drug-dealing, begging, and so on, are in fact rational responses to economic opportunities and constraints in poor communities. 'Expenditure statistics suggest that the shadow economy has to some extent protected the poor in Britain from the decline in their official income' (Jack and Jordan 1999: 200).

Children were also commodified. Although the decade of the 1980s and the early 1990s was characterised by increasing hostility to, and fear of, children constructed as 'criminal', the legal framework established under the Conservatives supported diversions from custody programmes (Goldson 1997). This apparent incompatibility with the neo-liberal 'tough on crime' agenda made perfect sense financially as community-based programmes were very much cheaper than custodial ones. Closing approved schools and other residential provision did not increase the overall crime rate, particularly when police and magistrates were persuaded to change their charging and sentencing practices. Local authorities' revenue expenditure became lower, and some were able to raise capital by the sale of large buildings and extensive acreage. Children in trouble could be managed more cheaply in the community than in custody. By 1993, however, legislation had caught up with rhetoric:

> Rapidly drafted legislation during 1993 [Criminal Justice Act 1993] shot great holes in the Criminal Justice Act 1991, which was shortly followed by the Criminal Justice and Public Order Act 1994. Where the 1991 Act had removed 14-year-olds from the prison system, the 1994 Act seeks to create a new generation of child prisons for 12-14 year-olds. This is not a return to the 1970s but to the period preceding the Children Act 1908. (Rutherford, cited in Goldson 1997: 131)

Despite the Children Act 1989, and the UK's adoption of the UN Convention on the Rights of the Child in 1990, children became increasingly constructed as the possessions of their parents. The Convention was not ratified until 1991, with the UK entering the maximum number of exemptions relating to child employment, child prisons and immigration. The Conservatives also pushed through a number of specific policies extending the dependency of children and young people on their parents. For example, benefits to unemployed 16- to 25-year-olds ceased, or were reduced on the assumption that young people would live with or be supported by their families. Additionally, parents were increasingly held financially liable for the criminal actions of their children, a measure aimed at 'motivating' parents to supervise their children more closely.

The introduction of markets in health and social care, brought about by the NHS and Community Care Act 1990, explicitly brought 'consumerism' into welfare. Much has been written about care-in-the-community and its dependency on the unpaid labour of women (Williams 1995, 1996). The Griffiths Report of 1988, *Community Care: Agenda for Action* (Griffiths 1988), on which the White Paper, *Caring for People* (DoH 1989) and the subsequent Act were based, was originally greeted with professional and, to some extent, cross-party enthusiasm. This was because of the emphasis on 'de-institutionalisation', greater flexibility of services and increased personal choice in welfare. These laudable liberal aims, however, were forged in the context of a welfare discourse that placed an economic value on the welfare subject (by now constructed as welfare 'consumer', 'customer' or 'service-user'). This aimed to enable the unfettered operation of the market so as to bring about economy, efficiency and effectiveness in welfare provision. Welfare markets have, of course, been shown to be at best 'quasi' markets (Le Grand and Bartlett 1993), with the service-user having little power as purchaser (apart from a few exceptions such as the Community Care [Direct Payments] Act 1996 – Petrie and Wilson 1999). However, the language of consumption, care manager, budget holder, mixed economy of care, and so on, entered, and has remained within, the discourse of welfare.

This discourse also implied that the normalised family would be able to care for its own members. Only families with some pathologised incapacity were constructed as needing to rely on state support. Yet, as has been amply demonstrated by many commentators, 'family' care is in reality unpaid care by women, sometimes in addition to child-rearing, domestic work within the home and employment outside the home:

> The community-care legislation in particular involved the largely hidden transfer of care responsibility from the public realm to the private sphere of the family, redrawing in the process the boundaries between the two. Community caring thus was to be resourced largely by women's unpaid domestic labour, consequently

entrapping many women even further and reinforcing their economic dependency on men. (Mooney 1997: 243)

Even though the Children Act 1989 did not explicitly bring welfare markets into children's services, as was imposed in social care by the NHS and Community Care Act 1990, these two Acts were designed to be 'consistent and complementary' (cited in Petrie and Wilson 1999: 185). The Children Act 1989 also had wide professional and cross-party support, and a long gestation period of nearly ten years. In the latter stages of its passage through parliament, however, it was influenced by the prevailing political climate and the then current child abuse controversies, such as the Cleveland Inquiry (Petrie and James 1995). The Act attempted to redress the balance between child protection and family support by defining the concept of 'need' in binary terms. A legal duty to support 'children in need' and their families in the community was imposed on local authorities. In reality, because no central government money for services was forthcoming (unlike the funding linked to the implementation of the NHS and Community Care Act 1990), little was available for families other than those whose children were believed to be at risk of abuse. Following the implementation of the Act, many local authorities restructured all personal social services into purchaser and provider arms (Petrie 1995), creating, in effect, internal markets. In some personal social services departments, for example, child protection workers were defined as purchasers, and foster-carers as providers, with few apparent benefits and a great deal of additional administration (Petrie and Wilson 1999).

There was an inexorable growth in private-sector provision too, particularly in specialist areas such as day-care, fostering and residential care, yet the contracting process, fraught with difficulty within services for adults, was barely recognised (Petrie and Wilson 1999). The impact of consumerising children's services, initially hardly noticed by many professionals, began to cause concern (Novak et al. 1997). Research revealed that a market approach was even more problematic in welfare services for children than for adults. First, it is more difficult to identify the consumer – is this the child, their carers or the local authority purchasing services on their behalf? Children are even more disempowered than vulnerable adults, despite the rhetoric of consultation and involvement laid down in statute. Second, many statutory services for children and their families, particularly those arising from the operation of child protection systems, are imposed and not sought (or even wanted) by the consumer.

Services they want, such as full-time, good quality, free day-care, are rarely available (Petrie and Wilson 1999). Last, the operation of the market rests on the idea of change. Consumers make choices which force poor providers out of the market and bring new providers into the market to meet unmet need. There is little evidence that poor provision fell by the wayside or that new providers filled the gaps in services (Craig et al. 1999). On the other hand, there is evidence to show that 'short-termism' became a common feature in the allocation of services to children and their families, denying children the very qualities of care they need for optimal development – quality, consistency and continuity (Novak et al. 1997). The concept of need enshrined in the Act meant that allocating scarce resources to those most in need, and reviewing the allocation regularly to ensure recipients were still in priority need, did not take account of the many ways of being and needing in postmodernity. The application of these constructs, however, had the effect of removing services that families found helpful as soon as they experienced their benefits:

> They'll only pay [for children's day-care] in an emergency and as soon as they think the family are climbing up the ladder a little bit they stop the child coming. (Novak et al. 1997: 14)

'Work' as a measure of worth is evident in the constructed pathologies of families under the neo-liberals. Normalised families are those whose fathers are in paid employment and support their wives and children. Only those families constructed as 'Other than' 'normal', therefore, cannot be self-supporting. The neo-liberals came to power, however, at a time of economic recession:

> In economic terms, the slump of the 1970s, and especially of the first half of the 1980s, international in scale and devastation, was the inevitable outcome of almost three decades of unprecedented economic growth within the advanced capitalist societies. (Jones and Novak 1999: 38)

During the first two years of Thatcher's first government unemployment, already at a post-war record high of 1.3m, rose to nearly 3m by 1982. Job losses occurred mainly in male employment, in heavy industries in the Midlands, North, Scotland and Wales (Jones and Novak 1999). The pattern of employment changed from permanent male employment to increasing numbers of part-time, short-term, low-paid jobs held by women, with consequences for household income and lifestyle. There was an increase in what became known as 'work-rich' and 'work-poor' households – that is, households where either both parents worked, impacting on child-rearing because of the need for (and lack of) out-of-family care (Craig et al. 1999), or households where neither parent worked, with an impact on family income (Howarth et al. 1998). As the state retreated from sharing responsibility with parents for children and young people, parents in work found it harder to spend time with their children, and parents without work found it harder to provide for them. Additionally, the burden of domestic work and childcare still fell most heavily on the shoulders of women, whether they were in paid employment or not (Summerfield 1998).

The neo-liberals were clear about the cause of poverty. In 1992, Peter Lilley, then Secretary of State for Social Security, pronounced 'Poverty is a result of people's idleness. Some people do not want work, they are simply scroungers' (*The Guardian,* 16 October 1992: 12). Income maintenance policies were gradually reduced in scope and amount. 'By making benefits paid to claimants more conditional, the government has tried to drive them into low-paid work or training' (Jordan 1996: 209). The change in state benefit terminology, at this time, reflected the supplementary discourse of 'work' as a signifier of moral worth which has constructed and deconstructed the welfare subject over time (Bauman 1998). For example, unemployment benefit was not only effectively cut under the Conservatives, no longer pegged to wages and living standards but to prices, but was also renamed the Jobseeker's Allowance, implying there were jobs available if only the welfare subject would seek them out. In general, there was a move away from universal benefits, one of the planks of the welfare state designed to reduce stigma and redistribute wealth, to selectivism, designed to target those who 'really' needed help. Universal benefits have been critiqued on the grounds they failed to deliver equity to women and racial minorities, but the move to selectivism worsened the economic situation for many children and their carers in the context of rising unemployment and changing labour-market patterns. As the Commission on Social Justice noted in 1994, 'means-tested benefits, which cannot prevent poverty, are also remarkably inefficient at relieving it' (cited in Pratt 1997: 204).

Older people became similarly excluded from work, acquiring both a personal invisibility and a public image of being a social and economic burden. Much of the welfare debate focused on the demands of an increasingly ageing population solely in epidemiological terms:

The number of people aged 65 and over is projected to rise from 8.4 million in 1985 to 9.0 million by 2001 ... Growth will be greatest among the very elderly who are also most likely to be disabled and in greater need of community care. (DoH 1989: 62)

Unlike the transition from childhood to adulthood, which is indistinct, the transition to becoming an elder is often dramatic and linked to exclusion from work (Hirsch 1999). During the neo-liberal governments, rising unemployment affected older workers as dramatically as it affected young people trying to enter the job market, creating competition between old and young for the right to work. Length of career shortened with the result that senior managerial positions were held by younger and younger people. The pattern of 'jobs for life' with promotion being linked to seniority and younger people learning from older workers also changed, not only in new industries but in traditional industries too. Within the workplace the age range reduced, with people in early adulthood and middle years being seen to be more productive and valuable to society as a whole than the young or the old.

Many elderly people lived alone while increasing numbers entered residential care, not only costly in resource terms but often institutionalising and damaging – an issue the NHS and Community Care Act 1990 purported to tackle. It is mainly racial minority groups, particularly Pakistani and Bangladeshi people, who retain multi-generational family units (Beishon et al. 1998) and whose voluntary welfare organisations continue to offer holistic services rather than services targeted on particular ages and needs (Butt and Box 1998). One consequence for these groups and communities trying to include elders in mainstream life has been the loss of income resulting from the switch from state grant aid to contracts. Contracts focus on specific services for target groups, those designated as being in priority need, and so inclusive services do not fit neatly within the contractual paradigm (Wenham 1993). The voices of older people were silenced in the public and private sphere, with two damaging consequences. First, the experience, skills and knowledge of several generations was discarded to our overall detriment. Second, those constructed as elders not only experienced social exclusion but were also constructed as a social burden, with the inevitable physical and psychological consequences this brings.

Disabled lives are also profoundly affected by the construct of 'work'. Carers work was not given the value of waged work. In 1998, for example, it was estimated that benefits for severely disabled children would need to be increased by between 20 and 50 per cent to meet minimum essential costs. Furthermore, most families were unable to increase their income through paid employment because of the demands of caring as well as the lack of suitable childcare (Dobson and Middleton 1998). The transition from childhood to adulthood for disabled people was also difficult. Young people found it almost impossible to access employment because of poor education, lack of health and support services, and disincentives to paid employment created by means testing of personal assistance (Morris 1999).

Despite the absence of an overarching policy or government department for families, neo-liberal discursive welfare practices profoundly affected the lives of many children and their carers.

The impact of neo-liberal 'family' policies

The lives of significant numbers of families in the UK were affected in destructive and damaging ways by neo-liberal policies, leading to levels of wealth inequality unprecedented since the great depression of the 1930s. The gap between the rich and the poor widened more quickly and more dramatically than in any other European country during the second half of the 1980s, when monetarist policies and de-regulation had begun to make a noticeable impact on the economy. Poverty as a whole increased, with children more likely than adults to live in poverty, and by 1992, more than 11m households were living on incomes below half-average, compared to 4m in 1982 (Howarth et al. 1998). In 1968, just 10 per cent of children lived in households with below half-average income, but by 1995-96 a third of the total child population (over 4.3m children) were doing so. The rise in child poverty has been associated with the rise in unemployment and between 1968 and 1996 the proportion of children with no working parent rose from 2 to 10 per cent in two-parent families, and from 30 to 58 per cent in lone-parent families (Greg et al. 1999). Since 1981 there has been a net loss of 500 000 jobs in the 20 biggest cities, particularly those in Scotland and the North-West (Turok and Edge 1999).

In 1991, 1453 households a week were experiencing mortgage repossessions, and between 1990 and 1998 a total of 454 280 households, containing 1.3m adults and children, had their homes repossessed with most moving into some form of temporary accommodation. Mortgage repossession was often the start of long-term poverty, especially for women and their dependent children (Nettleton et al. 1999). 'Step-families', a generic term covering a diversity of family arrangements, tended to have greater polarisation into 'work-rich' and 'work-poor' households than 'first families', and their children were more likely to have neither parent in employment (9 per cent compared to 4 per cent for first-family children) (Ferri and Smith 1998). In 1995, a study showed that children who had part-time employment, and were from families dependent on state benefit or lone-parent households, worked for longer hours and less pay than other children. Moreover, children in such households had learned to accept that they might not get what they wanted for their birthday, and to cover up their sense of disappointment (Shropshire and Middleton 1999).

The 19 child-abuse inquiries held in the decade 1980 to 1989 (DoH 1991a) drove welfare professional practice towards focusing on the inadequacies of parental care, with little regard for economic or environmental factors. The cost of child protection processes, in any case, often left local authorities with few resources to support children and their families in the community. The DoH's (1991b) own research review drew attention to the contradiction that, whilst social workers believed that they were removing children from their families to protect them from abuse, evidence suggested that poverty, ethnicity and family structure were closely correlated with decisions to remove. Large numbers of children were taken into state care in the 1980s, which was not only costly but proved to be damaging to many of these children, both as a result of abuse within institutions, and poor care and lack of continuity (DoH 1991c).

Britain's human rights record, as judged by international courts, has been appalling, particularly in relation to children. In January 1995, the UN reported violations of children's rights in the UK – 39 out of 43 paragraphs in the report were critical of Britain's performance. In particular, the report called for the abandonment of plans for secure training centres for 12- to 14-year-olds, an end to sanctioned parental violence in the home ('reasonable chastisement' being permitted by British law) and the raising of the age of criminal responsibility from ten years (Goldson 1997):

> Britain locks up more children in its prisons than any other country in Europe bar one ... The conditions to which children are condemned are inhumane, brutalising and abusive. Not only is the physical infrastructure strained and totally unsuited to guaranteeing basic standards of safety and welfare but everyday operational realities are underpinned by a culture of bullying, intimidation and routine self-harm ... It is not surprising that many children and young people detained in prison custody experience significant difficulties, struggling to cope

with their sense and experience of permanent fear and risk. The incidence of self-harm and suicide comprises the most striking reminder of the conditions to which children are exposed and directly connects with bullying and intimidation ... There were record levels of suicide and self-harm in youth custody during 1994. (Goldson 1997: 135)

The overall result of neo-liberal policies has been an increase in what has become known as the 'socially excluded', those whose participation in their own society is not wanted or facilitated. Their absence from the mainstream is not seen as a loss of richness, but rather their anticipated arrival is viewed with fear and apprehension. Whilst discursive practices arising from the dominant discourse of welfare did not cause the growth of poverty in the UK, it can be argued that they did not ameliorate the consequences for children and their families. On the contrary, the neo-liberal preoccupation with constructing difference as abnormality, and attempting to enforce a particular 'family' form as desirable, has had savage consequences for many.

New Labour, 'family' policies and welfare discourse

New Labour came to power with the stated aim of reducing child poverty and social exclusion, apparently an ideological return to some level of state responsibility for the well-being of citizens. However, for New Labour, like the neo-liberals, social exclusion is a manifestation of individual pathology and welfare dependency:

> Poverty is not really the problem. Rather, it is those 'who have lost hope, trapped in fatalism. They are today's and tomorrow's underclass, shut out from society'. (Peter Mandelson, cited in Jones and Novak 1999: 200)

As the election drew near Peter Mandelson, Labour spokesperson, made a distinction between 'deserving' and 'undeserving' families:

> New Labour stands for the ordinary families who work hard and play by the rules. ... New Labour's enemies include the irresponsible who fall down on their obligations to their families and therefore their community. (Barry Hugill, *The Observer*, 13 April 1997: 29)

Frank Field, as Minister for Welfare Reform, emphasised the distinction between 'work for those who can, security for those who cannot,' and also referred to those considered undeserving of welfare:

> I think there are real difficulties in improving benefit levels until our welfare to work strategy begins to work and we have much more ruthlessly rooted out fraud. (Frank Field, cited in Timmins 1998: 11)

New Labour's emerging policies aimed at, or impacting on, families will be examined in three main areas: policies aimed at bringing parents back into the labour market, including child care for young children as a way of reducing poverty (for instance, New Deal for Lone Parents and Sure Start); policies to do with the concept of need within families (such as Quality Protects); and policies aimed at youth offending. It will be argued that New Labour inhabits the same discourse of welfare as the neo-liberals, and that the supplementary discourses of 'work', 'consumption' and 'sexuality' construct 'Other than' normalised families in the same way.

'Families', 'work' and child care

New Deal is a typical example of how New Labour turn a correlation into a causality, producing programmes aimed at individuals derived from macro-level patterns and outcomes:

> Many preventive interventions seek to apply to individuals an understanding of cause and effect which can only be established at the level of the group ... In statistical terms, for example, poverty is associated with ill-health. But the relationship may or may not be valid for any specific individual; these are quite literally, general relationships, and even they are difficult to determine. (Freeman 1999: 235)

There is extensive evidence to show a correlation between the rise in unemployment and the growth of poverty during the neo-liberal terms of office (Jack and Jordan 1999). It does not follow, however, that the way to eradicate poverty is to force everyone into paid 'work'.

Influenced by workfare programmes in the US, particularly the Wisconsin approach, New Labour have established Welfare to Work as part of the New Deal. One of the target groups are lone parents through New Deal for Lone Parents. The rhetoric is softer and, as yet, compulsion is not part of the package, but New Labour's approach is remarkably similar to workfare in the US. In particular, 'Other than' families are perceived as needing a 'push' to ensure they do not become a drain on society and their children do not grow up to be 'welfare dependent'. The sub-text is a warning message conveyed to all:

> This message is of course not meant only, or perhaps even primarily, for those dependent on welfare ... Whether the purpose is to persuade the working poor to accept their lot or to construct particular forms of sexual and social morality, what happens to those who are dependent on the welfare system reverberates across the whole working population. (Jones and Novak 1999: 194)

There is little evidence from the US that workfare reduces poverty. It certainly reduced the numbers claiming benefit in Wisconsin where, between 1994 and 1997, the number of claimants fell from 14m to 10.5m, yet no one knows where these claimants went or how they live (Jones and Novak 1999).

There is a great deal of evidence to show that lone parents are no different from most parents as far as the well-being of their child is concerned. Whilst they want a decent income, they attach much more importance to the care their child receives whilst they are at work, and this is a major factor mothers consider before they enter the labour market (Craig et al. 1999). Ensuring adequate out-of-home care is what is expected from parents within the UK and European legislation. Indeed, as will be outlined later when New Labour's youth justice reforms are examined, parents can now be criminalised if their young children (below the age of criminal responsibility – still set at ten years) engage in behaviour deemed criminal. Lone parents are, therefore, caught in a double-bind, held accountable for their own impoverishment and the rearing of children destined to form the underclass if they do not work, yet potentially criminalised if their children are not sufficiently supervised whilst their parent works. Whilst affluent parents can choose whether or not to place their child in day-care, and have choice of day-care provision if they want to work, the choices of poor lone parents involved in welfare-to-work programmes are very limited.

New Labour recognised that childcare provision must go hand-in-hand with welfare-to-work programmes and established a number of Early Years initiatives. Shortly after coming to power, they attempted to bring some coherence into policy planning, particularly where policies might affect 'family' life, by establishing cross-departmental planning fora. This is an example of New Labour's commitment to 'joined-up thinking'. The Comprehensive Spending review that took place between 1997 and 1998 was charged with identifying the pattern and level of government spending, and recommending reforms in line with government priorities. Although most of the review was undertaken by individual departments, there were a number of 'cross-cutting' surveys, in particular that of children's services, led by the Treasury. This survey led to the Sure Start initiative (day-care and parental support for young children and their families), with £540m funding for 250 local programmes, made available until the end of this government's term of office in 2002.

Early Years services, particularly full-time day-care for young children, have been fragmented and piecemeal since the end of the Second World War. Women, constructed primarily as wives and mothers pre-1939, were reconstructed during the war as workers to replace men conscripted into the army. As part of the drive to bring women into the labour market, free and full-time day-care was made available for any mother wishing to work. A network of state nurseries, open from early morning until late evening, often providing transport for children to and from home, was established (Owen and Petrie 1997). Whilst with our current understanding of children's well-being such long hours may not seem to offer a child-centred regime, nevertheless 'good enough', and even exemplary, care for many children was provided while their mothers worked. Almost as soon as the War was over these facilities were closed as women were expected to return to their homes. In fact, many women remained in the labour market, but the level and quality of childcare provision was no longer available. Consequently, out-of-family day-care for young children has been problematic since the war years. Insufficient places, unevenly distributed and of variable quality, have been provided mainly by the independent sector. Furthermore, what has been available has had to be paid for by parents themselves, with only periodic low-level financial support for certain categories such as lone parents (Owen and Petrie 1997). The reconstruction of women as workers under New Labour is very different from that of the war years. Women were publicly honoured then for doing 'men's work' and rearing children, activities that were seen to benefit the wider 'community'. Now, women are being given a chance to 'redeem' themselves so that neither their child, nor themselves, continue to burden society. The government leaflet (LP 15 [version 3/99] September 99), urging women to consider New Deal for Lone Parents, lists many benefits. All are aimed at the mother, none refer to the well-being of children. None recognise the lone parent's contribution as a carer of children, nor as potentially carrying out two jobs (one at home, and one in the labour market).

A number of Early Years' duties and requirements have been placed upon local authorities. These are designed to increase accessible childcare by making a part-time place available for all 3- and 4-year-olds, and to improve the life chances of disadvantaged children. These duties include the establishment of Early Years Development and Childcare Partnerships and Childcare Audits, as well as Early Years Childcare and Development Plans based on these. There are also the Early Excellence Initiatives and Sure Start programmes. Most of these initiatives are expected to involve 'partnerships' between different local authority departments, the voluntary and independent sectors, and even parents. Other policies and programmes, such as the Working Families Tax Credit and Child Care Tax Credit, Working Time Directive, parental leave provision, the National Family and Parenting Institute, Youth Offending Teams, and so on, are meant to support these developments. These initiatives are also meant to be congruent with area-based initiatives such as Education Action Zones, Health Action Zones and New Deal for Communities. 'As an example of the "joined-upness" between these initiatives, all New Deal for Community pathfinder districts are Sure Start trailblazer districts as well' (Glass 1999: 258). The numbers of initiatives have certainly increased the administration, bureaucracy and confusion at local level without necessarily making it easier to improve childcare for children. Parents report great difficulty in finding appropriate day-care and usually have to establish a network of arrangements, partly paid for and partly informal (Craig et al. 1999).

Although most activities involve 'partnerships', there is no agreement as to the level of power-sharing in welfare 'partnerships' (Petrie and James 1995), and the level of power transfer rarely involves major decisions about resource allocation. Anyone attending 'partnership' meetings will note that the same individuals and agencies circulate from one meeting to another. Rather than widening the network to include 'Other than' normalised family members, or community members, the workloads of a few, particularly local authority managers, have simply been increased. Indeed, the level of cross-initiative planning required means that the same people have to be involved, or the administrative tasks associated with such an instrumental and positivist approach would not be accomplished. Furthermore, all of these initiatives remain firmly within a dominant discourse of welfare that constructs 'Other than' normalised families as undesirable. Welfare services and fiscal policies are developed within constructs of 'work', 'consumption', 'sexuality' and 'family' that combine to marginalise many women and their children. Evidence suggests, for example, that money paid directly to mothers is more likely to be used to meet the needs of children than money paid to a working father. For working parents, the minimum wage and Working Families Tax Credit (received in the main by fathers) replace Family Credit, which was usually paid to mothers. The amount available for children is, therefore, likely to be reduced because of New Labour's failure to recognise the impact of gendered fiscal policies (Goode et al. 1998).

'Other than' families are subject to a plethora of activities designed to turn them into normalised parents and children. They are constructed as needing interventions to change their lifestyle, such as outreach services and home visiting. An example of this is Sure Start, a scheme that 'is consciously intended to achieve long-term results such as better educational performance, lower unemployment, less criminality and reduced levels of teenage pregnancy' (Glass 1999: 258). Sure Start is based on the High/Scope programme in the US, one of the few 'edu-care' programmes for young children that has been subject to longitudinal research – covering 27 years by 1993 (Schweinhart et al. 1993). To date, this research shows that, for every $1 spent per child, $7 was saved by the taxpayer during the lifetime of the individual (due to such factors as lower rates of crime and higher average earnings). Whilst the research findings might be debatable, there is no doubt that the children involved experienced high quality pre-school education. New Labour's claim, however, to have initiated a similar scheme for young children in the UK is fallacious. Instead, what has been set in place is a programme designed to integrate existing welfare services aimed at families, rather than an intensive model of childcare like High/Scope. Despite this, New Labour are expecting the same results.

Given the emphasis that New Labour are placing on identifying those families needing early interventions to ensure that society, as a whole, does not pay the price later, it is necessary to examine how 'need' is constructed within the dominant discourse of welfare.

'Families' and children in 'need', or not in 'need'

'Need' has acquired a particular meaning since its incorporation into legislation and was conceived in housing legislation in 1949, when local authorities were encouraged to plan their programmes 'to meet the varied needs of the community' (cited in Macey and Baker 1973: 22). The NHS and Community Care Act 1990, and the Children Act 1989, both rest on the assessment of individual need as a passport to services. 'Needing' does not rest on what someone wants (such as more money or decent living conditions) or what may be beneficial but is determined by the state. Need as defined within the Acts is both specific and excluding. Although the definition in the Children Act 1989 (Sec 17 (1)) could apply to almost any child, it is linked to the assessment of individual parental failing rather than structural or environmental issues such as poverty. The difficulty for personal social services has always been how to separate poor consequences for children that are due to environmental factors such as poverty – for which, apparently, neither the state nor parents are to be considered culpable – from those due to parental action or inaction. Many homeless families, for example, live for long periods in appalling bed and breakfast accommodation which is highly unsuitable for children. Even though there is substantial evidence to show that the well-being of women and children in these circumstances is being undermined (Miller 1991), the state only provides the minimum it is required to do – temporary accommodation, with 'temporary' being left open-ended.

As has been shown in Chapter Three, needs arising from sexual or social behaviour constructed as 'abnormal' may not be recognised or met, either wholly or partly for fear that the social fabric of society will be undermined by the apparent approval this gives to 'abnormal' behaviour. In fact, the act of identifying those 'in need' simultaneously identifies those 'not in need' – an act of rationing as much as it is an act of giving; an act of exclusion as well as an act of legitimisation. It has been shown that during the period 1979 to 1997, welfare discursive practices and policies moved towards greater selectivism and away from universalism, towards assessing those in 'priority need' and away from services and benefits as of 'right'. New Labour remain firmly within the same discourse of welfare, and their discursive practices not only maintain these perspectives but develop them further. Neo-liberal condemnation of the poor as architects of their own downfall was crude and extreme:

'I think we'll have to go back to soup kitchens', she told him and paused. Then noting his reaction, she continued, 'Take that silly smile off your face I mean it'. (Margaret Thatcher to Patrick Jenkin, Secretary of State for Social Services, April 1979, cited in Jones and Novak 1999: 139)

New Labour are more 'modern' in the sense that they are firmly within the positivist tradition, believing that the application of 'true' knowledge to social problems will solve them. In some areas, they are also more brutal. New Labour are prepared to carry out what the neo-liberals talked of doing, but lacked the conviction or means to bring about:

> What distinguishes new Labour and its third way from the new right is principally their use of the state. For the new right state intervention was [an] anathema: at best dispensed with altogether, at most confined to the maintenance of the infrastructure of the economy, trade, law and order and security. Faced with growing poverty and social stress, all it could do was withdraw into an increasingly coercive role. The third way allows for a more interventionist state, taking on the authoritarian legacy of its predecessors, but adding to this the greater range of powers the state possesses to achieve its ends. (Jones and Novak 1999: 178)

This trend can be uncovered quite easily when welfare processes aimed at the most pathologised families are examined. For example, social workers are one of the main determiners of those in need of welfare. Although social workers have always been agents of social control and rationers of state resources to some degree, they have had their room to manoeuvre, on behalf of their clients, severely reduced as the welfare state has given way to the welfare market:

> The welfare state ... [drew] together these two modes – bureaucracy and professionalism – in combinations as 'bureau-professional regimes'. Such regimes involve different 'balances of power' between the bureaucratic and professional elements in particular settings (compare medicine and social work, for example) but the concept provides a general key to the organisational architecture of the welfare state in Britain ... This complex of bureaucratic, professional and political power was identified by the new right in the 1970s as a major stumbling block to a radical reconstruction of the state ... [and] underpins the intensity of the attacks on all three modes of power represented by the welfare state. 'Arrogant' professionals were arraigned alongside 'inflexible' bureaucrats and 'interfering' politicians. (Clarke and Newman 1993: 50)

New Labour also support a market approach in welfare and view welfare professionals with suspicion. The role and duties of social workers have become increasingly prescribed in statute and government guidance, leaving less opportunity for individual professional judgement. However dangerous 'professionalism' was to the vulnerable and disempowered, monolithic and prescriptive courses of action are even more so. These are now usually monitored by detailed checklists. The Looked After Children (LAC) forms, for example, contain a minimum of 38 pages to be completed within five days of a child coming into care. Siblings also coming into care are not uncommon and one worker will have to complete 38 pages for each child. Whilst the LAC forms identify issues that are pertinent and important, these requirements smack of the 'Emperor's New Clothes' when staff shortages and the reduction of resources to personal social services are considered (Powell 1999), particularly in the context of the appalling child poverty outlined earlier.

The projected demise of the Central Council for Education and Training in Social Work (CCETSW), the professional regulating body for social work qualifications, is also significant. Its responsibilities will be allocated to a number of new bodies, including the Training Organisation for Personal Social Services (TOPSS). One significant consequence of this change is the increasing emphasis on competency-based assessment of student social workers. Effectively, as 'training' replaces 'education', there will be fewer opportunities for critical reflection by social workers on the nature of their activity and its ever-changing role in society. Moreover, since the Children Act 1989, the tasks of social workers have been increasingly prescribed in legislation, and the policies of New Labour are continuing the trend towards markets and managers and away from professionalism and advocacy. Social workers are increasingly likely to merely implement actions and judgements decided by government in the context of managerialism, rather than responding to individual and collective situations within a flexible professional framework. As a result, this group of welfare workers are likely to move even further away from the lived experience of the poor and be incorporated, even more firmly, into the dominant discourse of welfare. New Labour's modernisation project and 'joined-up' thinking must inevitably lead towards a greater involvement of social workers in the assessment of welfare benefits, including income and loans. Their advocacy role, on behalf of the citizen, will finally disappear.

Like the initiatives for young children and their working (or soon to be working) parents, referred to earlier, New Labour have introduced a range of policies and programmes aimed at improving services for 'children in need', which are set out in their policy document *Quality Protects* (DoH 1998). This outlines government objectives for children's services (to be measured by specific performance targets) and details the role of elected members in delivering the programme and outlines the size and purpose of the new children's services special grant. It also lists the government's requirements for the Quality Protects Management Action Plans (MAPS) on which payment of the grant will depend. The set objectives are wide-ranging and comprehensive. There are eleven objectives and additional sub-objectives which are:

> [S]upported by performance indicators drawn from the Social Services Performance Assessment Framework (PAF) ... and additional Quality Protects Indicators which local authorities will be required to use in Quality Protects Management Action Plans (MAPS). By bringing these together in one document, we hope to make the process as clear and straightforward as possible for local authorities. (DoH 1999a, para 4: 2)

This positivist approach is evident throughout the DoH's publications in that these confidently transform what are complex human interactions and relationships into a set of management targets. These targets are then used to direct welfare organisations towards 'solving' problems that correlate with factors (such as the impact of poverty) that are outside their control. These objectives are also to include 'value for money' (VFM) considerations because they are to be linked to the Best Value programme which replaces Compulsory Competitive Tendering (CCT), discussed more fully in Chapter Six:

> DETR are about to launch a public consultation on the indicators to be used for Best Value. The significance of the label 'Best Value indicator' is that, through the legislation which underpins Best Value, local authorities will be required to set targets for improvements against each such indicator. We have proposed a number of indicators for children's services to be included in the DETR consultation. (DoH 1999a, para 19: 6)

For example, local authorities are directed to ensure that the children they are responsible for achieve well educationally, and receive a standard of health 'no worse than that which can be expected for the general population' (DoH 1999b, Annex 1, Objective 3.2: 13). The measure for educational targets are to be Standard Assessment Tests (SATs) and GCSEs, despite the criticism that can be made of these assessments in terms of their relevance or usefulness. For health and development objectives, measures such as rates of teenage pregnancies, access to information about health and healthy lifestyles, and rates of offending are to be taken into account. The emphasis is, therefore, on disciplinary and regulatory techniques aimed at the 'child in need' to ensure conformity to normalised models of living. Ultimately, the 'child in need' must 'work', acquire 'heterosexual' identity and consumer status, and live within a normalised family. Their 'Other than' lives have no value to themselves or society.

Local authorities are also required 'To ensure that children are securely attached to carers capable of providing safe and effective care for the duration of childhood' (DoH 1999a, Annex 1, Objective 1.00: 8). This objective relates to 'children in need' living with their families in the community, and 'looked after' children (the generic term within the Act for children in care or 'accommodated'). Sub-objectives include considering adoption as the first long-term option for a child not able to return to living with their birth family. Although the programme clearly draws on significant and useful research relating to, for example, the importance of attachment figures for a child's overall development (Wilson and Petrie 1998), translating this research into management objectives has meant that the constructs of the normalised 'family', 'sexuality', 'consumption' and 'work' are powerfully evident and, as a consequence, limit the choices available to children. For example, like the neo-liberals, New Labour do not wish to see adoptive families that do not conform to the normalised family, and so requiring local authorities to consider adoption as the first permanent alternative will limit the variety of lifestyle options for children. Much of the research highlighting the 'success' of adoption draws on the results of baby adoption or those children without challenging behaviour. The needs of children who are currently being put forward for adoption are very different. As most children who cannot live with their birth families are coming through the care system, they are likely to have multiple needs due to their (albeit brief) life experience. They need parenting from those with specialised skills, who understand exclusion and difference. Normalised families may not be able to meet these needs. Suitable adopters are also difficult to find and, in response to this, the commodification of children is becoming increasingly evident. Some local authorities now place photographic adverts of 'pretty' female children on the Internet in an attempt to 'sell them' to suitable adopters (*Daily Express,* 14 October 1999).

Part of the *Quality Protects* programme includes a new framework for the assessment of 'children in need'. This framework highlights the dangers of New Labour's emphasis on the relationship between individual pathology and socio-economic factors. The consultation draft (DoH 1999b) makes clear that *Quality Protects* is part of the government's strategy to end child poverty, tackle social exclusion and promote the welfare of all children. However, 'assessment', that is deciding who has 'needs' which are legitimate to meet, is identified as the primary tool through which this is to be achieved. Although it is stressed within the document that the guidance is not a practice manual and should be adapted to suit individual circumstances, it is, in essence, a blueprint for how poverty and the social exclusion of children are to be understood and dealt with.

The guidance presents a prescriptive top-down policy framework within which the construction of 'Other than' families can be clearly seen, despite earlier paragraphs outlining in some detail the extent of poverty in the UK and the requirement to consider the 'impact of wider family and environmental factors on parenting capacity and the child' (DoH 1999b: 17). Moreover, the wording of the document is occasionally chilling. For example, in relation to employment (in the context of high unemployment and changing labour-market patterns described earlier), social workers are required to identify 'Who is working in the household, their pattern of work and any changes? What impact does this have on the child? How is work or absence of work viewed by family members? How does it affect their relationship with the child?' (DoH 1999b: 24). Judgements are to be made on the basis of these value-laden statements. This is particularly ominous when the following extract is considered:

Local agencies, including schools and education support services, social services departments, youth offending teams, primary and more specialist health care services and voluntary agencies need to work together to establish agreed referral protocols which will help to ensure that early indications that a child at risk of social exclusion receives appropriate attention [sic]. (DoH 1999b: iii)

The networking of such many and varied services might be considered to be an efficient and effective way of responding to troubled children. The focus, however, is primarily on the culpability of the 'family' and, increasingly the child, for their own social exclusion. This is particularly evident when multi-agency offending teams are examined.

Multi-agency youth offending teams, introduced by the Crime and Disorder Act 1998, are being piloted in ten areas across the UK and are described as being at the 'cutting edge' of government youth justice reforms. 'Offending', like 'need', is understood to be a failing of 'Other than' families. The teams will tackle behaviour and issues that, it is alleged, put young people at risk of criminal activity, including poor parental supervision, domestic violence, peer-group pressure, truancy and school exclusion, alcohol, drug misuse or mental health problems. No mention of inadequately resourced schools with dilapidated buildings located in run-down neighbourhoods with poor housing conditions and few prospects, for many young people, of a worthwhile job or decent income. No recognition, either, that socially-constructed masculinity needs to be altered to shift the abusive power balance in gender relations. Young people are to be made to face up to the consequences of their behaviour for themselves, their victims and the wider community. No mention of the wider community facing up to the consequences for young people of the society that has been constructed for them. However, the Act itself, when implemented in full, has even more ominous and far-reaching consequences, as the following section will highlight.

Juvenile justice and the normalised 'family'

The legacy of the neo-liberals in relation to crime was a system which was heavily dependent on incarceration. The system was not only savage, but costly and ineffective. In 1995, the Howard League for Penal Reform observed that, although levels of offending had remained stable since 1990, there had been a 25 per cent increase in the use of imprisonment since 1993, with young people constituting a disproportionate percentage (Goldson 1999). Goldson points out that "Young offenders" became the new "enemy within", the language of punishment and retribution became ascendant and youth crime was effectively (re)politicised' (Goldson 1999: 7). Earlier in this chapter, it has been shown that constructs of the normalised 'family', 'consumption', 'sexuality' and 'work' pervaded neo-liberal policy and discursive practices in relation to young people in trouble with the law. The blame for their behaviour was placed with their 'Other than' families (usually lone mothers and absent fathers), lawless communities and their own individual pathologies (expecting to consume the good things of life without working for them). This social construction of 'juvenile crime' ignored the many facets of their lived experience, including the impact of poverty, exclusion from education, exclusion from employment and exclusion as consumers; this latter point being particularly significant in a society where being able to act as a consumer is a primary constituent of social status.

New Labour's construction of 'crime' and juvenile offending, both in opposition and in government, are not only similar to those of the neo-liberals, but could also be described as even more one-dimensional and simplistic. Jack Straw, Home Secretary from 1997, promised to be tough on crime. In his first speech as Prime Minister, Tony Blair talked of young people in epidemiological terms:

> Young people with nothing to do are sucked into a life of vandalism and drugs, and make life hell for other citizens. Our Youth Offender Teams are going to nip young offending in the bud. Children wandering the streets at night, getting into trouble, growing into a life of criminality, will be subject to Child Protection Orders. (cited in Jones and Novak 1999: 173)

Currently, England and Wales have one of the lowest ages of criminal responsibility than in the majority of European countries (Goldson 1999). As signatories to the UN Convention on the Rights of the Child (1990), the UK had been urged by the UN to raise the age of criminal responsibility and abandon plans for penal institutions for 12- to 14-year-olds. Nevertheless, New Labour has not only ignored these recommendations (adopting neo-liberal plans for secure juvenile training centres run by private contractors), but have also produced legislation and policies which have gone further than those of their predecessors. The Crime and Disorder Act 1998 has introduced a range of new measures which spring from a construction of 'a punitive vision of parental responsibility rooted in constructions of family pathology, "problem" families and "crime-prone" families which reach back into the previous century' (Goldson 1999: 12). The provisions in the Act for Child Safety Orders effectively draw children below the age of ten years into court proceedings that could lead to the making of a care order to the local authority for failing to comply with the imposed conditions. A care order made in such circumstances does not need to have regard to the welfare checklist of the Children Act 1989 (Part

1, Section 1(3)), and the court is not required to appoint a *Guardian ad Litem* to oversee the welfare of the child:

> Clause 12 Crime and Disorder will, when implemented, effectively criminalise those *below* the age of criminal responsibility … If such an order is breached, behaviour which, but for a child's age, would be deemed criminal, may result in a deprivation of liberty coupled with a suspension of parental responsibility. (Goldson 1999: 197 – original emphasis)

Not since the Children and Young People's Act 1969 (repealed by the Children Act 1989) has it been possible to deal with the offending behaviour of children in such a draconian way.

As far as child curfews are concerned (Sections 14-15, Crime and Disorder Act 1998) there is little evidence suggesting they are effective in relation to crime prevention. Moreover, substantial comparative research suggests that with such schemes certain sections of the community, particularly children and young people from racial minorities, will be 'more likely than others to be subject to imposed forms of exclusion' (Goldson 1999: 16). Other measures within the Act include abolishing the concept of *dolix incapax* which had previously required the prosecution to prove that a child between 10 and 14-years knew that what they were doing was seriously wrong. Thus, in criminal law, but not marriage or property legislation, children from 10-years-old are now regarded as adults. Constructed sexuality is also evident in the new Sex Offender Order, which can be made in respect of any child or young person not necessarily convicted but simply reprimanded, or warned, for an alleged sexual offence.

Parenting Orders (Sections 8-10 of the Act) contain two elements: a requirement on a parent or guardian to attend counselling or guidance sessions; and a requirement to exercise a measure of control over their children. Any parent failing to comply will be guilty of an offence and may be fined. None of the measures in the Act are supported by national or comparative research evidence, and the Act as a whole flies in the face of the philosophy of the Children Act 1989 (which itself fell below the standards required by the UN Convention on the Rights of the Child). It reflects a crude understanding of complex issues and a construct of normalised family life that appears not to be the lived experience of many people. The principles of decriminalisation, diversion from formal criminal proceedings, and decarceration from custodial institutions (the three D's) have not only been abandoned (Goldson 1999), but earlier and more punitive, less effective and more excluding approaches have been revived.

Conclusion

Signposts to future welfare discursive practices, including emerging 'family' policies of New Labour, have shown that both the neo-liberals and New Labour inhabit the same discourse of welfare. Within this discourse, the normalised family has acquired hegemony as 'Other than' families have been constructed as 'abnormal' and responsible for their own impoverishment and social exclusion:

> Under the conditions of late capitalism this location [the family] provides a site for the continuing promulgation ... of the *ideology of familialism*, a celebration of the virtues of the nuclear family, the nurturing roles of women, the subordination of children and other requirements of the social order. (Leonard 1997: 38 – original emphasis)

However, Beatrix Campbell (*Guardian Women*, 5 November 1998: .4), in addressing New Labour's 'family' policy proposals, highlights two crucial flaws in the government's thinking: first, research on cohabiting, married and lone parents does not prove that marriage is better for children – it merely shows that working-class and wageless parents are more likely to cohabit, while lone parents live on lower incomes. Consequently, if children in cohabiting or lone-parent families suffer from more material deprivation, then this is because they are poorer. In other words, it is the structural context in which relationships are played out – the social and economic context – that really matters (not whether parents are married or not); second, findings from research demonstrate that the 'family' can be a dangerous place for children (whatever the marital status of the parents) – particularly, because of physical, psychological and sexual abuse.

In contrast to New Labour's policy direction, Jack and Jordan call for a re-building of 'social capital' in order to promote the well-being of children. They define this as 'an environment in which adults interact as relatively equal members of a community which fosters trust, co-operation and individual initiative, and promotes strong associations and voluntary organisations for the common good' (Jack and Jordan 1999: 242). They argue that social capital is greatest in societies which have the most equal distributions of wealth, rather than those that are the richest. Welfare

282   *'Modernising' Social Policy*

practices and policies, when mediated through the supplementary discourses, or narratives, of 'family', 'work', 'consumption' and 'sexuality', combine to both ignore and undermine the inevitable changes taking place in 'family' life in postmodernity. This leaves many people excluded from participating in their own society, marginalising those, especially 'Other than' families, whose contribution is most needed to construct and reconstruct an inclusive society. The impact of long-term poverty on children and their families has been individually, as well as socially, destructive. Growing up without access to many resources, when these are available to others in view, combine to ensure some children are difficult to care for, within and outside their 'families'. Families merely adjust to the social conditions around them. It is these social conditions that must change. New Labour, like the neo-liberals, seem intent on developing welfare within a discourse that constructs a deficit model of 'family' life, where 'Other than' normalised families are constituted as 'abnormal', and where the increasingly authoritarian state regulates the minutiae of 'family' life. This will not reconstruct, but will further erode our meagre sense of social well-being, pitting the 'haves' against the 'have-nots' even more decisively.

References

Bauman, Z. (1998) *Work, consumerism and the new poor*, Open University Press, Buckingham.

Beishon, S., Madood, T. and Virdee, S. (1998) *Ethnic minority families*, Policy Studies Institute, Grantham.

Bell, M., Butler, E., Marsland, D. and Pirie, M. (1994) *The End of the Welfare State*, Adam Smith Institute, London.

Butt, J. and Box, L. (1998) 'Respect is the key', *Community Care*, 19-25th February, Issue No. 1210, pp. 22-23.

Campbell, B. (1984) *Wigan Pier Revisited*, Virago, London.

Clarke, J. and Newman, J. (1993) 'Managing to survive: Dilemmas of changing organisational forms in the public sector' in N. Deakin and R. Page (eds.) *The Costs of Welfare*, Avebury, Aldershot, pp. 46-63.

Cooper, C. (1987) *An Introduction to AIDS and Housing*, MA Dissertation submission, Polytechnic of North London, London.

Coppock, V. (1997) '"Families" in "Crisis"?' in P. Scraton (ed.) *'Childhood' in 'Crisis'?*, UCL Press, London, pp. 58-75.

Corteen, K. and Scraton, P (1997) 'Prolonging "Childhood", Manufacturing "Innocence" and Regulating Sexuality' in P. Scraton (ed.) *'Childhood' in `Crisis'?*, UCL Press, London, pp. 76-100.

Craig, G., Elliot-White, M., Kelsey, S. and Petrie, S. (1999) *An Audit of Children's Needs*, Policy Studies Research Centre/University of Lincolnshire and Humberside, Lincoln.

Daly, M (1997) 'Cash Benefits in European Welfare States', *Journal of European Social Policy*, Vol. 7, No. 2, pp. 129-146.

Dobson, B. and Middleton, S. (1998) *Paying to care: the cost of childhood disability*, York Publishing Services Ltd./Joseph Rowntree Foundation, York.

DoH (Department of Health) (1989) *Caring for People: Community Care in the Next Decade and Beyond*, Cmnd 849, HMSO, London.

DoH (Department of Health) (1990) *Children Come First*, Cmnd 1264, HMSO, London.

DoH (Department of Health) (1991a) *Child Abuse: A Study of Inquiry Reports, 1980-1989*, HMSO, London.

DoH (Department of Health) (1991b) *Patterns and Outcomes in Child Placement: Messages from current research and their implications*, HMSO, London.

DoH (Department of Health) (1991c) *Children in the Public Care: A Review of Residential Childcare*, HMSO, London.

DoH (Department of Health) (1995) *Child Protection: Messages from Research*, HMSO, London.

DoH (Department of Health) (1998) *The Quality Protects Programme: Transforming Children's Services*, Circular LAC(98), HMSO, London.

DoH (Department of Health) (1999a) *The Government's Objectives for Children's Social Services*, HMSO, London.

DoH (Department of Health) (1999b) *Framework for the Assessment of Children in Need and their Families*, Consultation Draft, HMSO, London.

DSS (Department of Social Security) (1998) *New Ambitions for Our Country: A New Contract for Welfare*, Cmnd. 3805, HMSO, London.

Farmer, E. and Boushel, M. (1999) 'Child protection, policy and practice: women in the front line' in S. Watson and L. Doyal (eds.) *Engendering Social Policy*, Open University Press, London, pp. 84-101.

Ferri, E. and Smith, K. (1998) *Step-parenting in the 1990's*, Family Policy Studies Centre/Joseph Rowntree Foundation, York.

Freeman, R. (1999) 'Recursive Politics: Prevention, Modernity and Social Systems', *Children and Society*, Vol. 13, pp. 232-241.

Glass, N. (1999) 'Sure Start: the Development of an Early Intervention Programme for Young Children in the United Kingdom', *Children and Society*, Vol. 13, pp. 257-264.

Goldson, B (1997) 'Children in trouble: State Responses to Juvenile Crime' in P. Scraton, (ed.) *'Childhood' in 'Crisis'?*, UCL Press, London, pp. 124-145.

Goldson, B. (ed.) (1999) *Youth Justice: Contemporary Policy and Practice,* Ashgate, London.

Goode, J., Callender, C. and Lister, R. (1998) *Purse or Wallet? Gender Inequalities and Income Distribution within Families on Benefits,* Policy Studies Institute, Grantham.

Greg, P., Harkness, S. and Machin, S. (1999) *Child development and family income,* York Publishing Services/Joseph Rowntree Foundation, York.

Griffiths, Sir R. (1988) *Community Care: Agenda for Action,* HMSO, London.

Hirsch, D. (1999) *Welfare Beyond Work: Active participation in a new welfare state,* Joseph Rowntree Foundation, York.

Home Office Ministerial Group on the Family (1998) *Supporting Families. A consultation document,* HMSO, London

Howarth, C., Kenway, P., Palmer, G. and Street, C. (1998) *Monitoring poverty and social exclusion: Labour's inheritance,* Joseph Rowntree Foundation, York.

Hudson, A. (1994) 'The Child Sexual Abuse "Industry"' in M. Langan and L. Day, (eds.) *Women, Oppression & Social Work: issues in anti-discriminatory practice*, Routledge, London, pp. 112-129.

Jack, G. and Jordan, B (1999) 'Social Capital and Child Welfare', *Children and Society*, Vol. 13, pp. 242-256.

Jones, N. and Novak, T. (1999) *Poverty, Welfare and the Disciplinary State*, Routledge, London.

Jordan, B. (1996) *A Theory of Poverty and Social Exclusion*, Polity Press, Cambridge.

Kennedy, M. (1995) 'Perceptions of Abused Disabled Children' in K. Wilson and A. James, (eds.) *The Child Protection Handbook*, Balliere-Tindall, London, pp. 127-149.

Le Grand, J. and Bartlett, W. (1993) *Quasi-Markets and Social Policy*, Macmillan, Basingstoke.

Miller, M. (1991) *Bed and Breakfast: women and homelessness today*, The Women's Press, London.

Mooney, G. (1997) 'Quasi-Markets and the Mixed Economy of Care' in M. Lavalette and A. Pratt (eds.) *Social Policy: A Conceptual and Theoretical Introduction*, Sage, London, pp. 228-244.

Leonard. P. (1997) *Postmodern Welfare: Reconstructing an Emancipatory Project*, Sage, London.

Macey, J.P. and Baker, C.V. (1973) *Housing Management*, 2nd Edition, The Estates Gazette, London.

Morgan, P (1995) *Farewell to the Family?*, Institute of Economic Affairs, London.

Morris, J. (1999) *Hurtling into a void: Transition to adulthood for young people with complex health and support needs,* Pavilion Publishing/Joseph Rowntree Foundation, York.

Nettleton, S., Burrows, R., England, J. and Seavers, J. (1999) *Losing the family home: Understanding the social consequences of mortgage repossession*, York Publishing Services Ltd./Joseph Rowntree Foundation, York.

Novak, T. (1997) 'Poverty and the "Underclass"' in M. Lavalette and A. Pratt, (eds.) *Social Policy: A Conceptual and Theoretical Introduction*, Sage, London, pp. 214-227.

Novak, T., Owen, S., Petrie, S. and Sennett, H. (1997) *Children's Day Care and Welfare Markets: research study funded by NHS Executive (Northern and Yorkshire)*, School of Policy Studies/University of Lincolnshire and Humberside, Hull.

Owen, S. and Petrie, S. (1997) 'Who pays the piper? Aspects of crisis in full-time day-care for young children in Britain' in R. Adams, (ed.) *Crisis in the Human Services: National and International Issues*, University of Lincolnshire and Humberside, Hull, pp. 246-251.

Petrie, S. (1995) *Day care regulation and support: Local authorities and day care under the Children Act 1989*, Save the Children, London.

Petrie, S. and James, A. (1995) 'Partnership with Parents' in K. Wilson and A. James, (eds.) *The Child Protection Handbook*, Balliere-Tindall, London, pp. 313-333.

Petrie, S. and Wilson, K. (1999) 'Towards the Disintegration of Child Welfare Services', *Social Policy and Administration*, Vol. 33, No.2, pp. 181-196.

Pilcher, J. and Wragg, S. (1996) *Thatcher's Children? Politics, Childhood and Society*, Falmer Press, London.

Powell, M. (1999) *New Labour, New Welfare State? The 'third way' in British social policy,* The Policy Press, Bristol.

Pratt, A. (1997) 'Universalism or Selectivism?' in M. Lavalette and A. Pratt (eds.) *Social Policy: A Conceptual and Theoretical Introduction*, Sage, London, pp. 196-213.

Schweinhart, I., Barnes, H. and Weikhart, D. (1993) *Significant Benefits: The High-Scope Perry Pre-School Study Through Age 27,* Monograph of the High/Scope Educational Resource Foundation Number Ten, Ypsilanti, USA.

Scraton, P (1997) 'Whose "Childhood"? What "Crisis"?' in P. Scraton (ed.) *'Childhood' in 'Crisis'?*, UCL Press, London, pp. 163-186.

Shropshire, J. and Middleton, S. (1999) *Small expectations: Learning to be poor?*, York Publishing Services/ Joseph Rowntree Foundation, York.

Smart, C. (1997) 'Wishful Thinking and Harmful Tinkering? Sociological Reflections on Family Policy', *Journal of Social Policy*, Vol. 26, Part 3, pp. 301-321.

Smart, C. and Neale, B. (1997) 'Good enough morality? Divorce and postmodernity', *Critical Social Policy*, Vol. 17, No. 4, pp. 3-27.

Song, M. and Edwards, R. (1997) 'Comment: Raising Questions About Perspectives on Black Lone Motherhood', *Journal of Social Policy*, Vol. 26, Part 2, pp. 233-244.

Summerfield, C. (1998) *Social Focus on Men and Women*, HMSO, London.

Timmins, N. (1998) 'Frank Field interviewed', *Poverty*, No. 100, pp. 10-13.

Turok, I. and Edge, N. (1999) *The jobs gap in Britain's cities: employment loss and labour market consequences*, The Policy Press, London.

Wenham, M. (1993) *Funded to Fail – Nuff pain, No Gain*, London Voluntary Services Council, London.

Williams, F. (1995) *Social Policy: A Critical Introduction*, Polity Press, Cambridge.

Williams, F. (1996) 'Social relations, welfare and the post-Fordist debate' in R. Burrows and B. Loader (eds.) (1996) *Towards a Post-Fordist Welfare State?*, Routledge, London, pp. 49-74.

Wilson, A. (1997) 'Social Policy and Sexuality' in M. Lavalette and A. Pratt (eds.) *Social Policy: A Conceptual and Theoretical Introduction*, Sage, London, pp. 121-139.

Wilson, K. and Petrie, S. (1998) 'No place like home: lessons learned and lessons forgotten – the Children Act 1948', *Child & Family Social Work*, Vol. 3, Issue 3, pp. 183-188.

9 'Modernising' Welfare

Critique

New Labour claims to herald new times, beyond the Left (Social Democracy) and Right (neo-liberalism) that characterised post-war politics in the UK. They offer a 'Third Way', believed to be best suited to confront the single most important force shaping our world – globalisation. They claim that national governments can do little to regulate domestic affairs, other than to adapt their people to the needs of the global economy. This refashioning includes New Labour's appeal to 'community values', civic responsibility, family solidarity and respect for the law, executed in the name of social inclusion and economic efficiency. It also includes New Labour's insistence that they represent a new project, pragmatic and beyond the ideology of both left-wing fundamentalism and market fundamentalism. They claim to be a government without adversaries in a country without enemies. In this final chapter we assess how valid these claims are, and to what extent the New Labour project is likely to succeed in delivering social inclusion. We then move on to offer an alternative welfare strategy founded largely on one single social policy initiative – the 'Citizen's Income'. After setting out the benefits of the Citizen's Income we suggest how political support for it might be won, including consideration of how the political environment in the UK can become more sensitive to the voices of groups and individuals presently excluded from decision-making processes.

As we have shown throughout the course of this book, New Labour's project during its first two years of government has centred on the 'modernisation' of welfare, designed around reciprocal rights and responsibilities in relation to 'work', 'consumption', 'the family' and 'sexuality'. That is, in return for inclusion in life's opportunities, the welfare subject is obliged to demonstrate that they are seeking to rejoin the labour market, taking responsibility for their own 'individualised' form of welfare consumption, looking towards a traditional family network for (or to provide) welfare support, and/or adopting a specific sexual orientation.

It is a highly moralising campaign, closely resembling the values of the libertarian right. However, the moral transformation envisaged under New Labour is only expected of welfare recipients, while those 'making it possible (civil servants and ministers, co-operating employers and the citizenry at large) ... need undergo no moral transformation themselves' (Birnbaum 1999: 438). Moreover, unequal power relationships and structural barriers to self-determination are side-stepped.

There have been some elements of wealth redistribution under New Labour. Gordon Brown's first budget in July 1997 did allow for some measured 'backdoor redistribution ... through stealth' (Powell 1999: 17). This included the windfall tax on privatised utilities (providing opportunity for some through New Deal) and reductions in tax relief on housing (MIRAS) and health insurance. The March 1998 budget distributed some help to working families on low pay, estimated at £500 per annum for the poorest fifth of households with children, through the Working Families Tax Credit, payable from April 2000 (*The Independent Budget Special*, 18 March 1998: 1). A new children's tax credit announced in the March 1999 budget, replacing the married couple's allowance and payable from April 2001, is also expected to leave households with children £200 per annum better off (*The Guardian Budget Special*, 10 March 1999). However, alongside these 'family friendly' reforms have been measures aimed at retaining the concept of 'less eligibility' to deter those perceived as part of a 'something for nothing culture' (*The Guardian*, 31 March 1999: 10). For example, proposals to abolish the severe disablement allowance and lone parent benefit – reflecting New Labour's emphasis on opportunity and inclusion through paid work – leave those unable or unwilling to enter the formal labour market further marginalised and excluded. Deconstructed, this is 'conditional' rather than reciprocal welfare, connected with work obligations and the belief that 'life on benefits is less attractive (or less eligible)' (Powell 1999: 22). As Dahrendorf argues:

> Third Way reforms of the welfare state [involve] above all the strict insistence on everyone, including the disabled and single mothers, working. Where normal employment – let alone desired employment – is not available, people have to be made to work by the withdrawal of benefits. (Dahrendorf 1999: 27)

Others who choose to live outside of capitalist labour relations – choosing strategies of survival such as radical community activism, caring for friends or relatives, or working in the alternative labour market – will be considered ineligible for welfare. Stuart Hall describes this element in New Labour thinking as:

> the remoralisation of the work ethic, and the restoration of that discredited and obscene Victorian utilitarian distinction between 'the deserving' and 'the undeserving' poor ... Not since the workhouse has labour been so fervently and single-mindedly valorised. (Hall 1998: 12)

To facilitate their programme of 'work friendly' reform, New Labour have focused on the concept of developing the human capital of the nation – or knowledge-based capital. They see that people are trapped in poverty because they lack the skills or motive to find 'paid work'. The solution is to make job opportunities available for everyone through education or training, increasingly likely to be compulsory, and 'work' linked to welfare benefits (effectively 'workfare'). Income support policies, for example, continue to reinforce obligations to work, with benefits kept well below wage levels or threatened with removal altogether (see Chapter Seven). However, these strategies are fundamentally flawed in postmodern societies now distinguished by uncertainty and risk. As Gorz argues, because social production in contemporary society 'demands less and less work and distributes less and less in wages, it is becoming increasingly difficult to obtain a sufficient, regular income from paid work' (Gorz 1999: 72). Many of those lucky enough to remain in work have largely seen the erosion of their job-status and income. For the low paid, the chances of falling back into unemployment are high (Oppenheim 1999). The absence of sufficiently secure, well-paid work, together with inadequate social protection for people outside paid work, is a key factor at the heart of the process of social exclusion. Yet New Labour still push the 'work is good, not to work is bad' mantra that has survived modernity. As we argued in Chapter Three, retaining allegiance to this supplementary narrative or discourse is important for the regulation of social order as, throughout modernity, the workplace has been an important site of social integration, where good habits and discipline are instilled:

> [I]n post-traditional, modern society ... work stood at the centre of the lifelong construction and defence of a man's identity. The life-project could spring from many ambitions, but they were all wrapped around the type of work to be chosen or be assigned to. The type of work coloured the totality of life; it determined not just the rights and duties directly relevant to the work process, but the expected standard of living, the pattern of the family, social life and leisure, norms of

propriety and daily routine. It was that one 'independent variable' which allowed a person to shape up and to forecast, with little error, all other aspects of their existence ... To sum up: work was the main orientation point, in reference to which all other life pursuits could be planned and ordered. (Bauman 1998: 17)

However, finding everyone permanent paid employment appears increasingly difficult in postmodern, post-industrial societies, highlighting the contradiction in New Labour's supplementary narrative on work.

As we have also shown throughout the course of this book, there has been little new investment in other areas of welfare under New Labour. There has been little new money for health, and the thrust of policy has been to remove bureaucratic processes in the (retained) internal market to achieve managerial efficiencies (see Chapter Four). Education policy has emphasised school 'values' and quality of leadership, with 'zero tolerance' for schools appearing to 'fail', rather than the social and environmental factors shaping the pupil's experience (see Chapter Five). In housing, the emphasis again has been on managerial effectiveness achieved through 'Best Value' (see Chapter Six). In respect of family policy, the personal social services are poised for another shift in the way in which they are expected to carry out their statutory duties, with detailed policies and procedures coming from the centre in a context of shrinking resources and increasing demand (see Chapter Eight). Under New Labour, we have witnessed the expansion of social engineering techniques, controlling the activities of both welfare professions and citizens to ensure conformity with behaviour desired by the government. In these respects, far from being a new and different project, there would appear to be little reason to dispute Hall's claim that:

> The framing strategy of New Labour's economic repertoire remains essentially the neo-liberal one: the deregulation of markets, the wholesale refashioning of the public sector by the New Managerialism, the continued privatisation of public assets, low taxation, breaking the 'inhibitions' to market flexibility, institutionalising the culture of private provision and personal risk, and privileging in its moral discourse the values of self-sufficiency, competitiveness and entrepreneurial dynamism. (Hall 1998: 11)

As we have shown in the preceding chapters, New Labour have produced a number of new initiatives and experiments – particularly through health and education action zones. Yet these are doing little to reduce the effects of poverty and the polarisation of rich and poor, or to bring about a more inclusive society. In the next section we set out an alternative welfare policy which we believe offers a more comprehensive strategy of inclusion.

An alternative 'welfare' policy?

New Labour's welfare modernisation programme centres on achieving social inclusion by getting people back into paid work. In the context of globalisation, where national economies are at the mercy of transnational corporations, this means generating the conditions favourable for maintaining inward investment. However, this policy emphasis is fundamentally flawed. Meeting the needs of global capitalism means lowering comparative real wages, taxation and public spending. The UK has already seen the proportion of employment paying subsistence wages decline significantly over the last 30 years, with many households now needing two or more wage-earners to subsist (Jordan 1998). In this environment, reliance on the labour market will not address social exclusion.

Pivotal to the proposed alternative welfare strategy is the notion that we need to deconstruct the dominant supplementary narrative of 'work' and to reconstruct a different understanding that will, in turn, lead to different notions of 'family', 'sexuality' and 'consumption'. More specifically, in respect of 'work', we agree with André Gorz's view, alluded to in Chapter Seven, that postmodern societies need to look beyond the centrality of a 'wage-based society' (Gorz 1999) and provide everyone with a guaranteed Citizen's Income, irrespective of social status and set at an amount deemed necessary to meet subsistence needs. Each citizen would receive the same basic amount, with extra supplements paid in line with higher living costs due to, for instance, child-care responsibilities or disability. Paid work would be taxable, at a rate sufficient to sustain the Citizen's Income Fund and other public spending. As people's incomes rise through involvement in paid work, their Citizen's Income would be 'taxed back'.

The concept of a Citizen's Income is not an entirely radical notion and similar ideas have been given consideration in the US recently (see *New Statesman*, 14 June 1999). Bill Clinton, considering a newly proposed universal savings account as part of his social security reform, gave some thought to giving people a capital stake rather than handouts. Under this scheme, families below a particular income ($40,000) would receive an annual $600 tax credit, plus another $700 if they deposit $700 of their own money into a bank account – providing an annual nest egg of $2,000. Higher income families would receive a smaller subsidy. The estimated cost to the taxpayer of this scheme is $30bn per year.

Senator Bob Kerrey has suggested giving every new born child a $1,000 savings account, to which $500 would be added each year until the child's fifth birthday. Compounded interest would give the child an estimated $20,000 start to their life at the age of 21. This would cost the taxpayer an estimated $15bn per annum.

Ackerman and Alstott have argued for giving every 21-year-old a flat-rate $80,000 (costing the tax payer an estimated $255bn per annum). The original stake could be paid back with interest at death, or through a 2 per cent increase in the tax of the wealthiest 40 per cent of American society.

Lipietz's treatment of Citizen's Income links it to radical work strategies and the development of a 'third sector', a permanently subsidised new employment sector offering jobs that were stable, dignified and socially recognised. Such jobs would specialise in activities that other sectors do not carry out to avoid the effect of displacement. Such activities may include, for instance, neighbourhood and environmental services managed by a range of organisations, such as community enterprises and co-operatives, financially assisted from tax exemptions and wage subsidies paid from savings in unemployment benefit allowances (Dunford 1997).

Beck also argues the need to rethink and redefine work, and to see that there is life beyond waged work:

> We need to see that the lack of waged work can give us a new affluence of time. We need also to see that the welfare state must be rebuilt so that the risks of fragile work are socialised rather than being borne increasingly by the individual. (Beck 1999: 27)

He supports the argument for a Citizen's Income and the introduction of self-organised citizenship work, an alternative labour market similar to Lipietz's 'third sector', embracing such activities as parenting, working with children, and artistic, cultural and community work. This comes close to the ideas of William Morris, who distinguished between 'useful work and useless toil, seeing the former as an essential human activity, at once a prime source of personal fulfilment' (Purdy 1999: 2). Moreover:

The work that makes the world go round includes unpaid caregiving, voluntary service, labour-only bartering, subsistence farming and non-vocational learning. Why not, then, include these activities in the New Deal programme? Why the fixation on the labour market? Would it not be better for us all to recognise the role of unpaid work and permit able-bodied claimants to fulfil their obligations to society by participating in any useful activity which has been duly vetted and approved? (Purdy 1999: 4)

This would require a new role for the Employment Service, one that moved beyond career counselling, and training and work placement schemes, to encouraging and seeking:

proposals from groups of citizens and non-profit making organisations for projects designed to fulfil unmet public needs and extend the range of options open to benefit claimants, including people with disabilities. Projects would have to be properly managed, provide value for money and pose no threat to existing jobs ... Such a system of 'liberal workfare' would build on New Labour's welfare to work programme, yet would challenge prevailing ideas about the nature of work and the primacy of the market. It would enable claimants to live more productive, less stigmatised lives. (Purdy 1999: 4)

A Citizen's Income would overcome a number of structural problems inherent in our present welfare system. It would address:

administrative complexity, bureaucratic tutelage, gaps in coverage, incomplete take-up rates and the various disincentives, uncertainties and indignities visited on recipients of means tested benefits. (Purdy 1999: 3)

A Citizen's Income would replace all other forms of income maintenance – family allowances, housing subsidies, unemployment benefit, sickness and disability allowances, and state pensions – and, therefore, be administratively simpler and more cost effective. Additionally, because it would be paid in advance and adjusted later in line with earnings through the pay-as-you-earn tax system, a Citizen's Income would avoid the poverty trap in which many people find themselves. It would also encourage more people to save by being non-means-tested. A Citizen's Income would also be equitable, with each recipient getting a rate based on their living costs regardless of 'race', class, gender and sexuality. It would also target need in a non-stigmatising way (Jordan 1998).

A Citizen's Income would also emancipate us all from what has been perceived as a growing imbalance in our culture between personal freedom and the pressure we experience as workers:

> Beset by job insecurity, family responsibility and consumerist fantasy, those with full-time jobs dedicate our lives to working and spending and have little time left for personal growth, relationships, and communal fellowship. (Purdy 1999: 3)

Beck shares this concern and sees the need to reduce working time for all, partly so that work can be shared, but also so that we can all be free to choose how we spend our time between different priorities: family, waged work, leisure, political activity, and so on. Genuine social inclusion is achieved through giving people autonomy to shape their own life experiences (Beck 1999). This notion echoes Doyal and Gough's views on the basic human needs that we require to be fulfilled to enable us to fully participate in our social world. These include not only physical and mental health, but also autonomy and social opportunities (Doyal and Gough 1991). A Citizen's Income would help to achieve these opportunities. It would recognise the importance of unpaid work, offering security to people who choose to opt out of the labour market in order to care for relatives, or to embark on a training or education programme, or to become involved in local community-development activities. It would give people time for political participation, which most rarely have, a prerequisite for genuine involvement in policy-making and building a democratic society. It would also allow people to form household structures in ways consistent with their own desires and choices, reflecting the changing trends in family patterns discussed in Chapter Eight.

Gorz, also sharing some of these concerns, presents a strong case in defence of a sufficient social income, based on unconditionality, that gives:

> individuals and groups increased resources for taking charge of their own lives, further power over their way of life and living conditions. (Gorz 1999: 83)

Gorz justifies the unconditional right to a sufficient basic income on the grounds that linking it to an obligation or duty to perform some type of work is too problematic. For example, those advocating that the right to payment should be linked to a duty to do 'voluntary' work leads to the absurd situation of making voluntary work 'compulsory'. Others who advocate the obligation of recipients of a social income to perform domestic work (such as caring for children or other relatives) undermine the private character of behaviour between people, behaviour that often has an emotional value. Such an obligation would also lead to greater state regulation of activities within the home (Gorz 1999).

There are, no doubt, difficulties in getting a Citizen's Income policy accepted as part of an alternative political programme. As Jordan acknowledges, the 'moral argument against this approach – that it rewards laziness, and gives no real encouragement to any social virtue – seems as stubbornly persuasive as ever' (Jordan 1998: 159). In particular, opponents of a Citizen's Income argue that it would be economically and socially damaging by generating a disincentive to work. However, in response to this, Gorz presents a persuasive counter argument. He suggests that a sufficient Citizen's Income would free people to:

> develop capacities (of intervention, creation, conception and intellection) which give them a virtually unlimited productivity, and this development of their productive capacity, which can be equated with the production of a fixed capital, *is not work,* though it produces the same outcome as work 'from the standpoint of the direct production process' … It is this 'time freed up for their own development' which makes it possible for them to take as their goal 'the free development of individualities', their 'artistic, scientific etc. development'. And it is this free development of individualities which reappears in production as the capacity to create an unlimited variety of wealth with a very small expenditure of time and energy. (Gorz 1999: 92 – original emphasis)

This is, according to Gorz, 'real economy' (Gorz 1999: 93). Moreover, in addition to increasing the productive capacities of individuals, replacing the 'work' ethic with opportunities for personal development will liberate people from exploitative, low-paid hazardous work:

> The basic social income must enable [people] to refuse work and reject 'inhuman' working conditions … The aim is not to enable people not to work at all, but rather to give genuine effect to the right to work: not the right to that work you are 'employed' to do, but to the concrete work you do without having to be paid for it, without its profitability or exchange-value coming into the equation … [It will] enable and encourage self-activity to take place, the resources with which individuals and groups can satisfy by their own unshackled efforts part of the needs and desires they have themselves defined. (Gorz 1999: 83)

The benefits from a Citizen's Income include prospects for large-scale developments in the collective or self-provision of facilities and services. In addition, Gorz shares Lipietz's argument that a Citizen's Income will allow people the time to develop multi-active lifestyles, engaging in voluntary work, artistic and cultural activities, family support and mutual aid, political and community action, education and training, and so forth (Gorz 1999).

Gorz also argues that if people are so easily disincentivised to work, as the critics of a Citizen's Income suggest, then we need to change society's notion of 'work':

> To change it by divesting it of all its reifying constraints (hours, hierarchy, productivity), which reflect its subordination to capital and which, so far, have determined the essence of what is currently known as 'work'. To change it by reconciling it with a culture of daily life, an art of living, which it would both extend and nourish, instead of being cut off from them. To change it by the way it will be *appropriated* from childhood onwards, when it will be possible no longer to suffer it as a penance, but to live it as an activity merged in the flow of life, a path to the full development of the senses, towards power over oneself and the external world, and as a bond with others. To change it from childhood onwards by linking the acquisition of knowledge with a pride in being able to do things. (Gorz 1999: 98-99 – original emphasis)

Jordan, critical of the coercive nature of Labour's New Deal policies aimed at forcing people into paid work, highlights the benefits of 'chosen participation' in economic activity over 'unchosen participation'. 'Chosen participation' is defined as that which someone has an interest in doing rather than merely does, thereby 'generating the most efficient feasible productive relations under minimally exploitative conditions' (Jordan 1998: 172). It is a concept that extends to all other areas of people's lives, not just economic activity. For instance:

> Chosen participation implies that individuals make rational decisions about with whom they will live and bring up children, as well as where they will work, and how they will spend their incomes. In order to be able to make such choices, they require some fundamental autonomy, so that they can recognise alternatives and select between them. (Jordan 1998: 172)

A Citizen's Income would not only extend people's autonomy over their economic sphere, it would also contribute to their ability to live in household formations reflecting their own desires and of their own choosing. Women and their children, for example, would not be forced to remain in violent relationships because of their economic dependence – a situation underpinned by inadequate and stigmatised benefits (Jordan

1998). This change is not feasible under New Labour's insistence that genuine autonomy is only achievable through involvement in the labour market.

Winning the comfortable middle classes over to a Citizen's Income may be politically problematic, but not impossible. Research evidence now overwhelmingly points to the links between violence, crime, low self-esteem, mortality and morbidity, and the scale of income inequality in society. For instance:

> The crucial determinants of population health and health inequalities turn out to be less a matter of medical care or the direct effects of exposure to hazardous material circumstances, as of the effects of the social environment as structured by social hierarchy. Increasingly it looks as if the most powerful influences on population health in the developed world are psychosocial. (Wilkinson 1998: 38)

It is now acknowledged that there is a strong correlation between trends in ill health and insecurity in the labour market, the lack of control we feel over our work environment, the fears and effects of unemployment, and low social status. These factors contribute to chronic anxiety and poorer immunity. Additionally, evidence suggests that healthy societies are less to do with stages of economic growth, but more to do with the distribution of wealth. Moreover:

> Societies which were unusually egalitarian and unusually healthy were also unusually cohesive ... [T]he index of civic community is closely correlated with income distribution. (Wilkinson 1998: 38)

Wide income differentials would appear to have a direct bearing on the nature of social relationships throughout society, including lower levels of trust and social support, and higher levels of hostility and conflict. Widening gaps in social status exacerbate notions of 'difference' and access to essential resources, fragmenting society into competing groupings and encouraging more aggressive social interaction (Jordan 1996). Low self-esteem can increase hostility between groups and individuals as they attempt to ward off feelings of ineptitude and lack of power. Consequently, the 'psychosocial welfare of the population is determined by structural factors' (Wilkinson 1998: 39). It becomes clear, therefore, that the benefits of a Citizen's Income for all embraces both health and crime factors, and anxieties about loss of self-determination, equally appealing to 'Middle England'.

A final argument in favour of a Citizen's Income is that it is both universal and reflective of the nature of a society's common wealth. In the case of the latter, a Citizen's Income represents the distribution of society's collective wealth built on past labour and ingenuity (Jordan 1998), as well as the pooling of socially-produced wealth created collectively by the labour force of the present, from which it is difficult to assess each individual's own contribution (Gorz 1999). In the case of the former, a Citizen's Income avoids selectivity based on moral judgements about 'difference'. It is based on universal distributive principles that recognise the real experiences of people, and avoids giving moral force – such as the morality of 'family' and 'sexuality' – to transactions between state officials and welfare subjects. Universality is also crucial to social inclusion. As Hall observes, William Beveridge understood that:

> 'universalism', despite its costs, was essential to binding the richer sections of society into collective forms of welfare... [T]he whole system would be in danger as soon as the rich could willingly exclude themselves from collective provision by buying themselves out. Why should they go on paying for a service they had ceased to use? (Hall 1998: 12)

Furthermore:

> No one perhaps fought more passionately against the gradual yet relentless replacement of universalist ambitions with selective practices than Richard Titmuss and Peter Townsend. In his desperate attempts to stem the rising tide, Titmuss reminded his readers ... that 'services for the poor were always poor services' ... Only when social services are aimed at the community as a whole and so are seen as benefiting everybody, could they 'foster social integration and a sense of community'. (Bauman 1998: 49)

We would also add, however, that a Citizen's Income offers a model of universalism distinct from the patriarchal and racialised universalism characteristic of the post-war welfare state. As Williams argues:

> the post-war welfare settlement depended upon women's unpaid caring work in the home (and to that extent welfare was never entirely state-provided) and reinforced both this and their economic dependency. Furthermore the development of mass provision was also made possible through the availability of low-paid labour from the colonies and ex-colonies. At the same time the 'universalism' of many of the post-war services and benefits was based on the norm of the white, British, heterosexual, able-bodied Fordist Man, and often

excluded women and black people upon whose paid and unpaid labour it depended. (Williams 1994: 61)

The cost of welfare in the UK was kept down by drawing in cheap labour, largely women and black immigrants. In the case of the latter:

> When black migrants did use welfare services they were often portrayed as scroungers, as in the case of council housing or income maintenance, or, in health, education and social services, treated as 'problematic' with little sensitivity to different social and cultural experiences or, subsequently, as pleading for 'special' treatment. (Williams 1994: 62)

Plans to 'modernise' welfare need to be reflective of these issues. They need to question the assumptions behind the dominant discourse of welfare that has informed the policies of the governments of both New Labour and the neo-liberal Conservatives, ensuring that policies reflect people's lived experiences.

Having established the benefits of a Citizen's Income, and set out some of the arguments to secure its political support, the next section moves on to consider how we can establish a new political environment that encourages active inclusion. While a Citizen's Income will assist marginalised groups and individuals to achieve some degree of economic security and autonomy, active inclusion also requires access to the policy-making process. Only then can the conflicting interests of different social groups and individuals be mediated in democratic ways. Central to this discussion is the notion of radical community development and conflict.

Community development and conflict

The struggles of people against processes of domination are more complex and diverse than the structuralist or functionalist accounts of welfare suggest, as discussed in Chapter Two. Movements in defence of freedoms have organised, and continue to organise, around 'work' campaigns, rights to access key areas of welfare 'consumption' (health, education and housing), rights to determine one's own sexual identity, and rights to live in household structures of one's own choice. Social justice around these areas offers possibilities for a truly 'New' political direction and for building a liberating strategy for inclusion built on 'diversity'. The mobilisation of new forms of collective action, in support of recognising diversity and difference, are possible within current discourses of welfare. For example, as Williams suggests, in relation to the restructuring of health and social care under the Conservatives, there emerged:

> at least three discourses around diversity and differences: one based upon notions of the exercising of consumer choice; another based on the creation of services based on the assessment of different individual needs; and a third rooted in difference as a form of political identity and a challenge to existing relations of power and inequality. (Williams 1994: 70)

The discourses of 'collective consumer rights' and 'empowerment' have also been strong under New Labour, particularly in relation to housing policy (discussed in Chapter Six). Organising around these discourses, it is clear that there are new possibilities for community involvement in welfare that, through local groups articulating their demands in their terms, create 'spaces for the involvement of groups in ... operating with a more politicised notion of diversity and difference' (Williams 1994: 70). Communities need to organise and campaign around the contradiction between the rhetoric of New Labour's discourse of welfare and the actuality of their experiences of what New Labour delivers. In particular, under New Labour, market welfare is failing to meet needs while state welfare is increasingly residualised and second rate; significant 'Others' – disabled people and lone parents – are losing benefits and social inequality is widening. In other words, policies from above 'do not appear ... to match the diverse needs articulated by the users below' (Williams 1994: 72). Here we see the seeds of Foucault's 'reverse discourse', touched on in Chapter Three, a 'competing' discourse around diversity and difference.

Jordan highlights the contradiction in Blair's orthodoxy of 'community', with its emphasis on traditional family values and civic responsibility (Jordan 1998). It is a brand of communitarianism that differs little from that of the American social scientist, Charles Murray (author of the underclass thesis that demonised lone parents for raising 'work shy' delinquents), and described by Hoggett as appealing to 'a lost age when neighbourhood ties were strong and families socialised their offspring more effectively than they are held to do today'; it is a notion of 'community' that is 'suffocatingly homogeneous and intolerant of difference' (Hoggett 1997, cited in Cooper and Hawtin 1998: 71-72). While communities can be supportive they can also be oppressive, with neighbours and extended families exercising control over children and young people, gays and lesbians, ethnic minorities, sexually-exploited women and teenage mothers, through the use of curfews, tagging, neighbourhood watch, resident associations and police-liaison groups (see Chapter Six; Cooper and Hawtin 1998; Jordan 1998). New Labour's 'New Deal for Communities' is aimed at criminal justice rather than social justice, consistent with its moral discourse of welfare:

> [New Labour's] orthodoxy leads to a politics of welfare that is moralistic, authoritarian and intolerant; that divides the working class on lines of perceived 'deservingness' and moral worth, and mobilizes the self-righteous and judgemental majority against those they neither know nor understand; and that it drives up enforcement costs, and ends by spending most of the welfare budget on control, surveillance, compulsion and correction. This is not social justice; it is not even liberalism. (Jordan 1998: 189-190)

In contrast, we advocate a different vision for communities, built on notions of tolerance, solidarity and equality of opportunity, achieved through radical community development. While it is not our intention here to conduct a detailed evaluation of radical community development (for an in-depth analysis of this, see Popple 1995), we summarise its key principles and values.

At the heart of radical community development is Paulo Freire's notion of 'conscientisation', whereby 'different' communities – comprising, for instance, gays and lesbians, ethnic minorities, the homeless, young people, and so forth – are enabled to comprehend the nature of the dominant discourse that 'subjectifies' and oppresses. Freire believed that it was the role of community development workers to assist, through education and training, 'oppressed' communities to gain a 'critical consciousness' – that is, to reflect and make sense of their lived experience (Freire 1976). Community development is about allowing people to recognise that the existence of unequal power relationships in society is both a personal and political issue. Once this has been achieved, communities can engage more effectively in critical dialogue with power holders. To be effective in this, community development workers need to have regard to the 'process' of involvement. This requires a mutual acceptance of certain key values, including a non-directive approach to community involvement where individuals and groups are empowered, prejudices are challenged, and there are full rights of equal access to the involvement process. This way, different interest groups within communities can come to define their own objectives and, through engaging in collective action, work towards changing their circumstances (Cooper and Hawtin 1998).

Concrete examples of community development in action can be found in experiments in 'participatory democracy' that appear to have transformed the political culture of cities in Brazil and Uruguay. These initiatives have been founded on extensive citizen involvement and the decentralisation of services and budgets to local neighbourhoods. These schemes had three objectives: first, to promote direct citizen involvement in urban management; second, to facilitate greater political awareness and the empowerment of residents and their organisations; and third, to create a genuinely democratic culture. As Chavez argues:

> Decentralisation and participatory budgeting challenge neoliberalism. They increase the accountability of local government and introduce decision making and negotiation from below in place of the traditional centralised and secretive process. This model seeks to transform powerless urban residents who, after decades of authoritarianism were used only to casting an obligatory vote every five years, into active subjects with growing power over the decisions that affect their daily lives. (Chavez 1999: 1)

These experiments have been encouraged by leftist parties seeking to address extremes of political, social and economic inequality in Brazilian and Uruguayan cities. They evolved out of city-wide seminars on different themes in urban management – transport, education, culture, health care, economic development, housing, and so forth – that aimed to define 'an integrated vision for the whole of the city' (Chavez 1999: 2). Two new administrative structures have been introduced: Regional Assemblies and the Participatory Budget Council (PBC). The PBC is made up of delegates from the Regional Assemblies, from the thematic seminar groups, from the municipal workers' union, from neighbourhood associations and from local government. Regional Assemblies consist of representatives from each neighbourhood association. Decision making is organised around two *rodadas* (rounds) of meetings where the local population, through its representatives, express their demands and needs, leading to the establishment of priorities for urban policies and municipal investment. According to Chavez, these changes have led to qualitative improvements in urban planning and management, with public resources now being allocated for the benefit of the majority rather than the few.

Empowering citizens requires a transformation of the 'consumerist' discourse that characterises both New Labour and the neo-liberals in favour of one that seeks to empower 'communities'. This needs what Barnett calls 'a profound and important shift in the character of political power in Britain' (Barnett 1998: 44). In contrast to Blair's gratuitous attacks on the 'sneer squad' – those who disagree with him – we argue that a healthy and democratic society should welcome criticism and conflict. Debate and disagreement are crucial to democracy, otherwise how can we become aware of the different lived experiences of different 'communities'? Discourse should be conceptualised as a generative process, involving negotiation between power interests. This way, as Jordan argues, a society's concept of 'social justice' represents the negotiated outcome of dialogue between these interests, constructed within a political process that allows democratic compromise. 'The whole project of democratizing society ... relies on this notion – that unequal partners can construct common interests through dialogue and negotiation' (Jordan 1998: 192). Radical community development offers the means to enable this to happen.

Conclusion

It could be argued that Tony Blair's success to date rests on fragile foundations. Unlike previous great coalitions in UK politics, such as Thatcherism or 'Old' Labour, New Labour has not, after two years in government, created a coherent political project. Rather:

> In place of an ideology or myth it has a rhetoric [that] implies that there is no rational alternative to the policies it favours. But it lacks emotional and moral resonance ... The underlying message is curiously apologetic. The world is changing, we are told. We may not like the changes; we may think them harmful or even wicked, but we can't stop them. All we can do is to adapt to them as gracefully as possible. It is the rhetoric of a management consultant, advising a company to redesign its products, not of a political leader, mobilising his followers for a rendezvous with destiny. (Marquand 1998: 26)

Part of the confusion lies in New Labour's attempt to rebrand both neo-liberal Conservatism and social democracy into a Third Way. Due to this, there appears to be no inherent respect for those actual, or potential, welfare subjects behind Blair's 'modernisation' project. Indeed, there does appear to be a stronger leaning towards the neo-liberal position on greater means-testing and targeting, promoting managerial effectiveness, and the abandonment of a redistributive tax system, thereby constructing the welfare subject as in need of coercion and control. Those without the means for personal insurance will be left to compete for scarcer and qualitatively inferior services provided by either a residualised welfare sector or a paternalistic voluntary movement. However, the thrust of Blair's policy developments – economic dynamism alongside a largely privately-insured welfare system – may well come unstuck in a less favourable economic climate. These are not measures that will heal the growing social divide in the UK. Indeed, the fragmentation of society in the UK will worsen, with severe social costs, and Blair may well find the electorate sceptical of his claim that New Labour represents a new era in politics.

New Labour's particular Achilles' heel is its commitment to tackling social exclusion. Blair's insistence on 'consensus', rather than conflict, in politics can only prove counter-productive to achieving this because it silences the 'Other than'. New Labour will fail to achieve social inclusion exactly because it fails to acknowledge the lived experience of welfare subjects, particularly those who fail to conform to the dominant supplementary narratives of 'work' and 'family'.

There is an alternative. If New Labour wants to establish a new era in British politics it needs to recognise diversity and celebrate difference. It needs to challenge the bastions of privilege perpetuated through class, 'race', gender and sexuality, mediated through public schooling, private medicine, housing consumption and so forth. This requires a pro-active state, investing in the essentials of life for everyone, and promoting real opportunity through redefining and redistributing work, providing economic autonomy, and encouraging genuine community involvement in the ways we have suggested above. It requires a new political environment within which conflicts can be harmonised through constructive dialogue and resolution. This requires acceptance of the notion that conflict itself can not only be constructive, but also that it is necessary for a healthy democracy. This all adds up to a different concept of reciprocity and democracy to that held by New Labour, one that includes mutual respect in negotiation and the accommodation of different values within the political process.

The proposals put forward in this chapter are not particularly revolutionary. Indeed, they acknowledge the concerns of current political and economic orthodoxy, and take these into account; for instance, a Citizen's Income is affordable (Purdy 1999). However, what these proposals do is challenge the dominant discourse of welfare, discussed throughout the course of this book, because they are not framed around notions of 'difference' that construct 'abnormality' and 'normality', 'deserving' and 'undeserving'. Consequently, they offer very real prospects for deconstructing and reconstructing the welfare subject to include rather than exclude, and to recognise and value difference and diversity. In such circumstances, there will be greater potential for eliminating poverty and tackling social exclusion. In contrast, the old ways of tackling poverty and exclusion are not working. By placing an emphasis on the way policies are framed, privileging values over prescription, we can start to reverse the processes whereby welfare divides and marks out the boundaries between individuals. In its place, we can seek to build security, freedom and choice in society through policies that enable different lifestyles, economic opportunity and cultural diversity to flourish.

References

Barnett, A. (1998) 'All Power To The Citizens', *Marxism Today*, November/December, pp. 44-46.

Bauman, Z. (1998) *Work, Consumerism and the New Poor*, Open University Press, Buckingham.

Beck, U. (1999) 'Goodbye to all that wage slavery', *New Statesman*, 5 March, pp. 25-27.

Birnbaum, N. (1999) 'Is the Third Way Authentic?', *New Political Economy*, Vol. 4, No. 3, pp. 437-446.

Chavez, D. (1999) 'Cities For People', *Red Pepper Archive*, http://www.redpepper.org.uk/xcities.html, 23 October 1999, pp. 1-5.

Cooper, C. and Hawtin, M. (eds.) (1998) *Resident Involvement and Community Action: Theory to Practice*, Chartered Institute of Housing/Housing Studies Association, Coventry.

Dahrendorf, R. (1999) 'Whatever happened to liberty?', *New Statesman*, 6 September, pp. 25-27.

Doyal, L. and Gough, I. (1991) *A Theory of Human Need*, Macmillan, Basingstoke.

Dunford, M. (1997) 'The hour-glass society: The sharing of work versus the disintegration of society', *City*, 8, December, pp. 171-187.

Freire, P. (1976) *Education: The Practices of Freedom*, Writers and Readers Publishing Co-operative, London.

Gorz, A. (1999) *Reclaiming Work: Beyond the Wage-Based Society*, Polity Press, Cambridge.

Hall, S. (1998) 'The Great Moving Nowhere Show', *Marxism Today*, November/December, pp. 9-14.

Jordan, B. (1996) *A Theory of Poverty and Social Exclusion*, Polity Press, Cambridge.

Jordan, B. (1998) *The New Politics of Welfare*, Sage, London.

Marquand, D. (1998) 'Can Labour kick the winning habit?', *New Statesman*, 23 October, pp. 25-27.

Oppenheim, C. (1999) 'New life for the welfare state', *The Guardian Society*, 29 September, pp. 2-3.

Popple, K. (1995) *Analysing Community Work: Its Theory and Practice*, Open University Press, London.

Powell, M. (ed.) (1999) *New Labour, New Welfare State? The 'third way' in British social policy*, The Policy Press, Bristol.

Purdy, D. (1999) 'Controlling the waves', *Red Pepper Archive*, http://www.redpepper.org.uk/xwelfare2.html, 23 October 1999, pp. 1-5.

Wilkinson, R. (1998) 'Why Inequality Is Bad For You', *Marxism Today*, November/December, pp. 38-39.

Williams, F. (1994) 'Social relations, welfare and the post-Fordism debate' in R. Burrows and B. Loader (eds.), *Towards a Post-Fordist Welfare State?*, Routledge, London, pp. 49-73.

Index